AF575619

Photographs: Together & Alone

Karlheinz Weinberger

Edited by Ben Estes

Introduction by Collier Schorr

The Song Cave

The Song Cave
www.the-song-cave.com

ISBN: 978-1-7340351-1-7
Library of Congress Control Number: 2020935454

FIRST EDITION

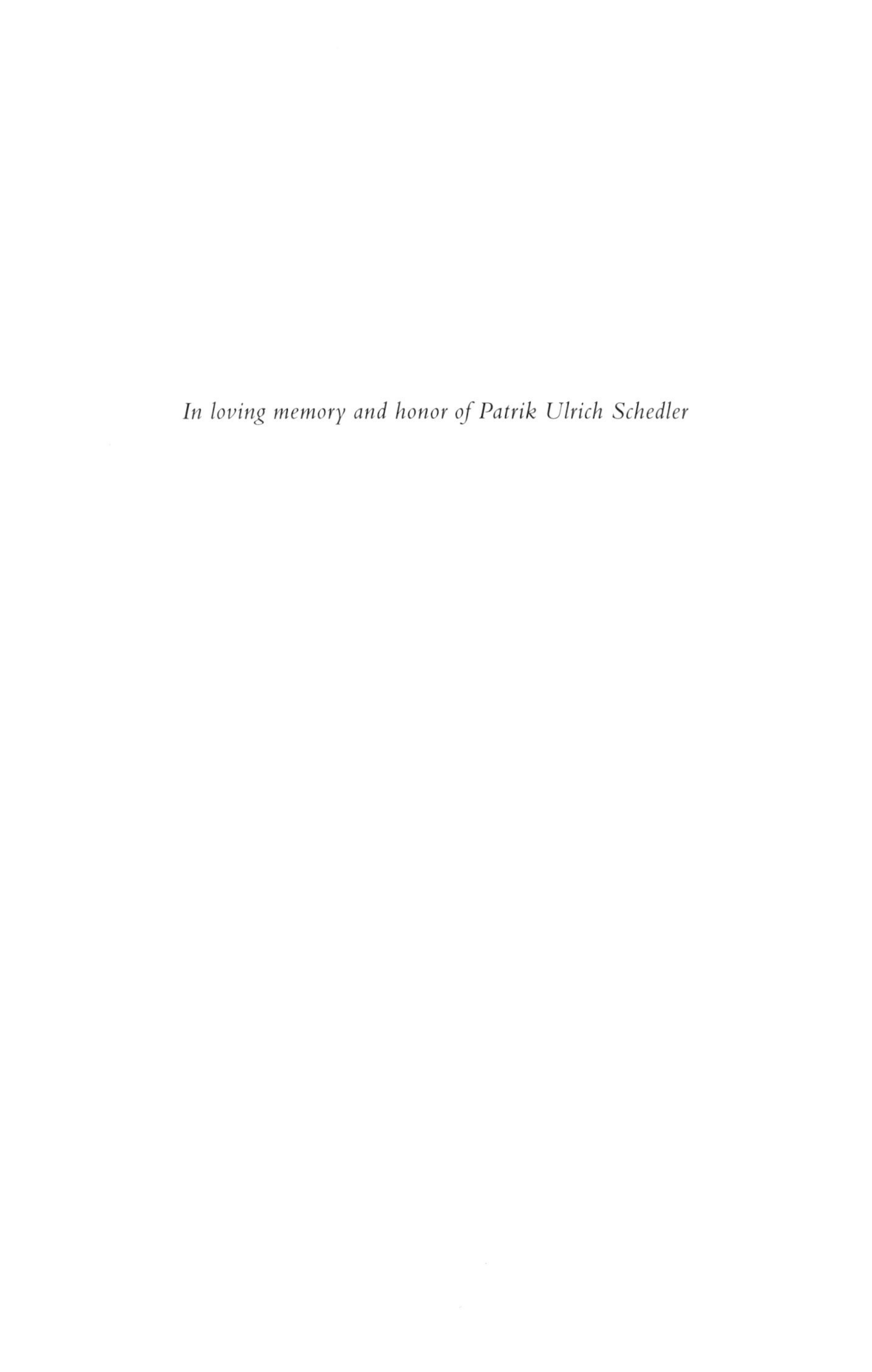

In loving memory and honor of Patrik Ulrich Schedler

Contents

It Must Commence

Collier Schorr

Once upon a time in Zurich, a camera found a population that lived on the outskirts of town. These people also gathered in city squares and by the caravans of traveling circuses, a proving ground for lounging and posing and making out. Cigarettes and hairspray clogged the air and tin foil was a quick way to shine metallic. There is nothing more perfectly symbiotic than the relationship between the outsider with a camera and the outsiders themselves.

It's pretty evident that only a leper, a loser, or the locked out Jew or homosexual especially, would have great success with 16 year olds who try to look intimidating and want to be looked at. It's like a god of good times made photographers for juvenile delinquents to keep them a bit less murderous and criminal. The delinquent dresses himself to preen, fully aware of his beauty, no way to succeed in the confines of society. He is literally waiting for the camera to acknowledge his existence.

Karlheinz Weinberger was not killed by hoodlums or Nazis or bikers, which suggests that flattery will get you everywhere and that he did not shit where he ate. Or were the hoodlums actually just a bunch of homosexuals who grew up to become Nazis; the kind who rubbed each other's shoulders in tents and in front of campfires? I, a woman, have often wondered what it would be like to be both a hoodlum and a male photographer. To rub shoulders with, or to rub shoulders covered in, stained denim. Weinberger's early images smell of hair lacquer and the later ones smell of whiskey and sweat. The latent adolescence of the closeted homosexual gives way to manhood. In a sense they—photographer and subjects—grew up together. It's a constant question—how to exist inside. Is it as simple as difference making a gap for other differences? The French word *écart* comes to mind. A distance, a deviation—*rester à l'écart de* (to keep out of, to steer clear). Here we have both a warning and an opportunity for something creative.

While these images are black and white, I crave the colors of the sweaters and bandanas in the color photos of young gang members. Like candies in leather wrappers. The color, like in *The Wizard of Oz*, makes them queerer. But in black and white, the boys and girls are tougher, more masculine. Much has been made of the way these Swiss boys dressed, taking all the liberties of Elvis, even as it made them look like pretenders. The fantastic fetishism left over from military marches throughout Europe made them look uber-gay. Hard soft top bottom. When you thread nuts and bolts through the fly of your jeans, you have crossed over into a realm most people can't even process. There is no understandable reference for this kind of fashion mutilation (in public at least), and it predates Gunther Brus' bloodletting performances by at least two decades. The giant medallions predate hip hop and RUN-DMC, the belt buckles paying homage to Elvis, but bowing towards a Texas rodeo rather than a Tennessee jukebox. Male domination so accessorized it almost becomes Dr. Frankenstein's experiment, a foreshadowing of Andy Warhol's film of the same name (Andy Warhol's *Frankenstein*.) Let us not forget Frankenstein is the creator. And the creation, the subject, is the monster. Dirty boys abound. The outcast, the monster in gothic literary conventions, akin to the homosexual, pushed to the edges of society. He is a monster because his sexual expression disturbs the heteronormative town folk. And then there is the camera. An outsider approaches. A man with a camera who thinks they are not demons and also thinks they are.

I used to go up to boys at a local pool in Germany and ask "Kann ich macht eine builder auf Dich?" and they would stare at me, shrugging their suntanned shoulders, and then say something I didn't understand. And then I did it. And bowed my head with a bit of relief and walked away.

I hate to talk about love in photography, because as a practitioner who has been *in love* I know this kind of love fades like the writing on a candy heart left in one's pocket. The *I love you* disintegrates. It seems particularly male, of the moment, in penetration and ownership no matter how feminine and maternal I might feel. Loving has a use value. Keeping a subject in front of you. A camera is a dick. It is not a vagina, though in another essay I could argue that it's a tunnel the subject is compelled to enter. Truthfully, it's more a thing that punctures the ego of the person in front of it. Stabs them in their sudden need to be adored. What Weinberger did, however, was to not move on so fast. His camera stroked the boys it commandeered. It must have, because they seemed to stay around. Having dressed up and done their hair and laced their crotches, Weinberger was their screaming chorus of girls. The fanbase. In his apartment the lights made a stage, the stage of white boards supported the performance. I imagine the photographer's elbows worked the camera while young hips swayed to the rhythm.

Weinberger is best known for his images of the younger rebels. They have been copied in countless fashion shoots, irresistible to stylists. Mostly the studio shots. In looking through the edit in this book, the countryside images, there is a looseness and a nice level of distance. Less static than in the artist's homemade studio (in the same house where his mother lived), here you clearly feel a life is being lived by faraway minds. Weinberger is not with them, but is in on it. There is a dichotomy between the close-up and the voyeuristic landscapes. A boy perched on the knees of a girl, who could be a boy, because you see such similar jeans. These pictures make me feel wistful. The way the camera celebrates the thing it isn't. It's a strength, and it causes a romantic illusion. At one point the boys Larry Clark photographed were his age. They were kind of gross and fucked up. Then he got older and the boys felt younger, chosen for a kind of cuteness, in fact chosen period. And Ryan McGinely was in his pictures looking much the same as the other kids, his friends. Now he is not. Was Weinberger ever young with his subjects? Was he ever just one of them?

That illusion of the *dreamy pal* fractures in the second part of the book, a series of recently found prints of nude men and boys. Most of the clothes are gone and most of the "pretty boys" are gone. There is a change of cast. Shot from the '50s-'70s, these pictures have a catch-as-catch-can feel. The men are a little more real, less *pirate fairies* with extremely crafted hair. They are in the studio/house, white cardboard flats, and beds, and white-walled corners. I confess I prefer spectacle in a cock photo. I know this about myself. I'm less interested in "collection," like critic Vince Aletti. So my take on these is prejudiced. I really got to know about cocks from the Moroccan boy penises of Baron Wilhelm von Gloden photos, and the grown-up African American men Robert Mapplethorpe cruised. So, the male versions of the mother and the whore. I want it to be extreme or barely there. Weinberger's nudes are actually poignant. The flesh is usually small, white. Illusions and expectations are a bit lost. For me, it's a search but I don't know the dialogue. The before-and-after that results in these almost shy, tender images. I always found nudes challenging because the skin lacks a contrast. No clothes make no identities. White bodies make blanks (blanc). Perhaps these images are closer to who Weinberger was? They certainly speak to the future compulsions of Bruce Weber, and the contemplations of Jack Pierson. But they also dismantle the fantasy. Photographers are promiscuous and their modern medium with rolls of film means they could make a lot of pictures. Hunt for the one, own the many. Souvenirs—the symbol of experience, and for a photographer, also the proof of being acknowledged. The studio portrait proves the person was there, and that he looked at the photographer. My favorite image is of a young blond man, with almost a gymnast's short thick body, one knee cocked. His hand is covered by the aluminum globe of a studio light, which feels as open as an orchid.

For a few days I owned a Karlheinz Weinberger image of a biker in a Nazi helmet wearing a denim vest. It cost $900. I put it in a show I curated called *Overnight to Many Cities*. It was mine. Every day I saw this image on the wall, and became more and more anxious. I finally canceled the purchase. I worried what wanting that image said about me. And what it said about all the fabricated Nazi pictures I had made in Germany. How I had wanted it felt directly connected to how Weinberger might have wanted it. Theatrical danger. *Instant character*, as Susan Sontag wrote of immediate connections. You look at them and they look at you, and it must commence.

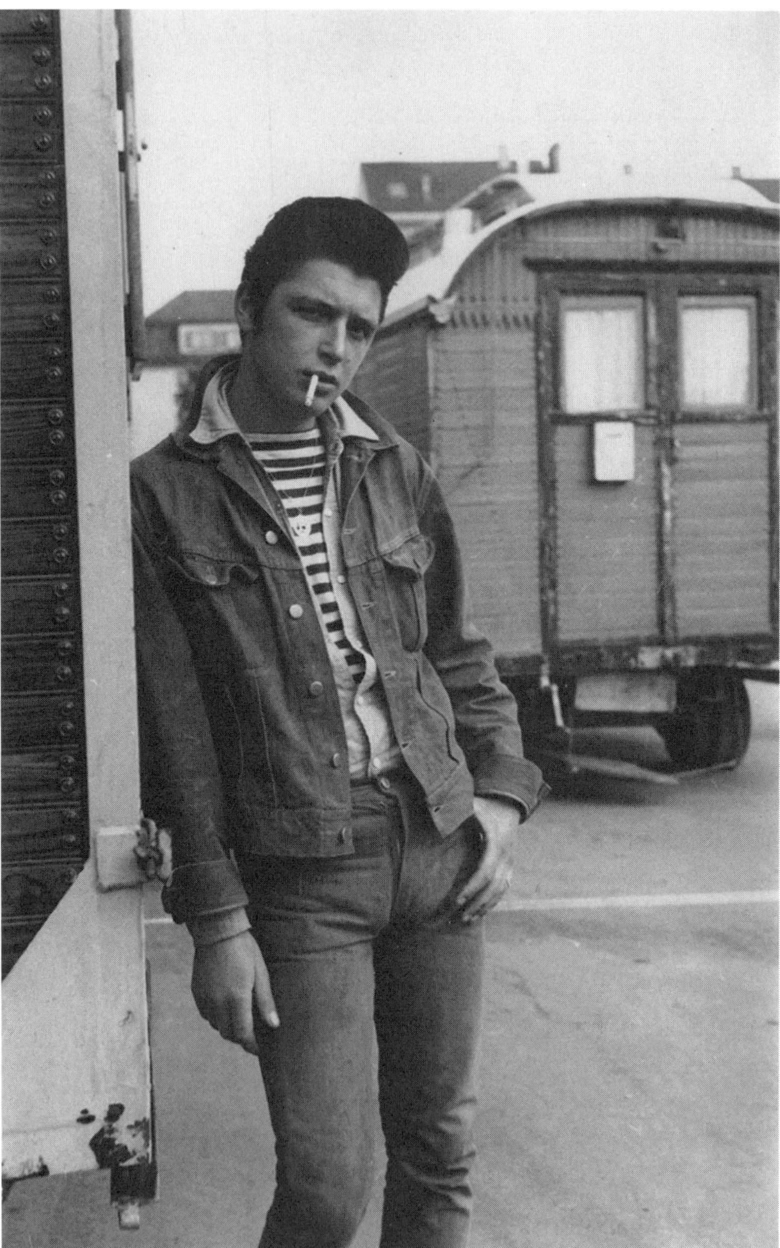

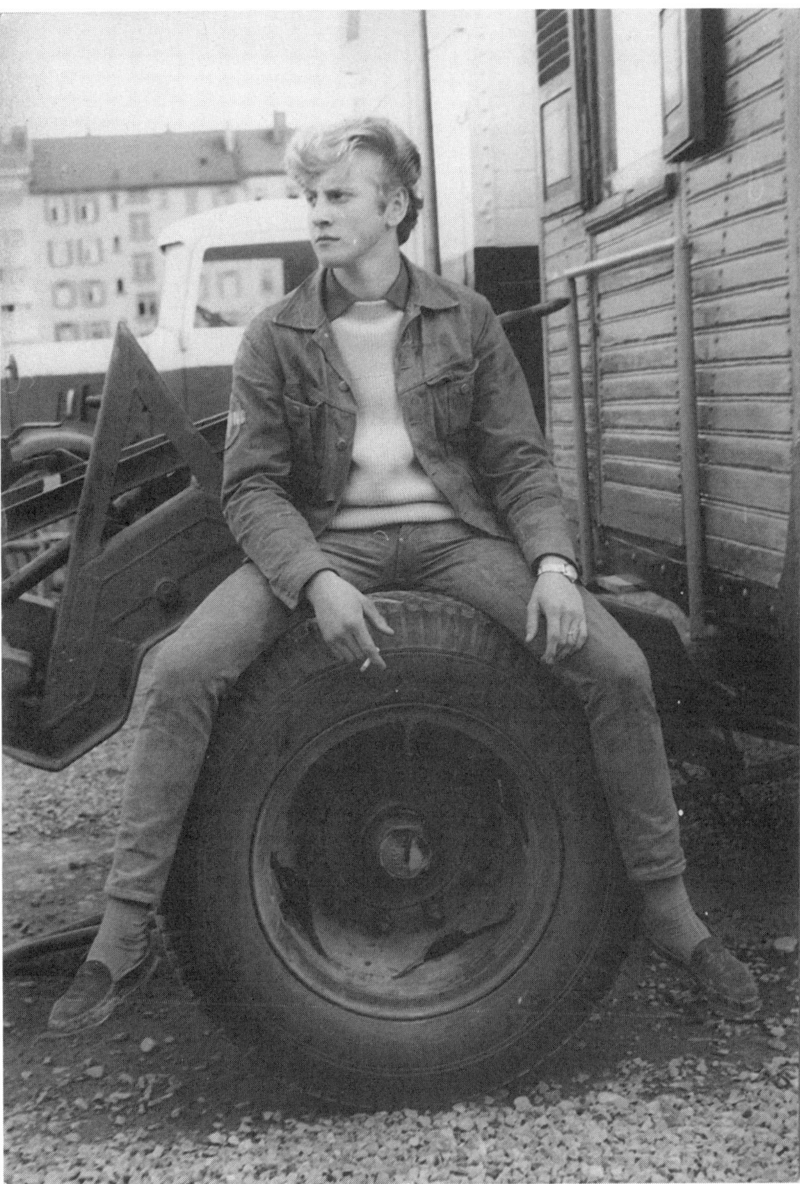

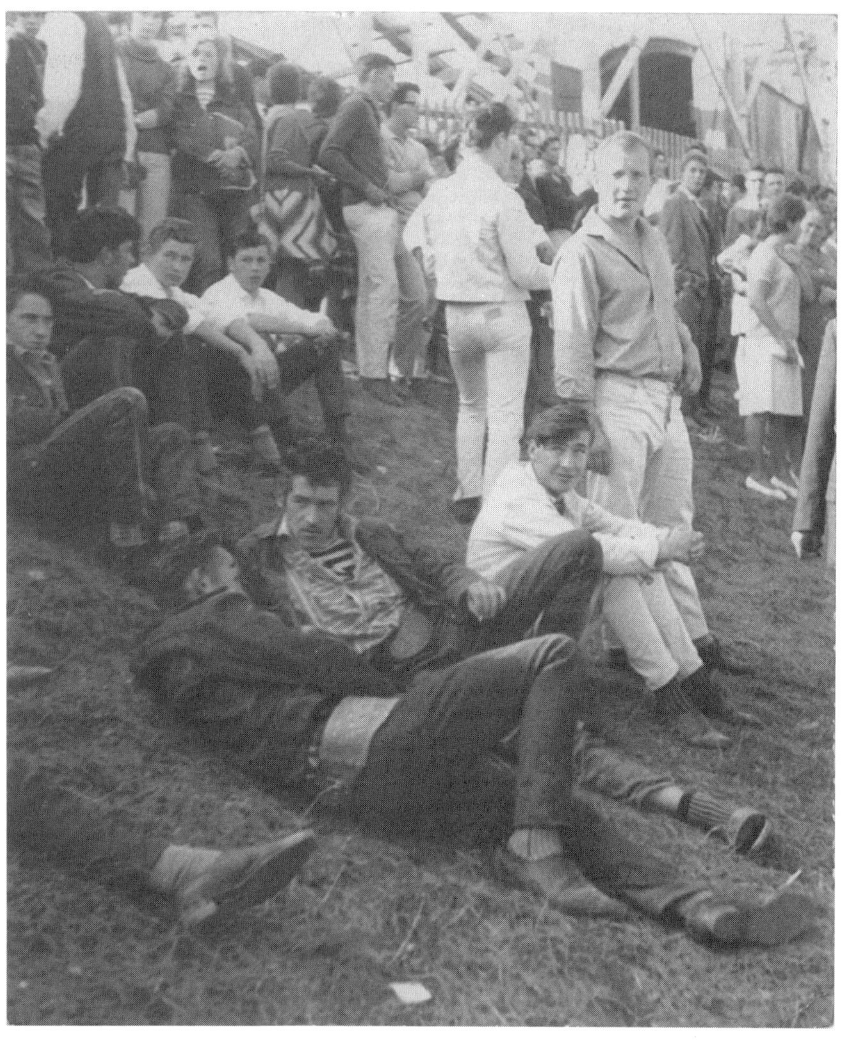

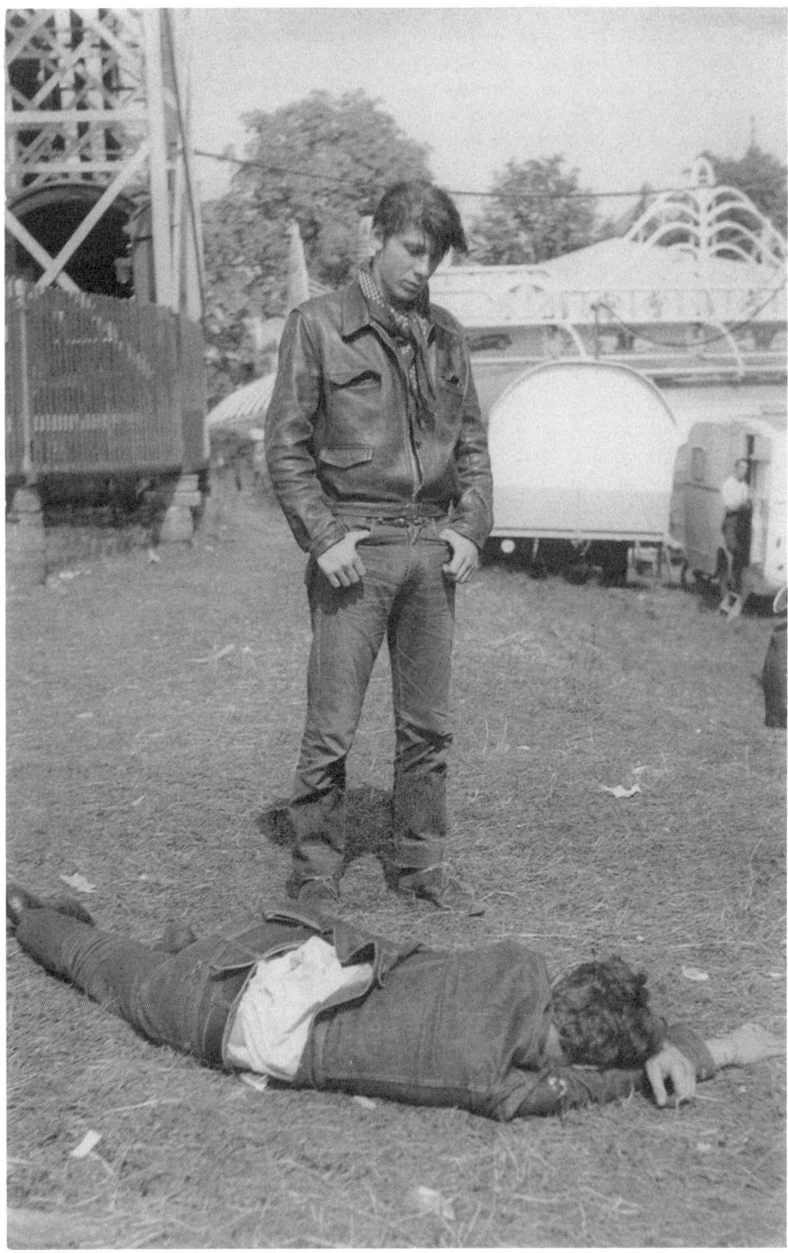

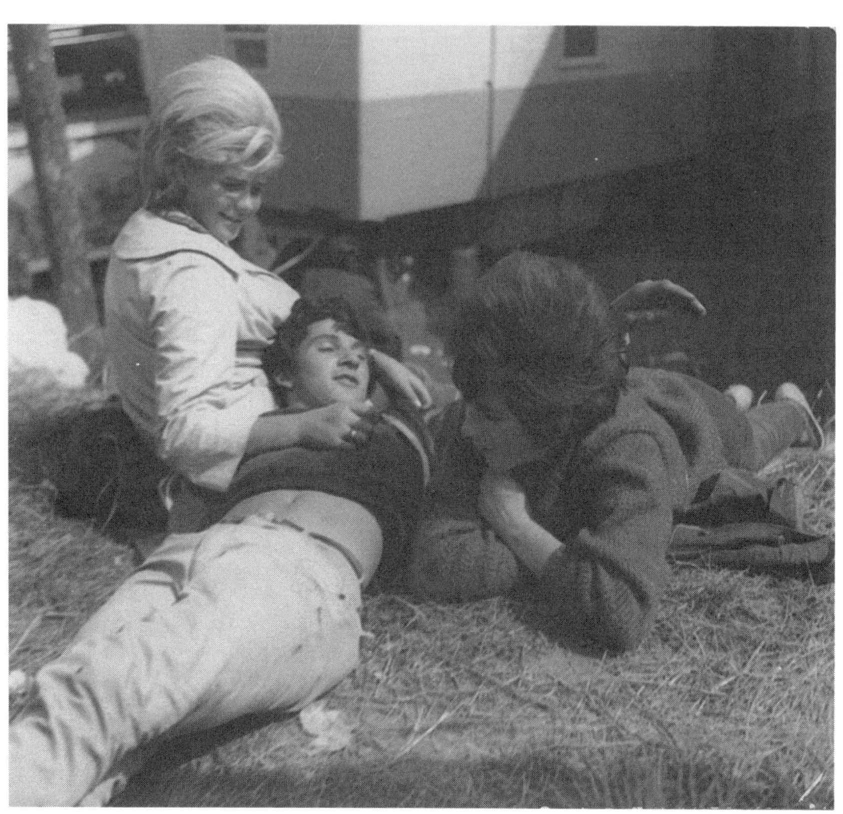

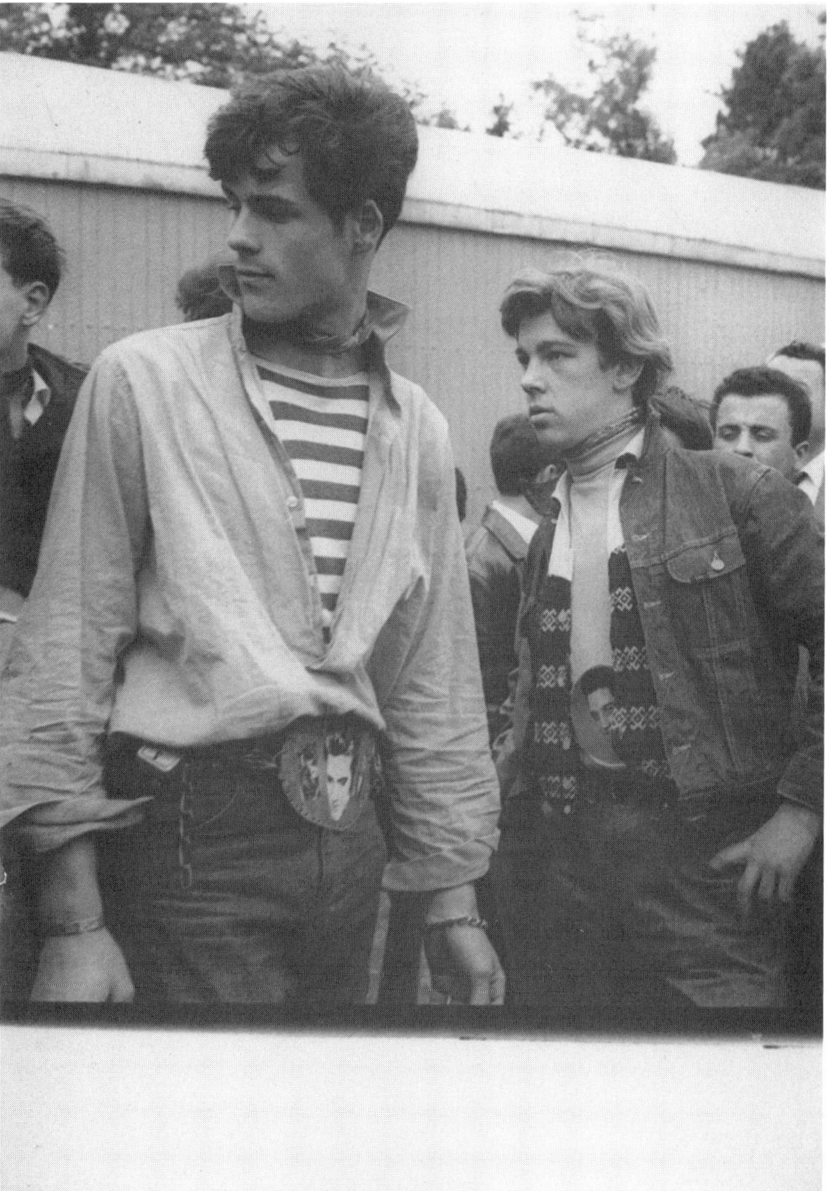

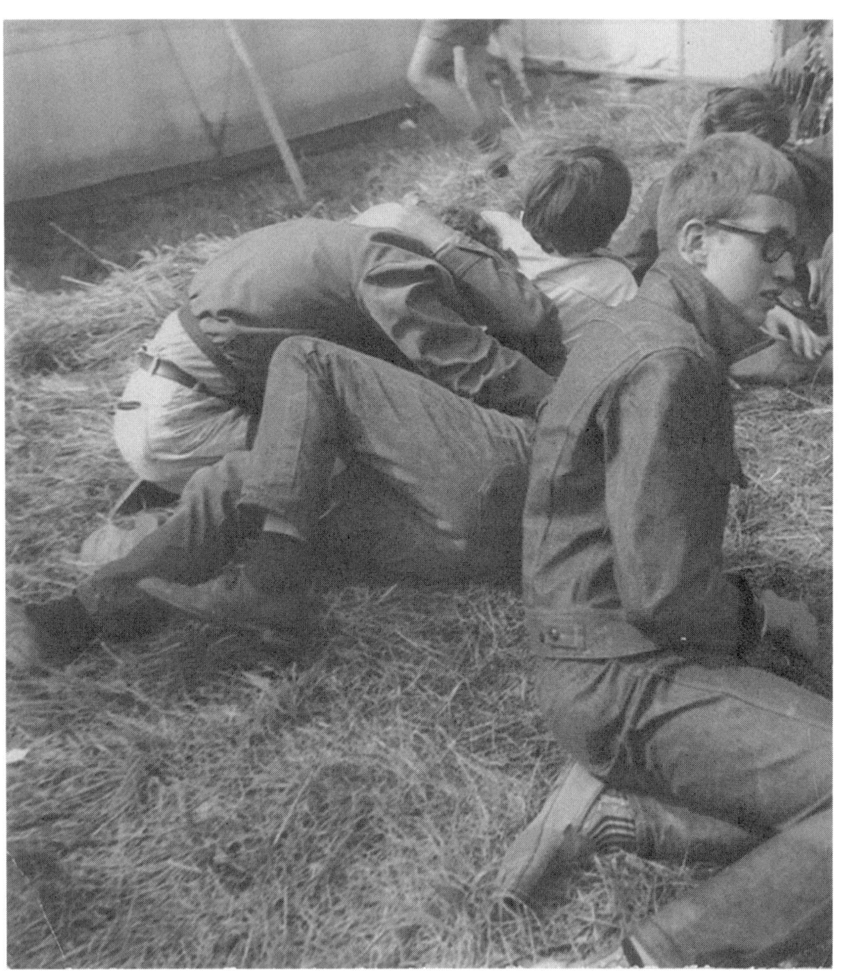

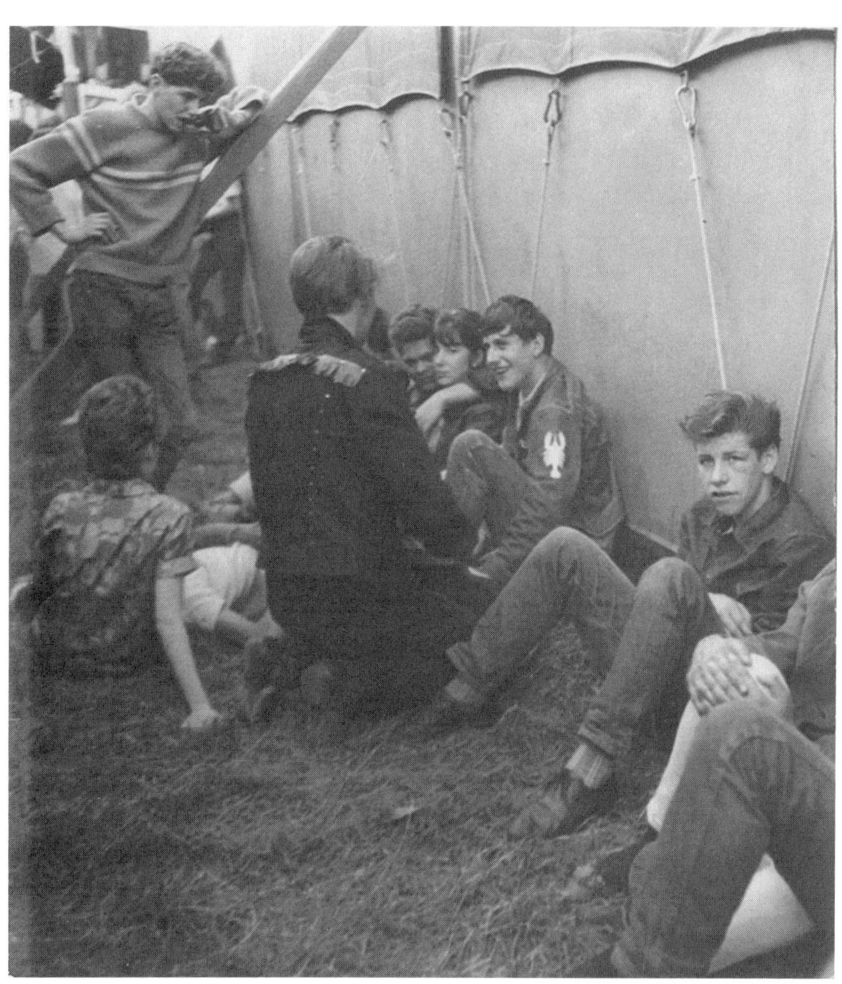

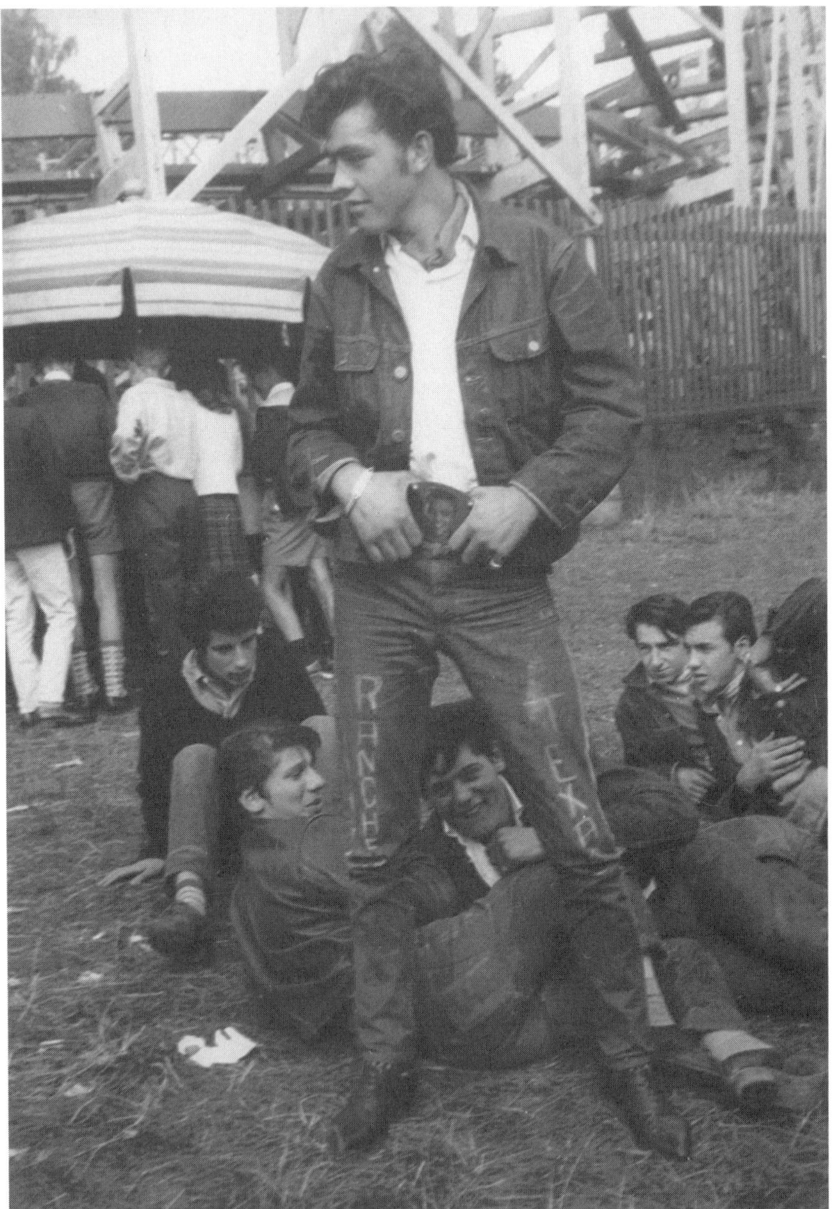

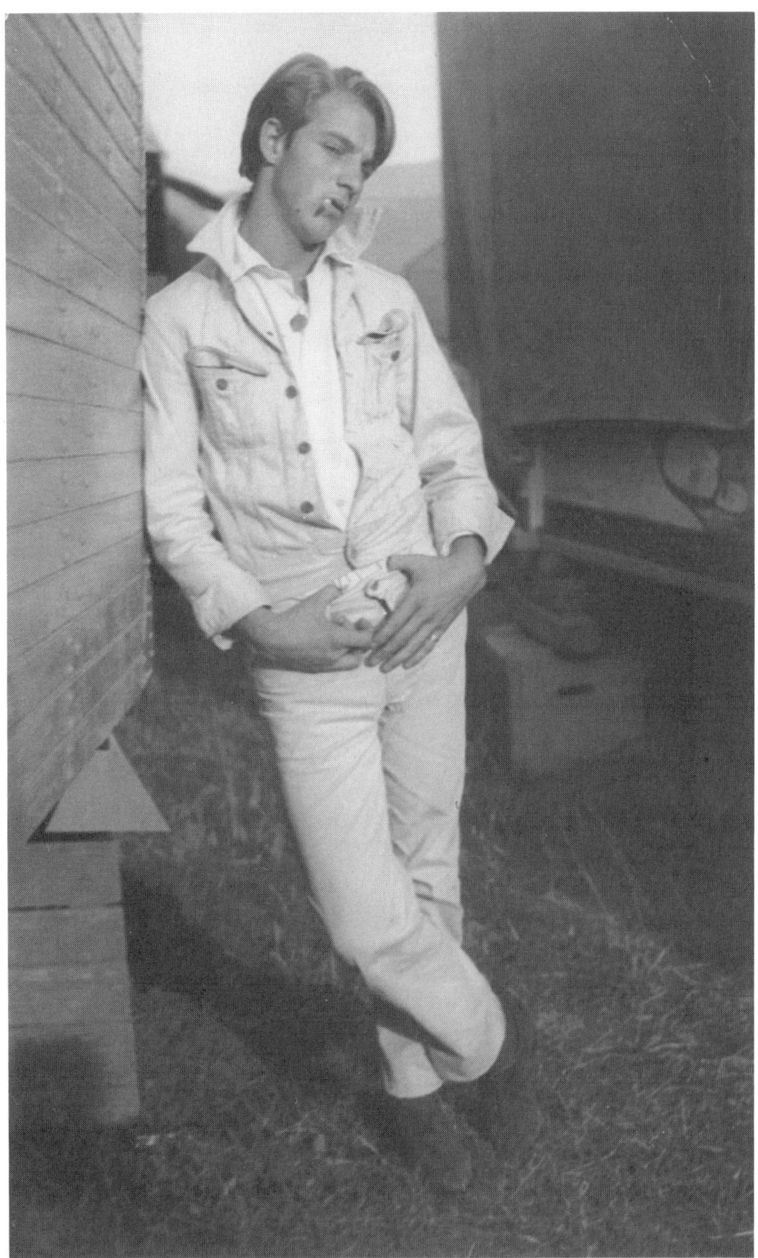

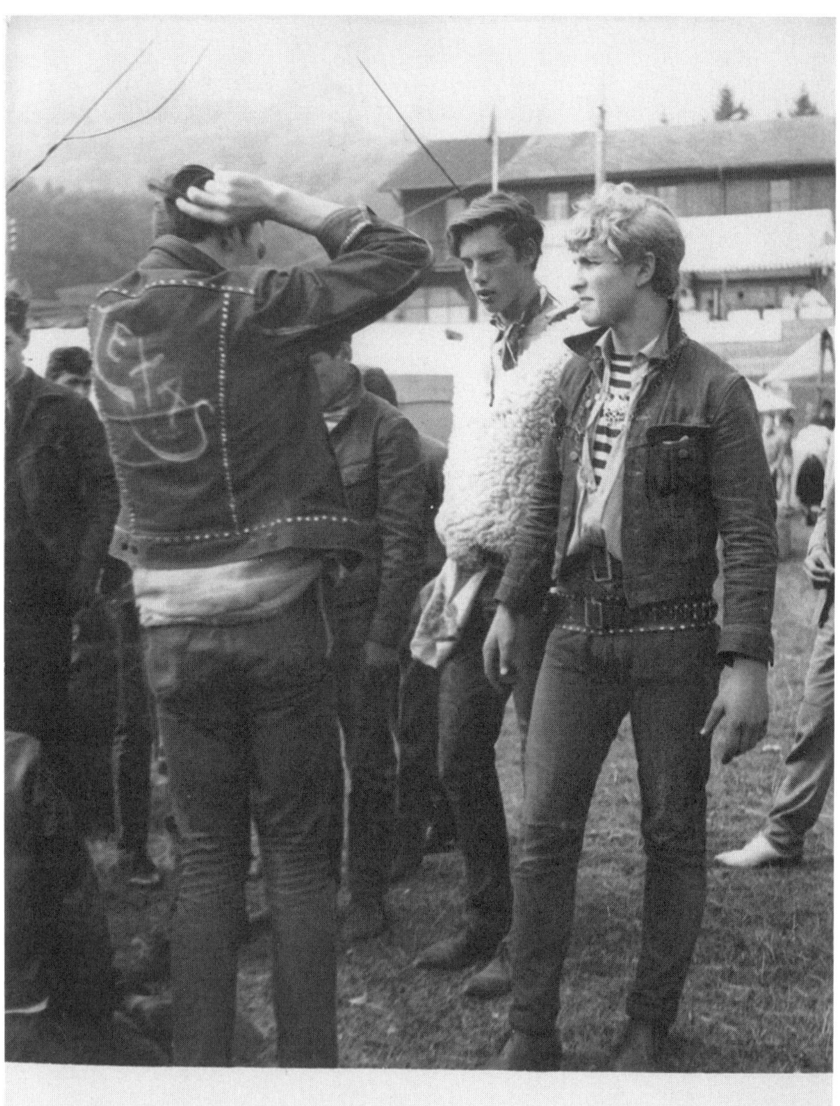

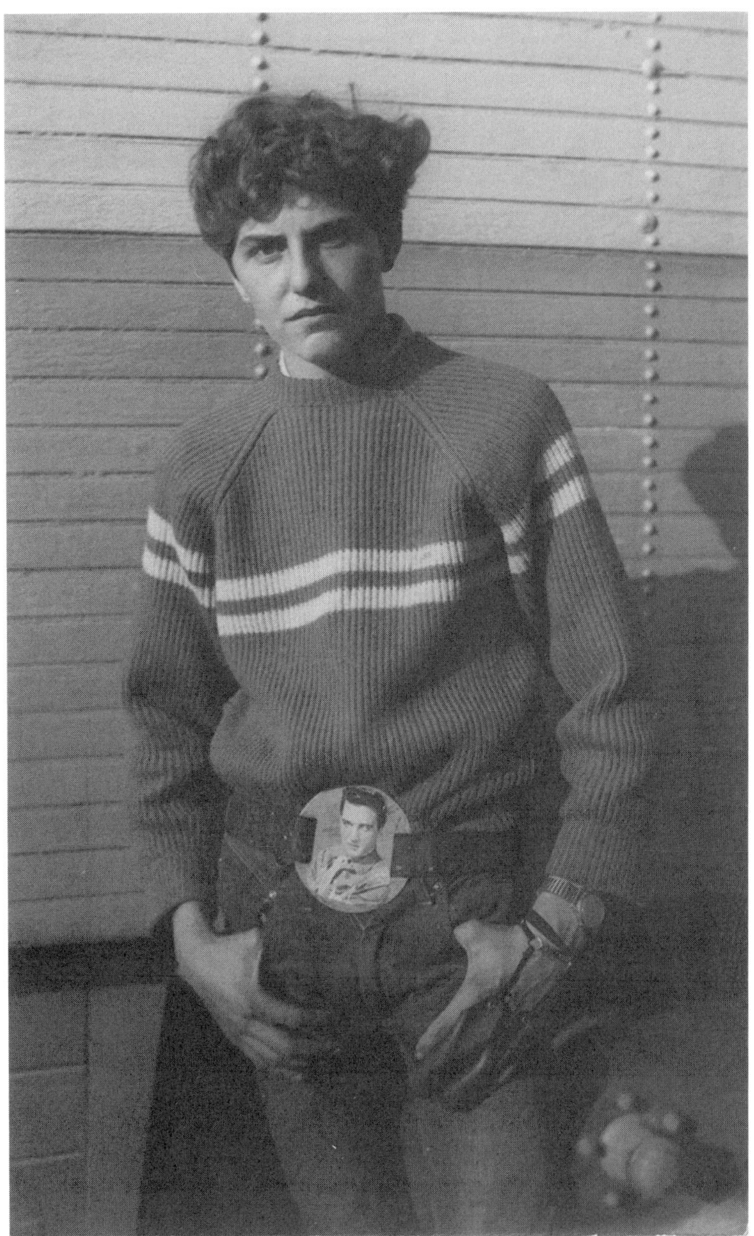

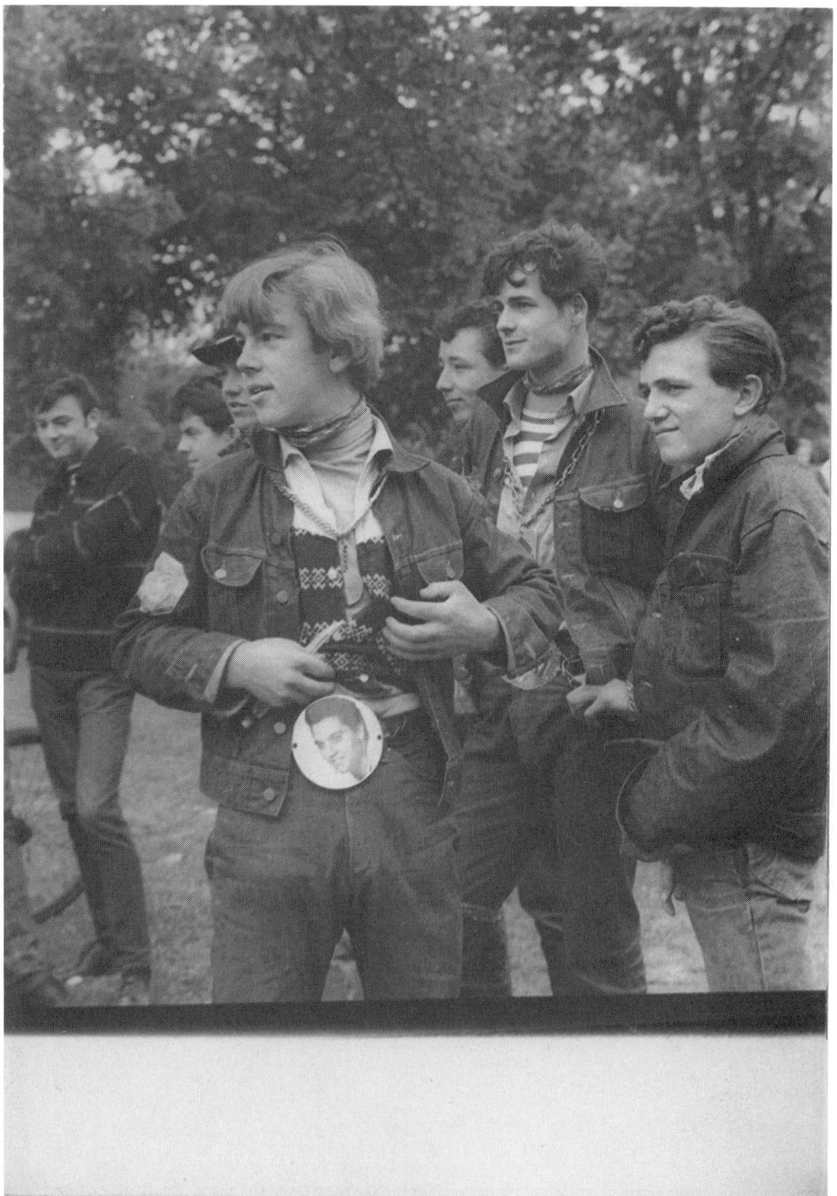

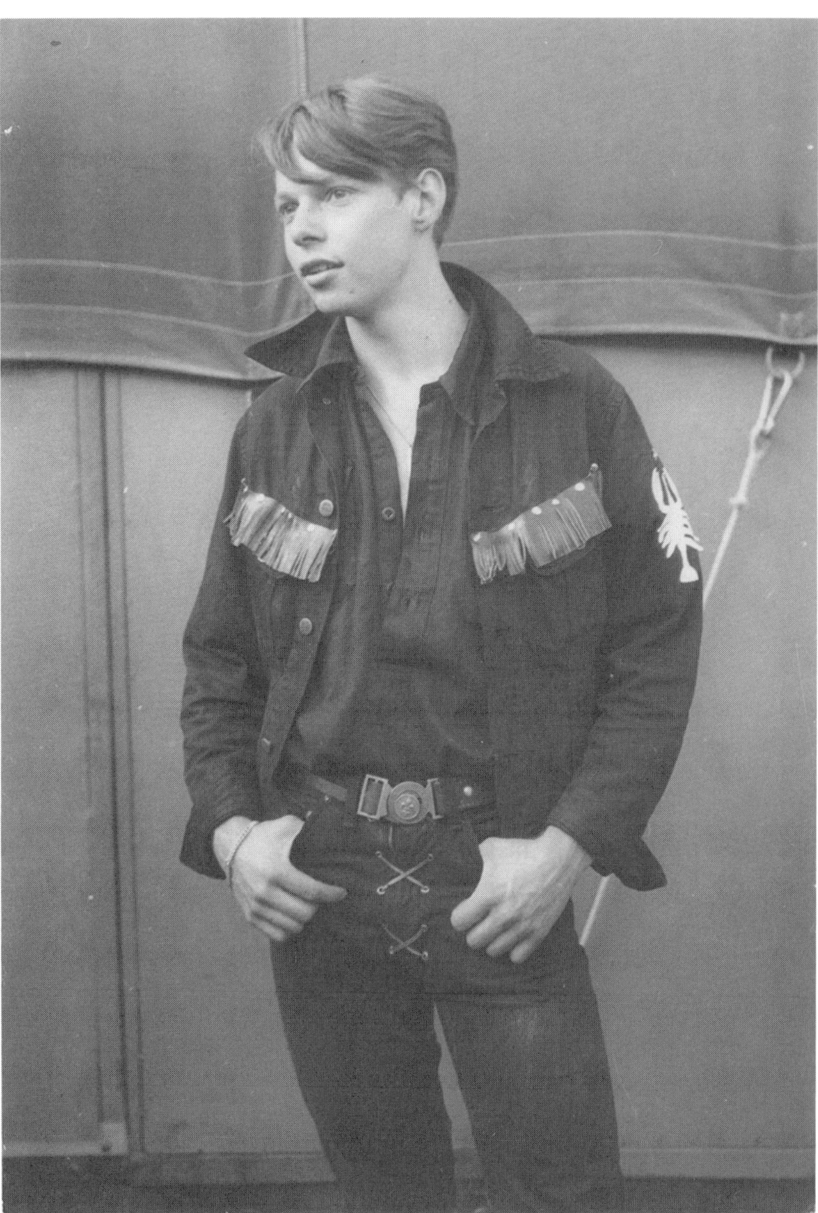

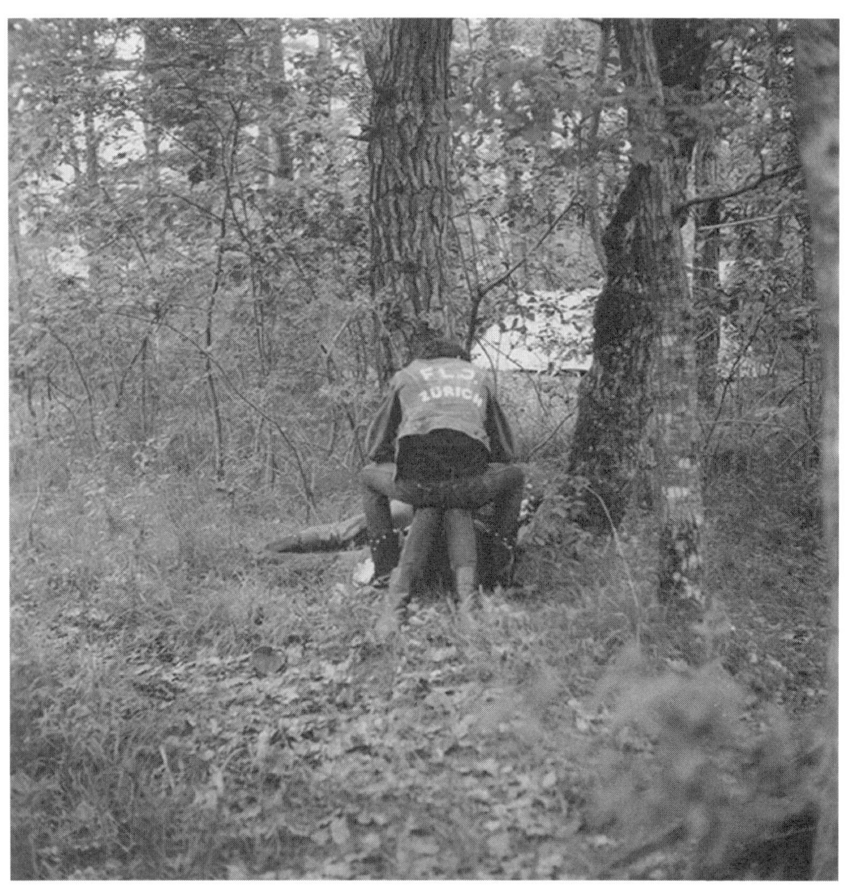
ZURICH

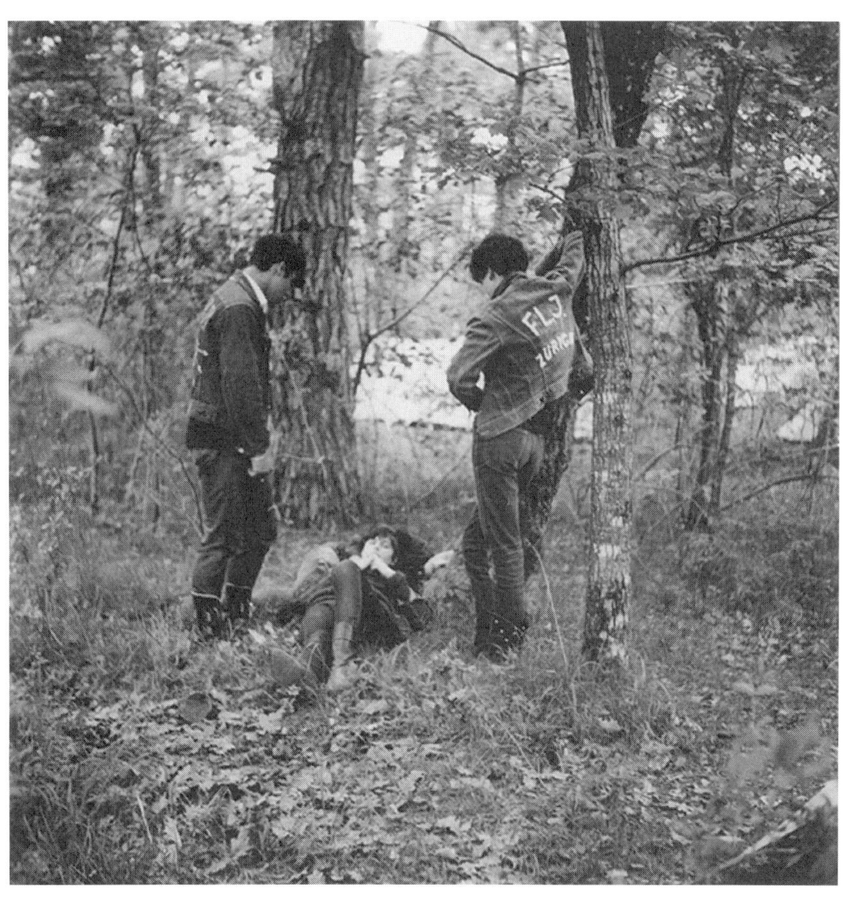
F.L.J.

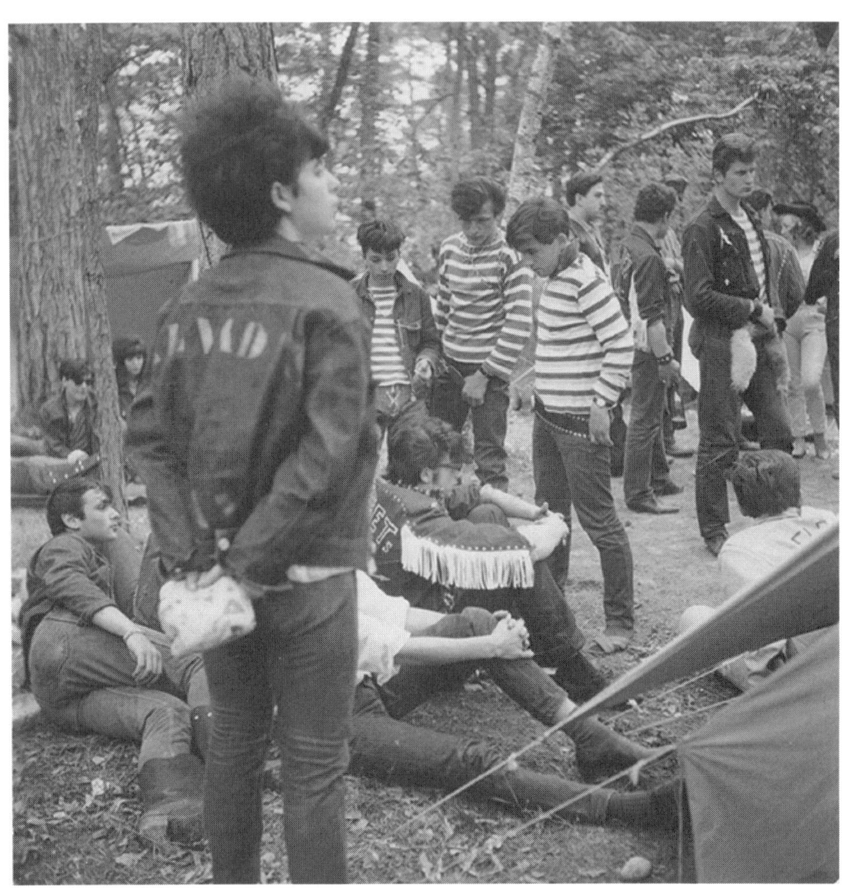

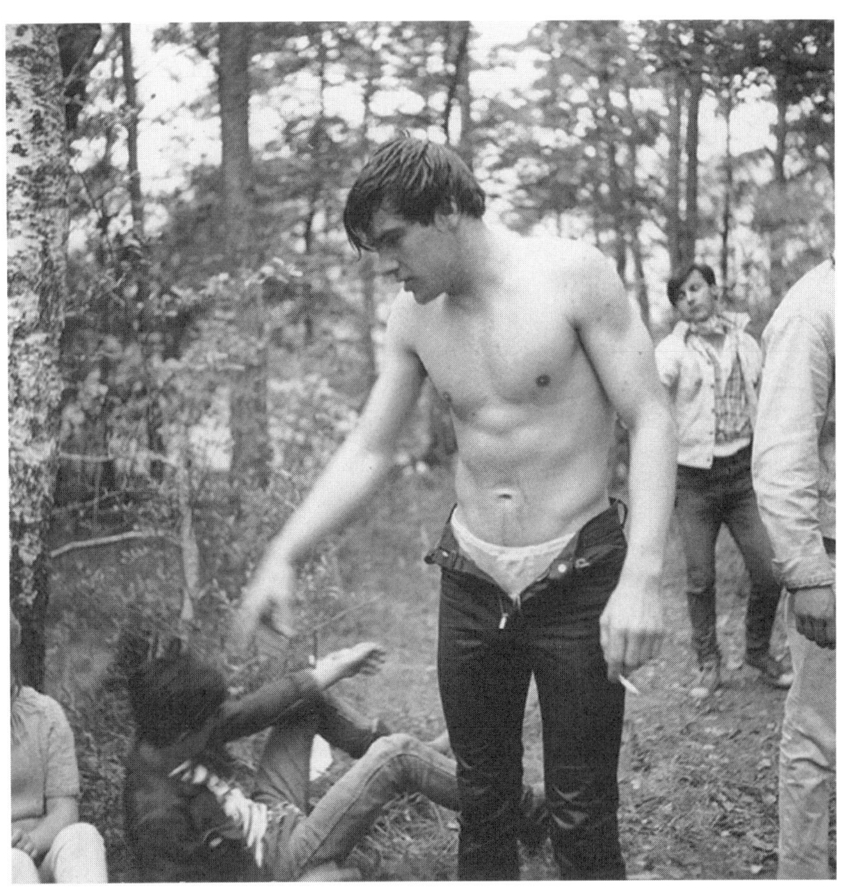

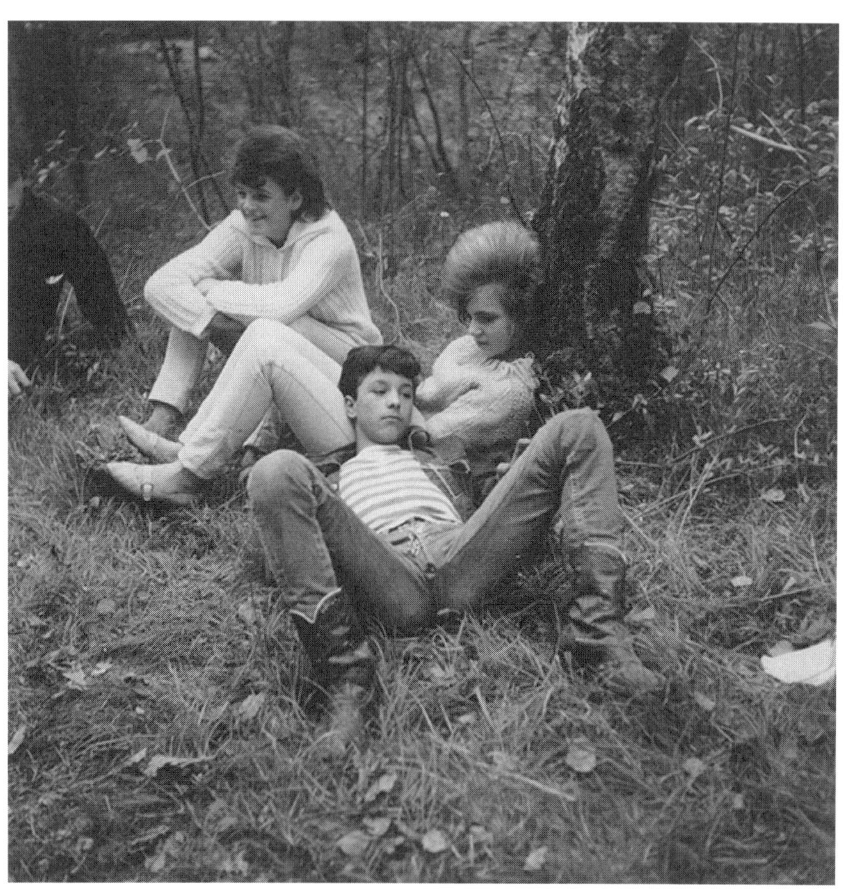

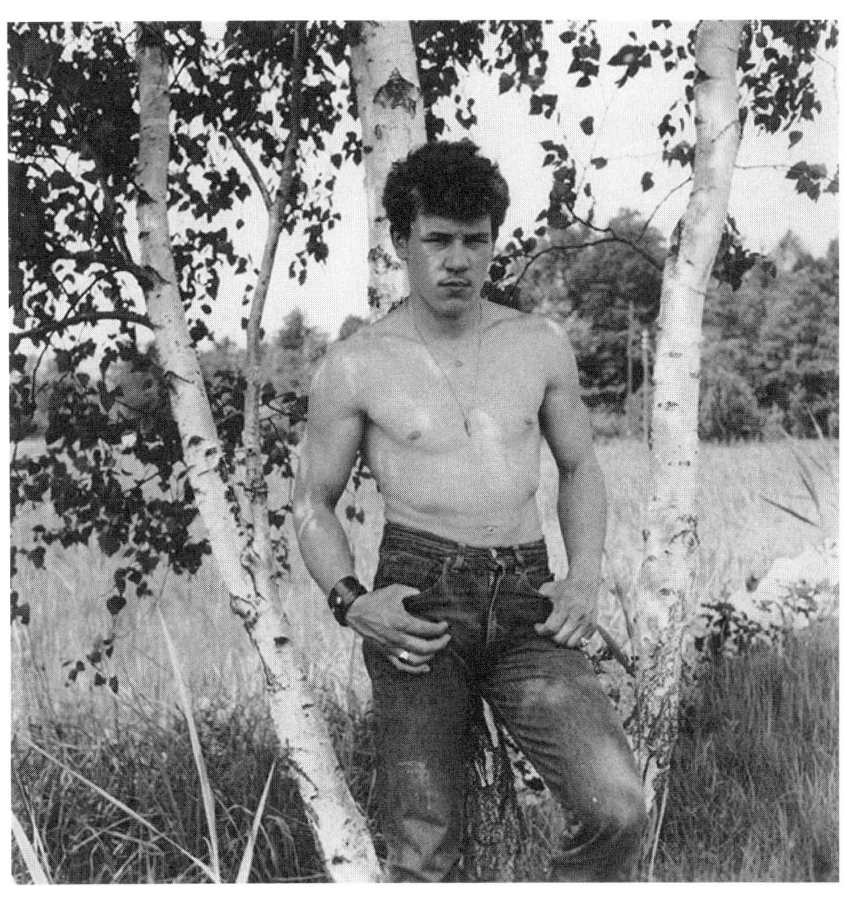

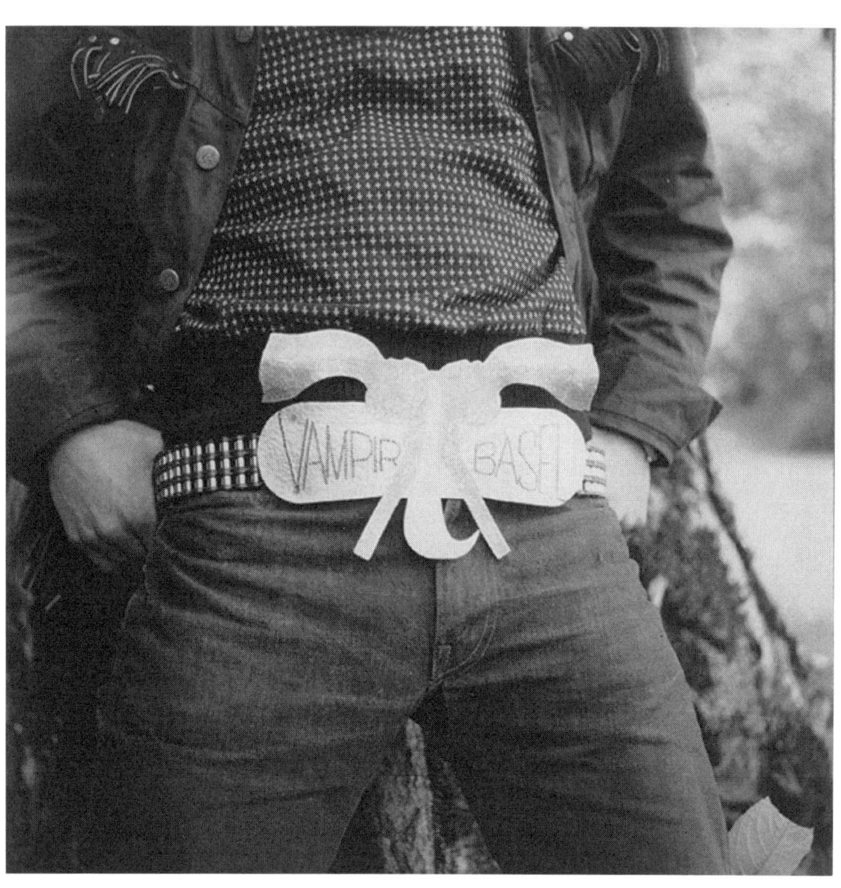
VAMPIR
BASEL

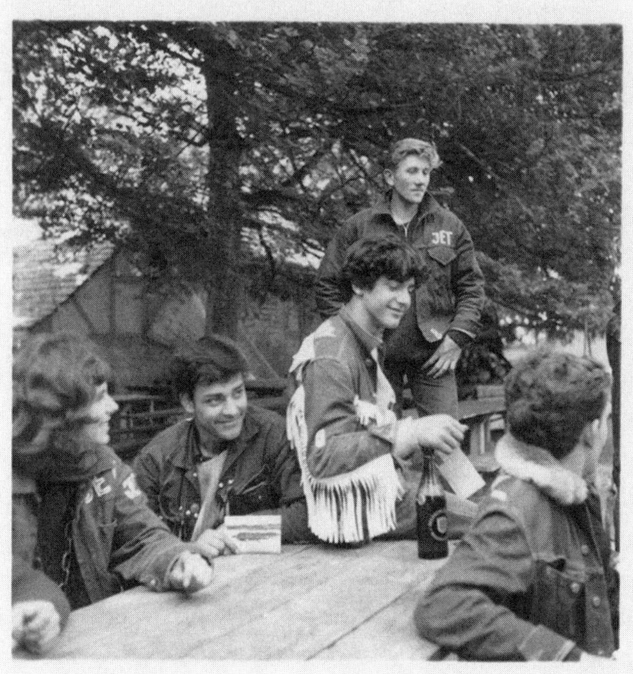
JET

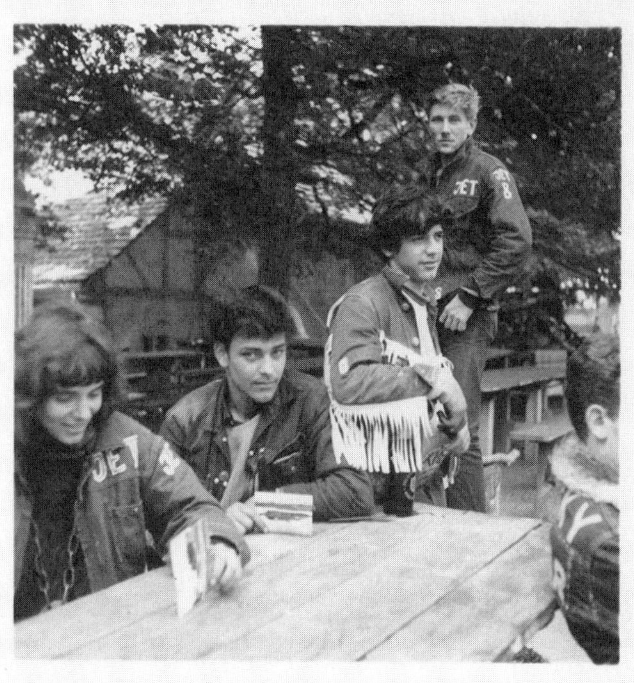
JET
8

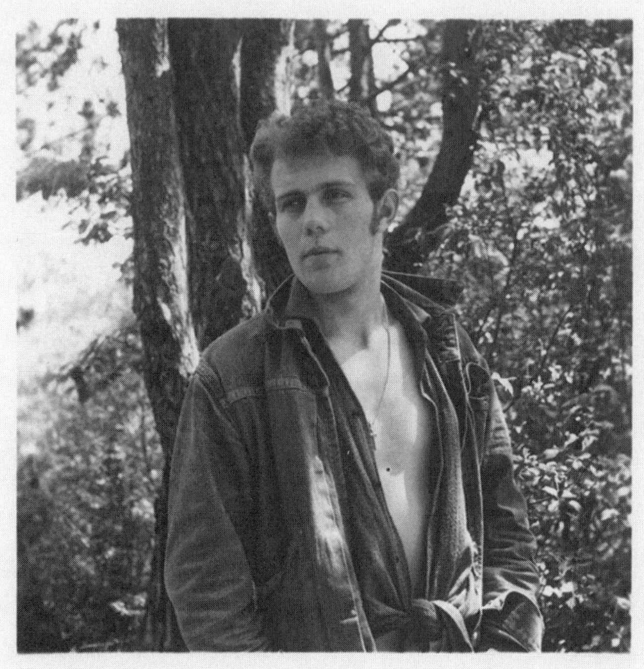

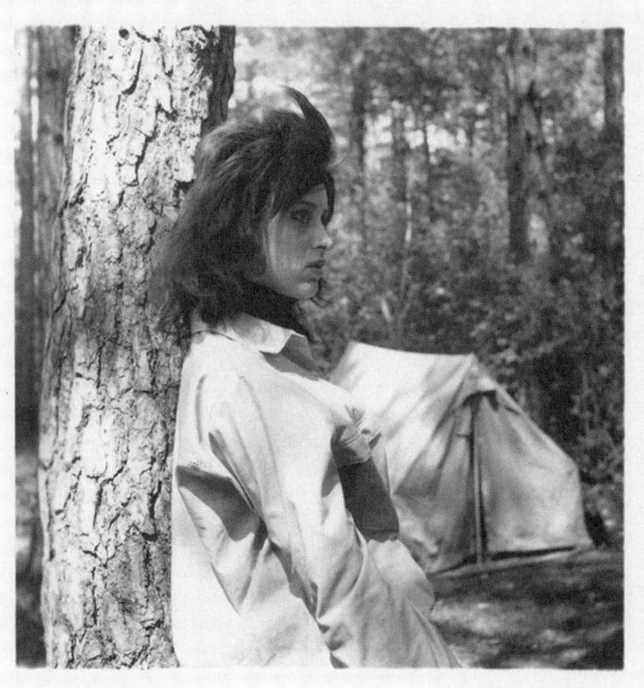

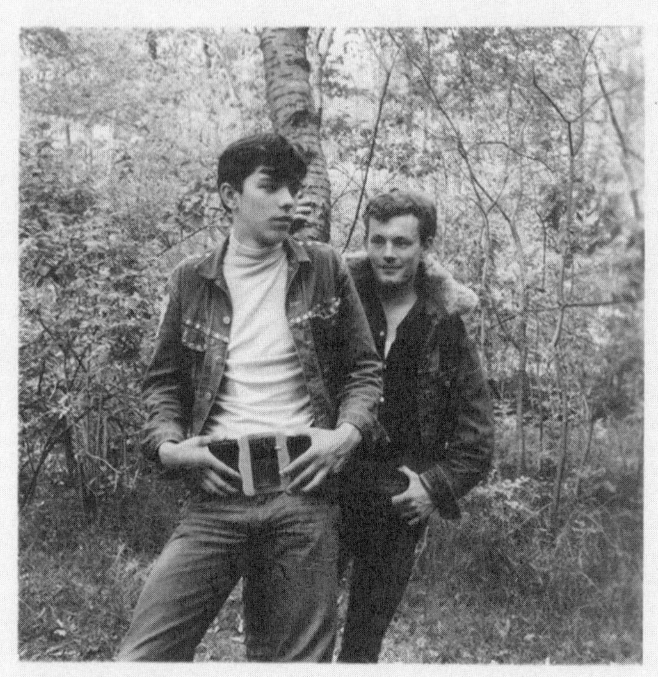

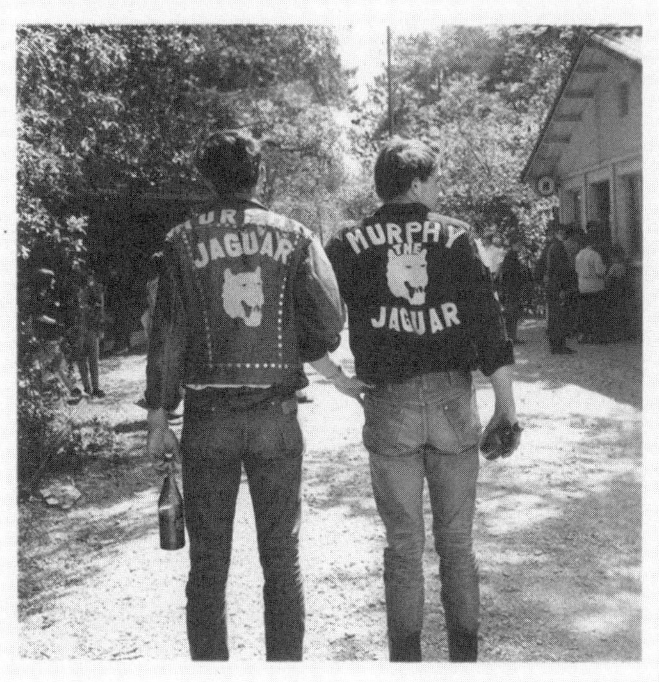
JAGUAR
MURPHY
THE
JAGUAR

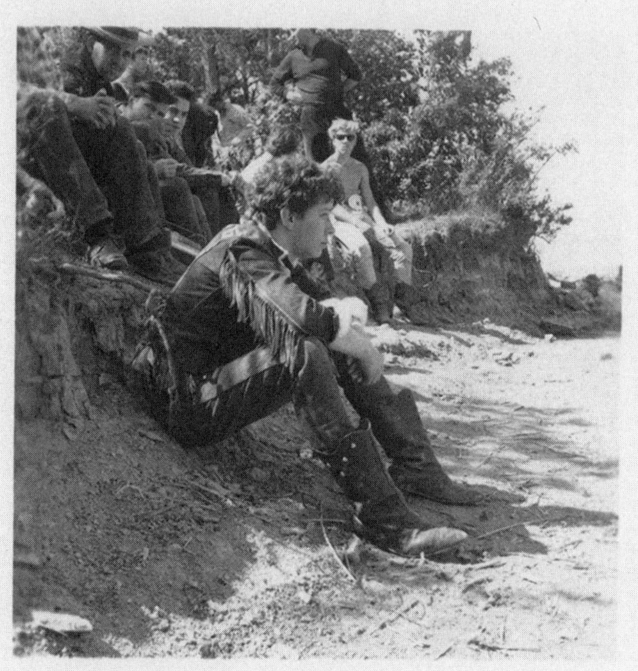

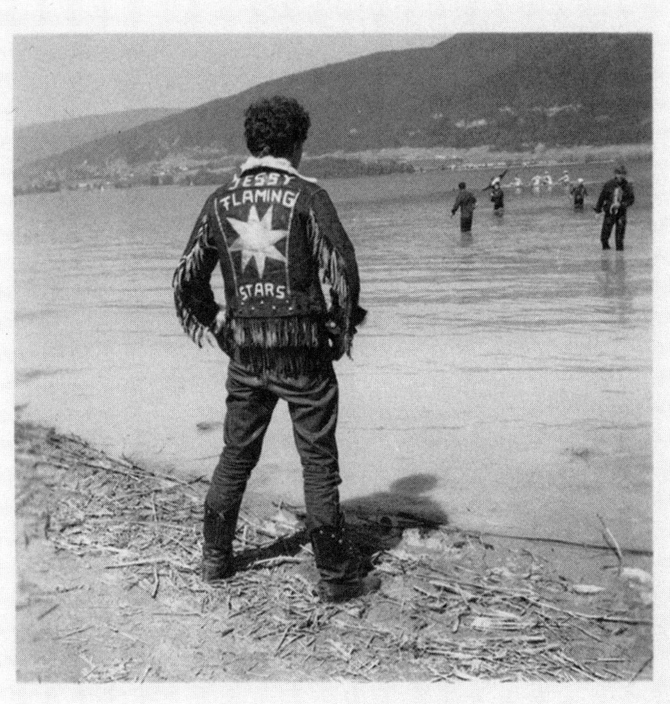
FLAMING
STARS

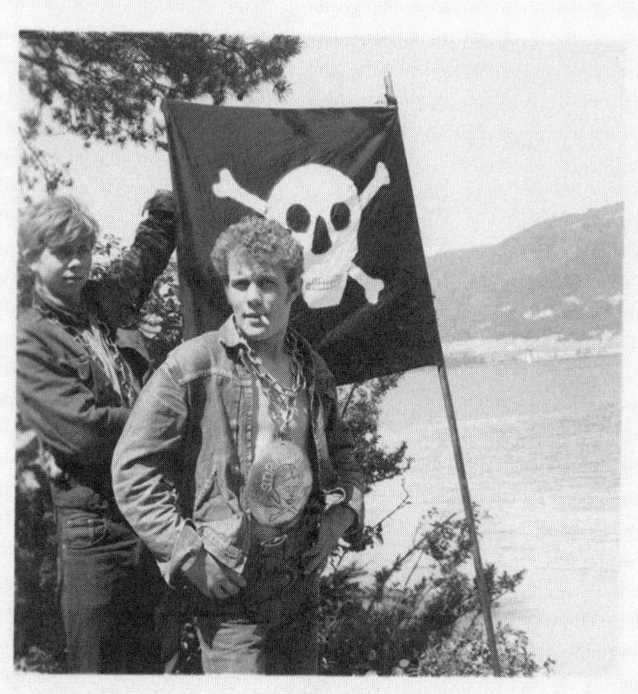

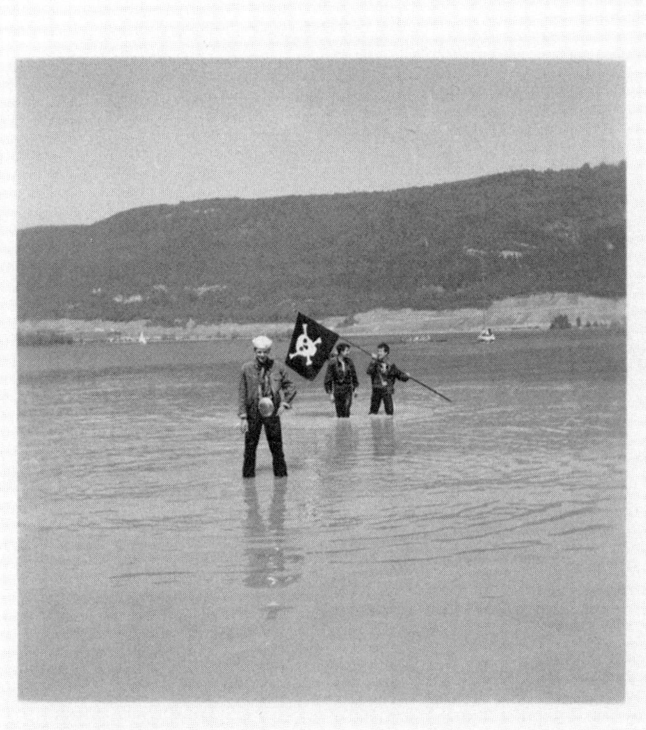

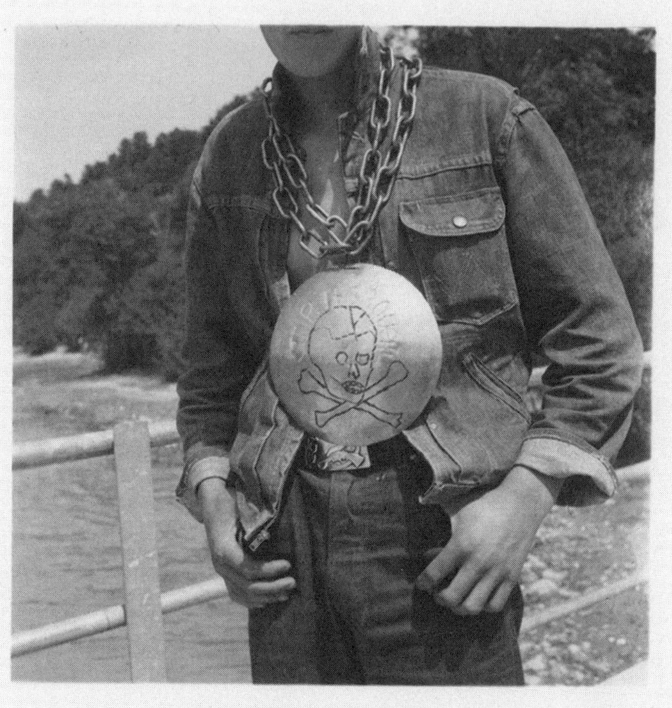

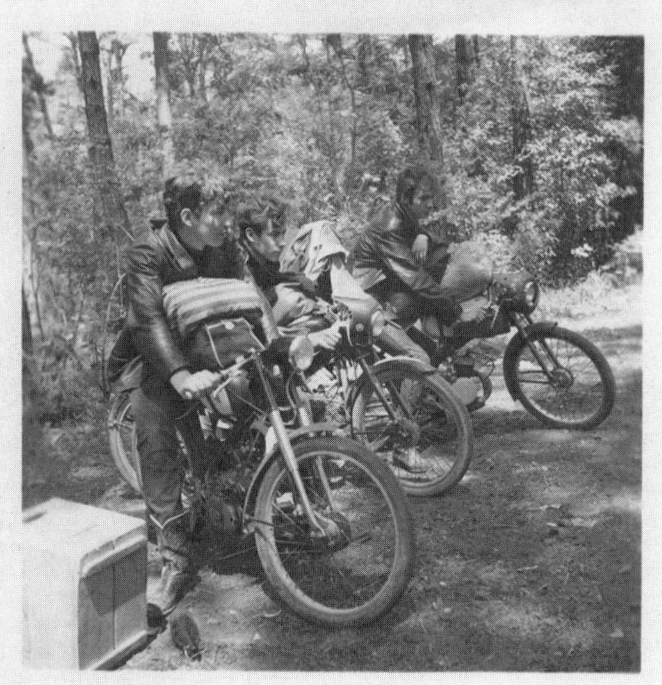

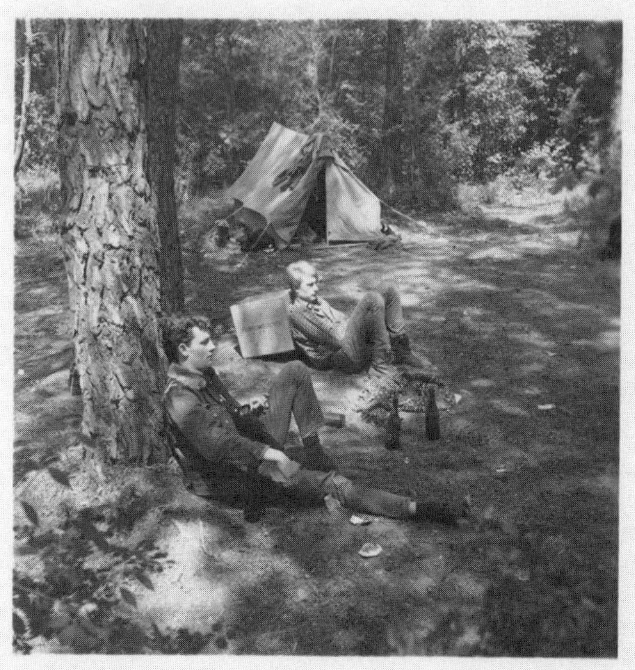

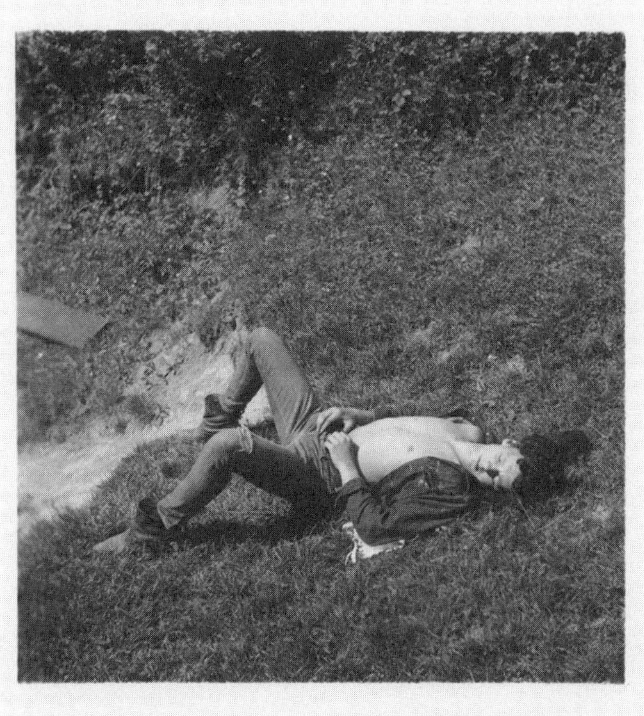

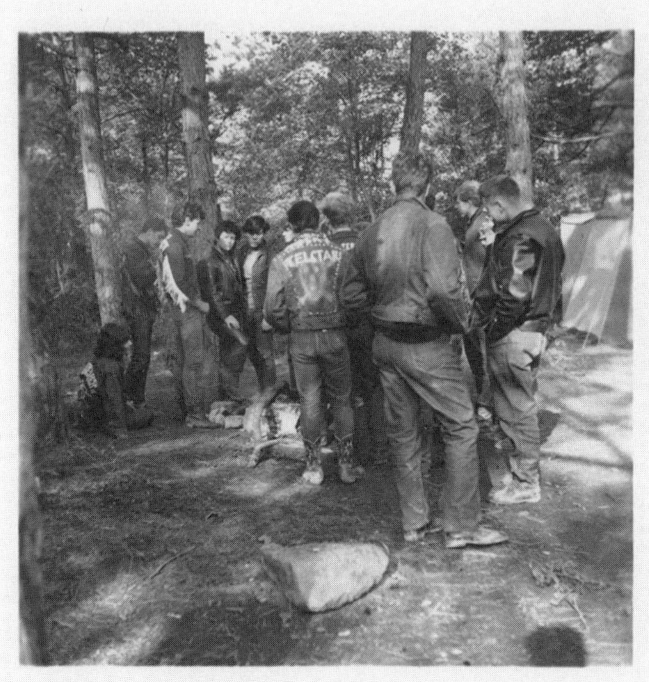

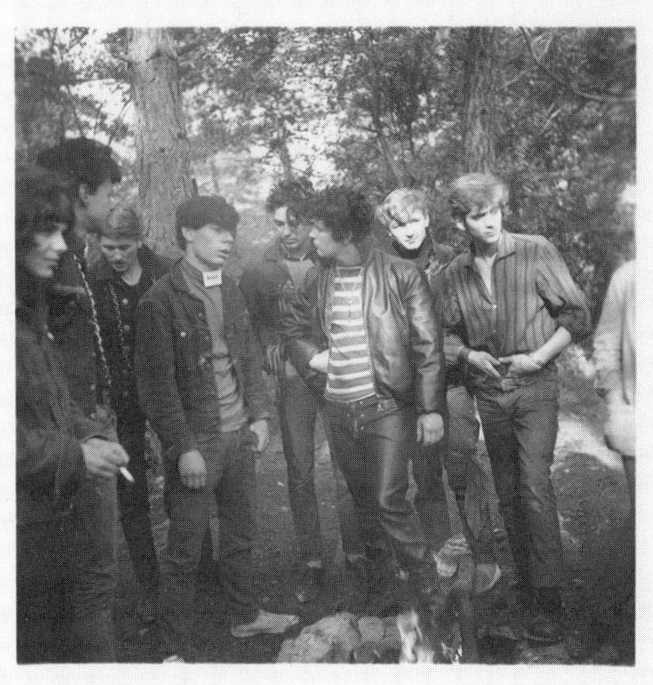

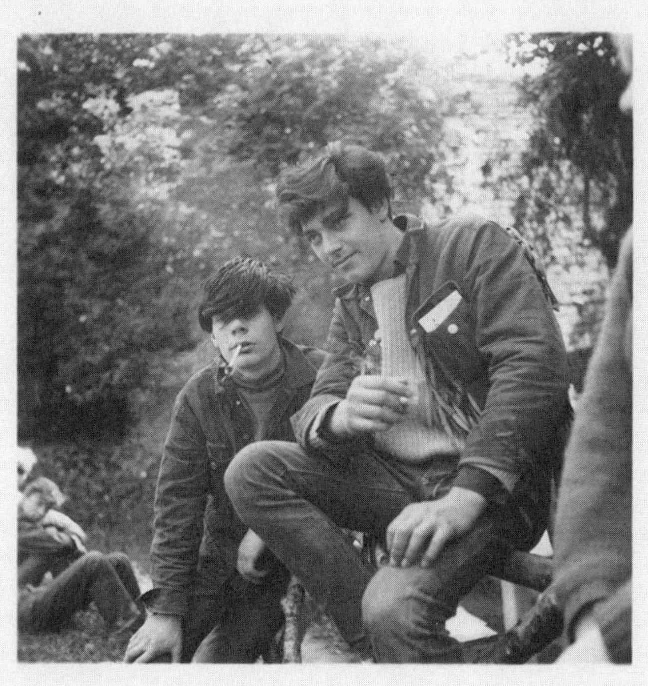

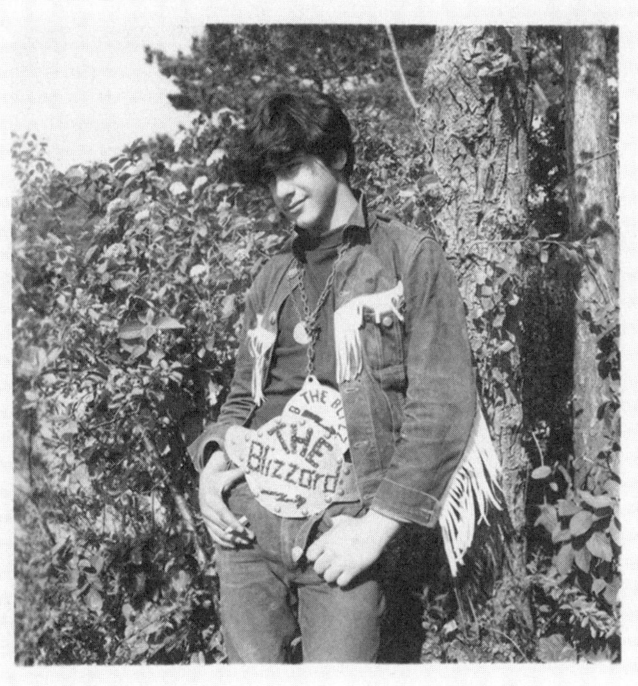
THE
Blizzard

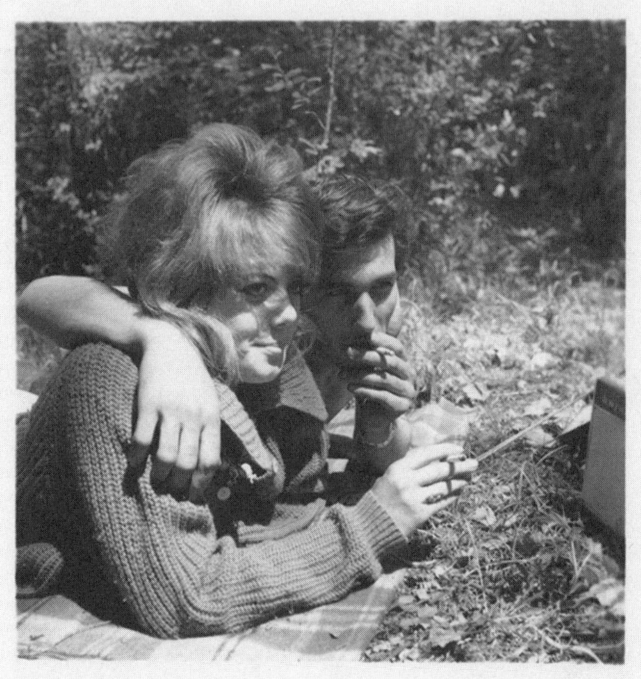

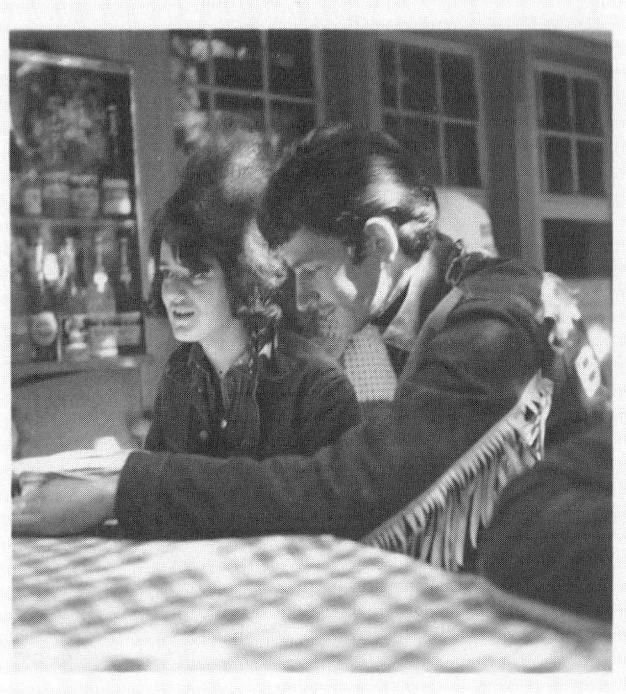

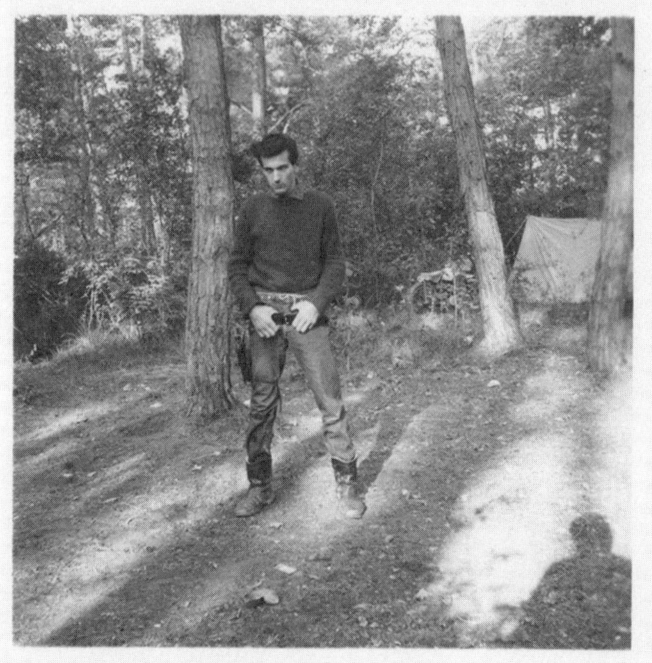

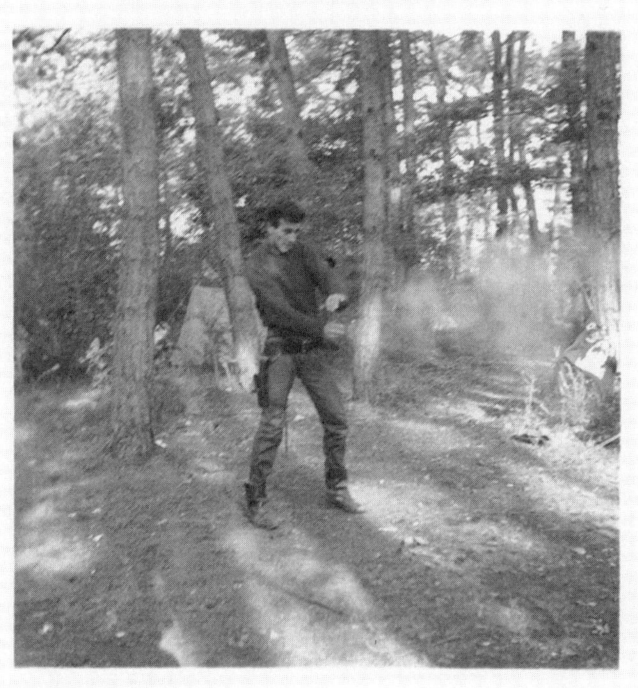

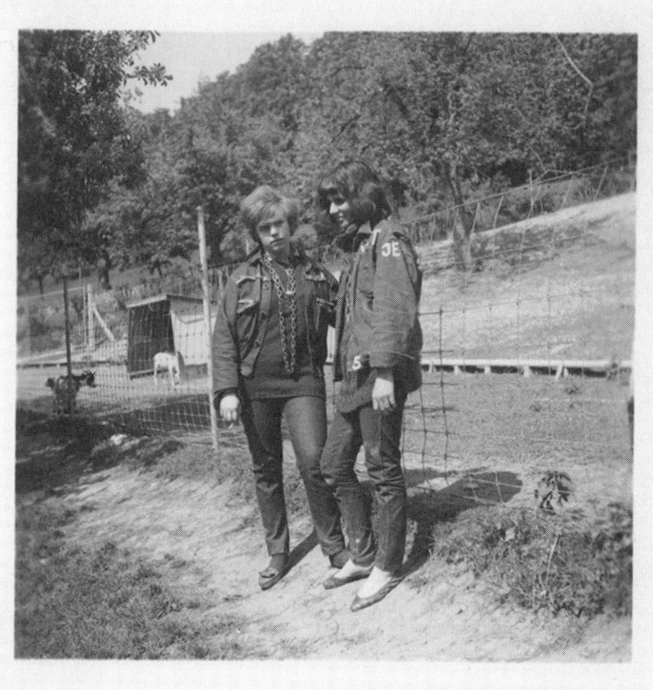

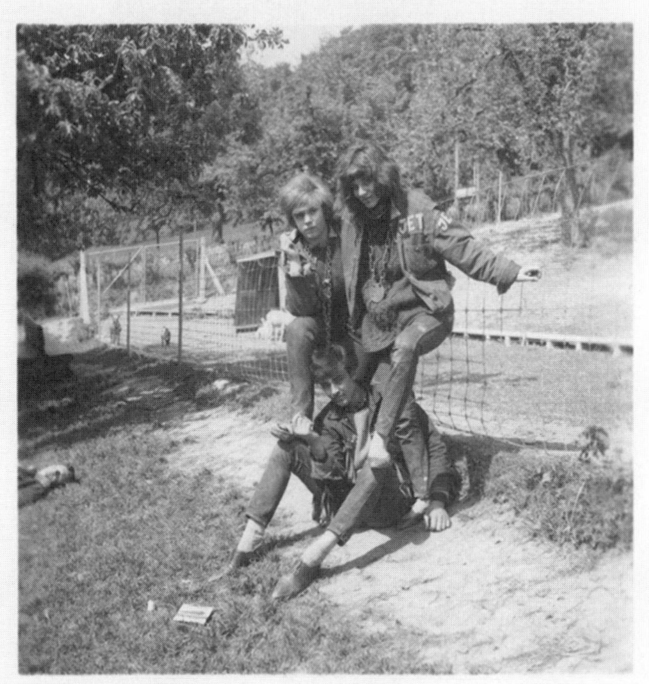

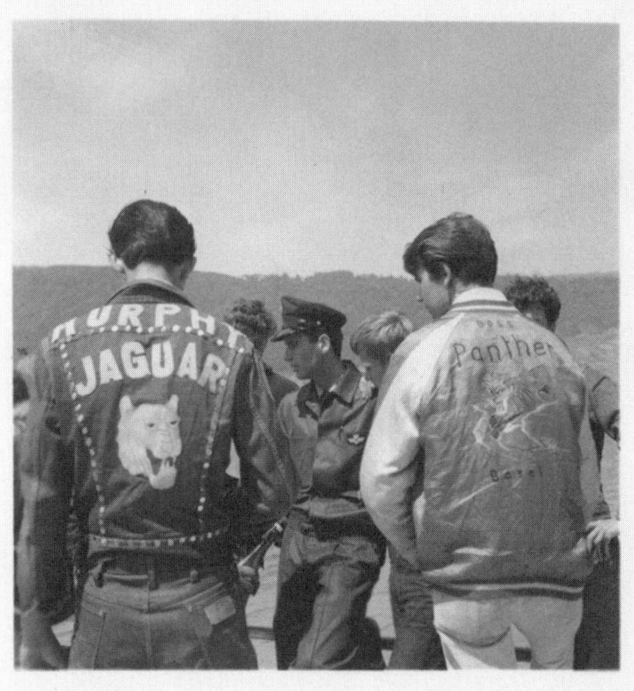
JAGUAR
Panther

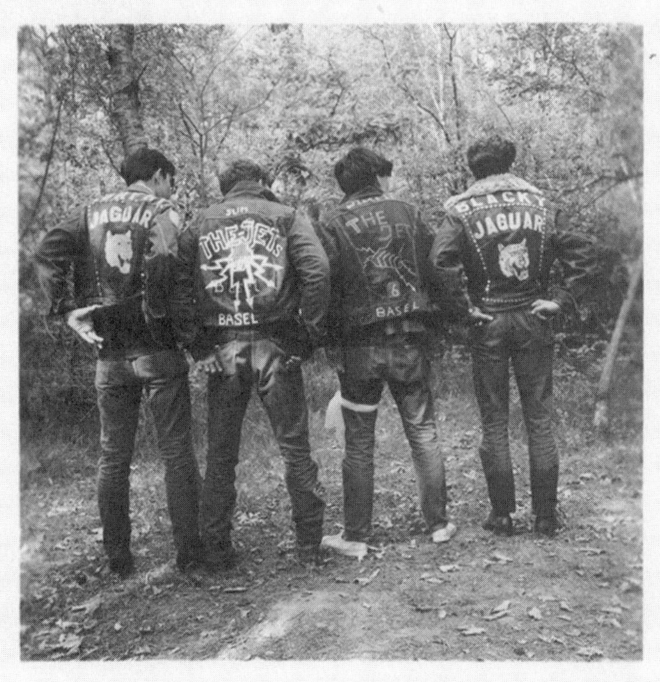
JAGUAR
THE JETS
BASEL
THE
BASEL
BLACKY
JAGUAR

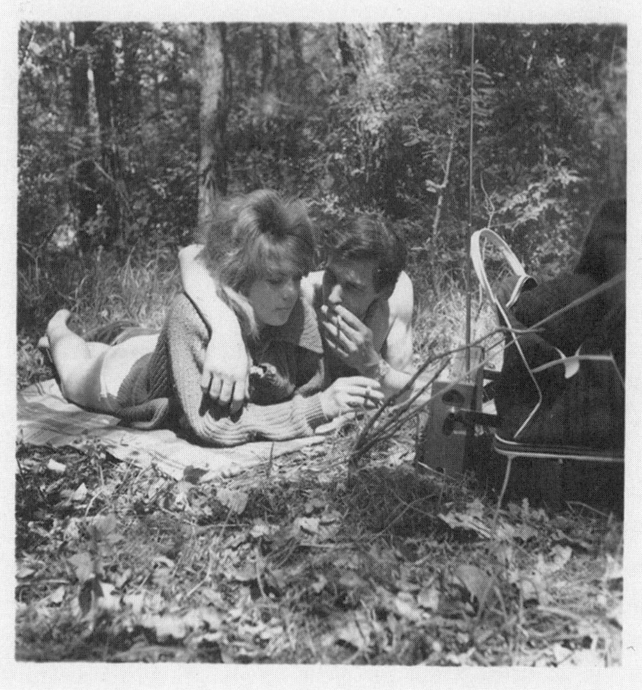

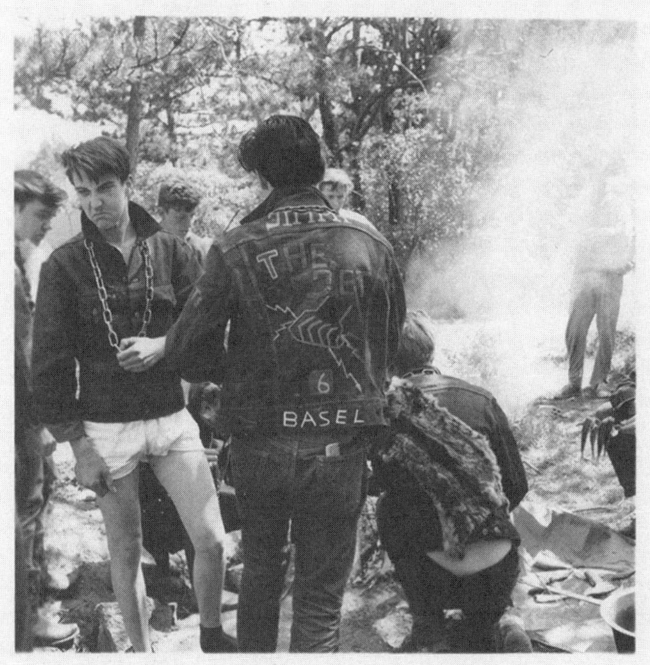
THE
6
BASEL

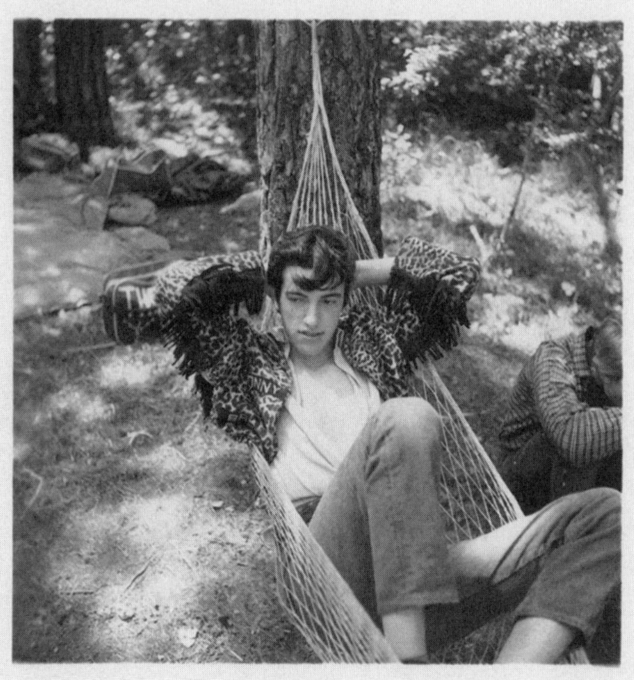

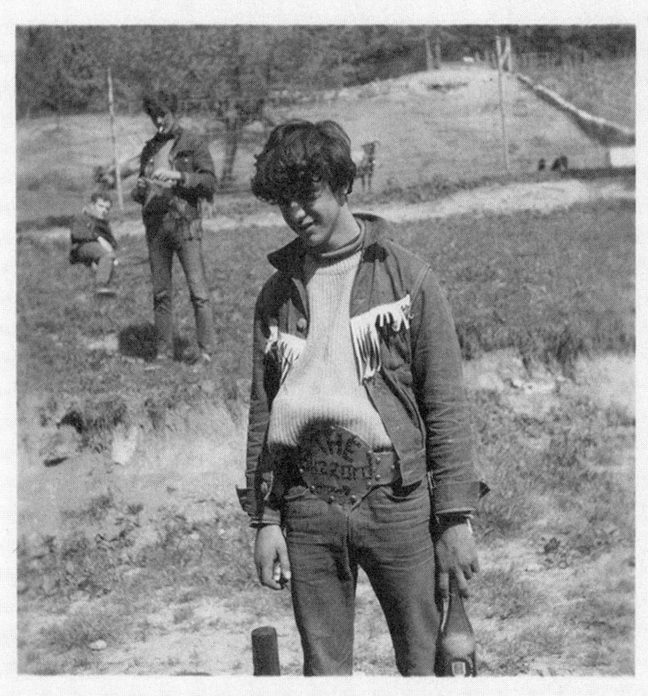

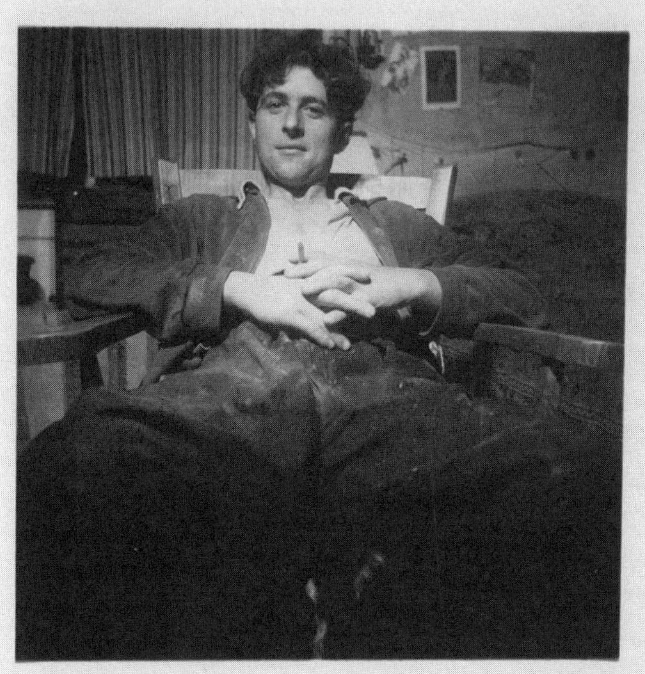

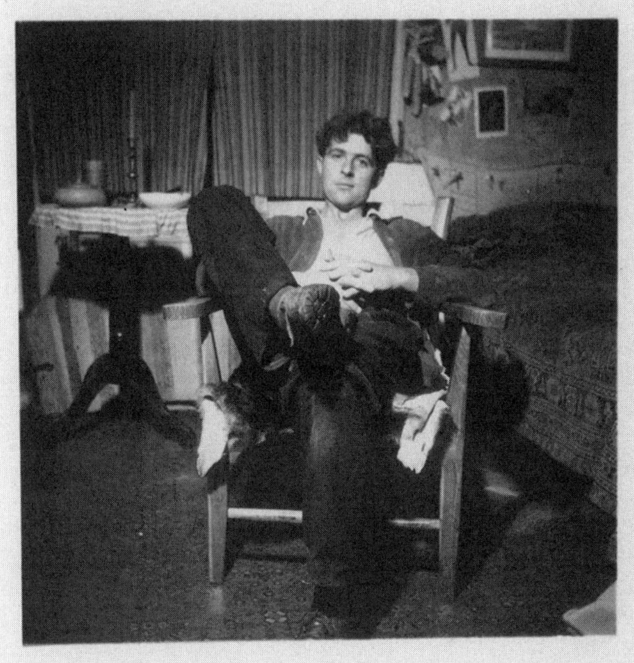

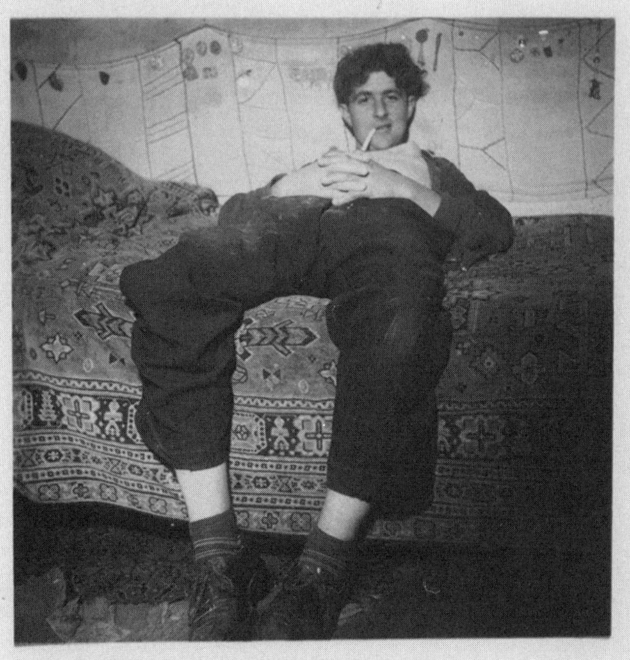

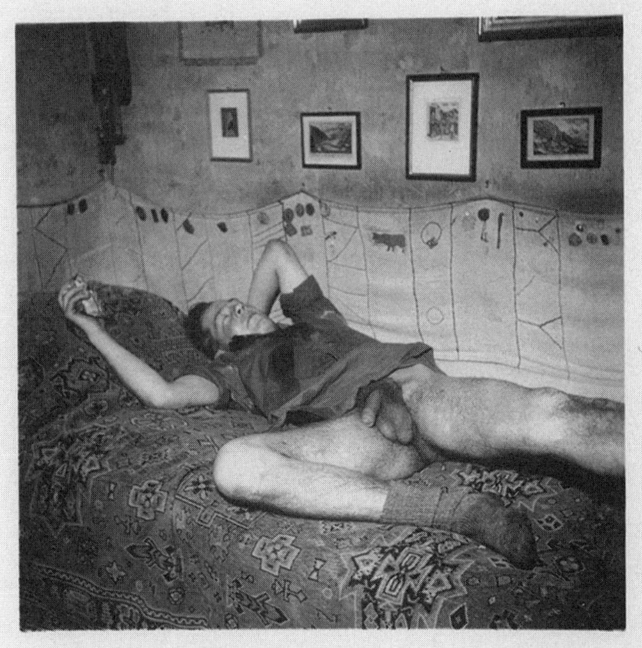

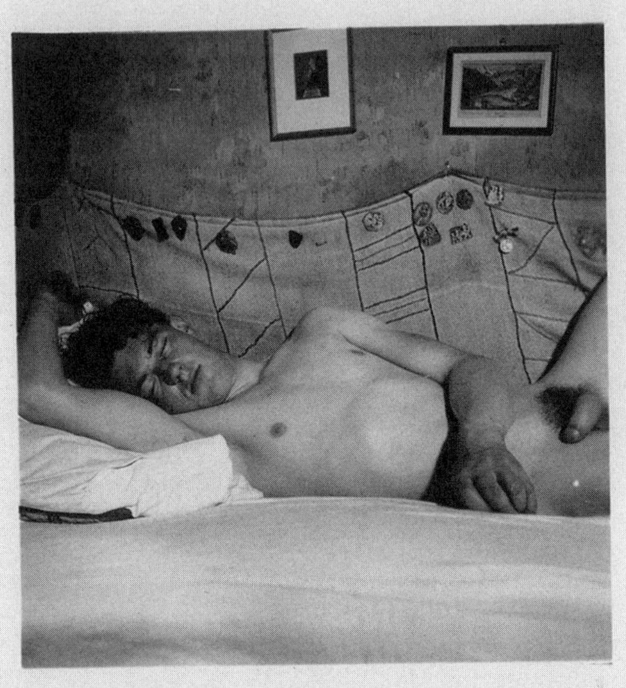

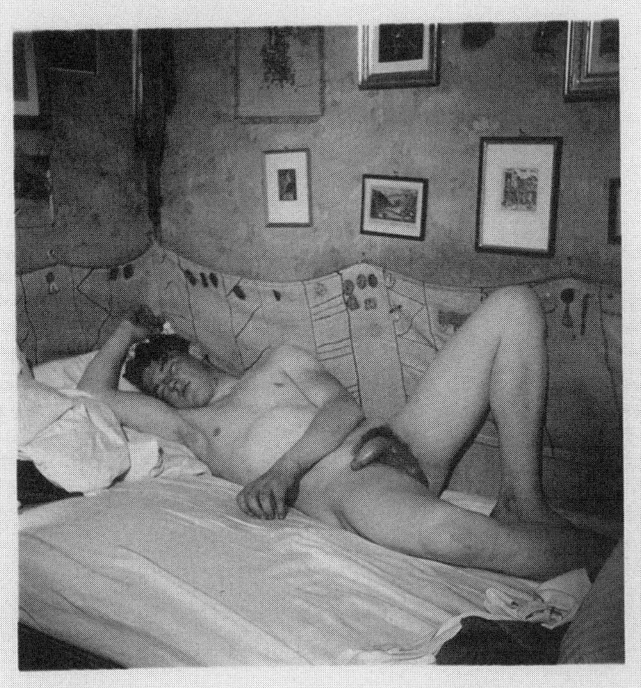

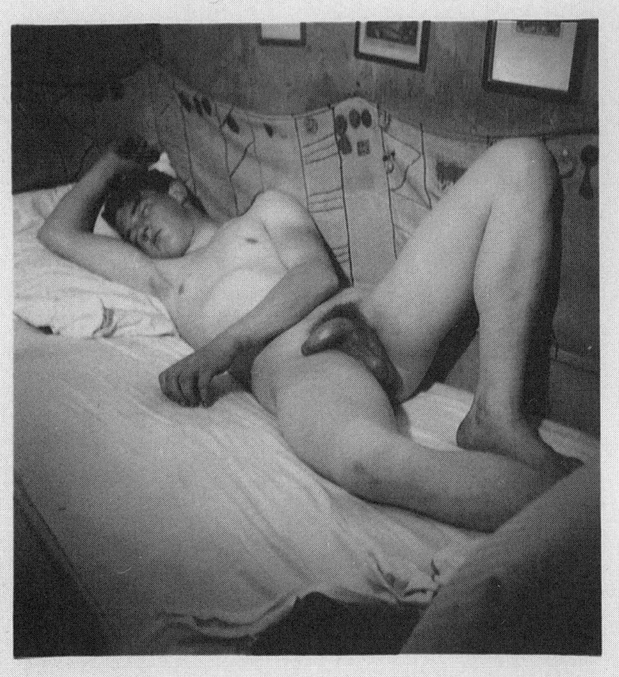

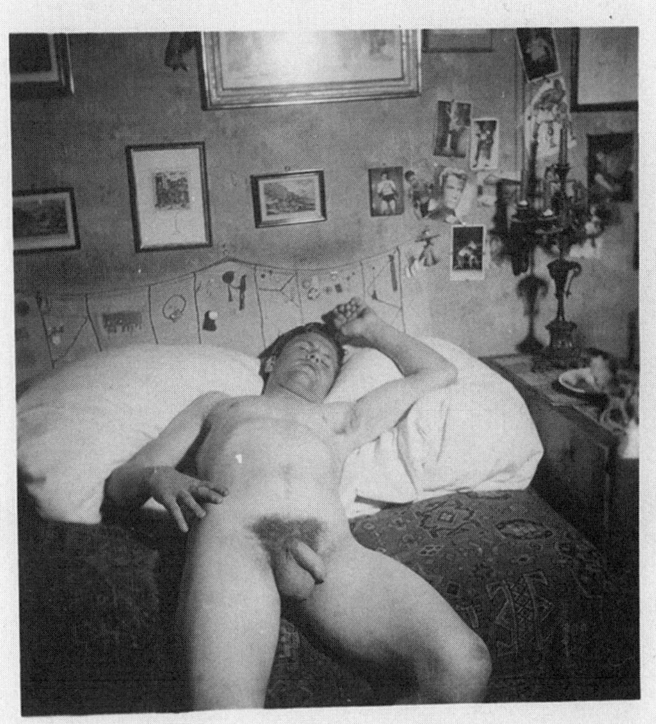

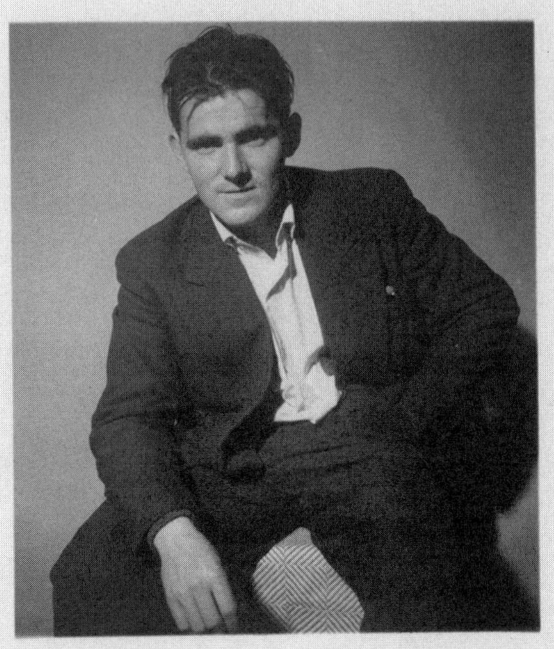

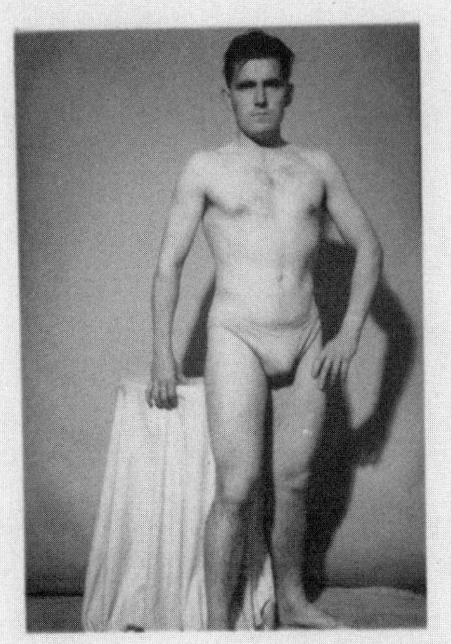

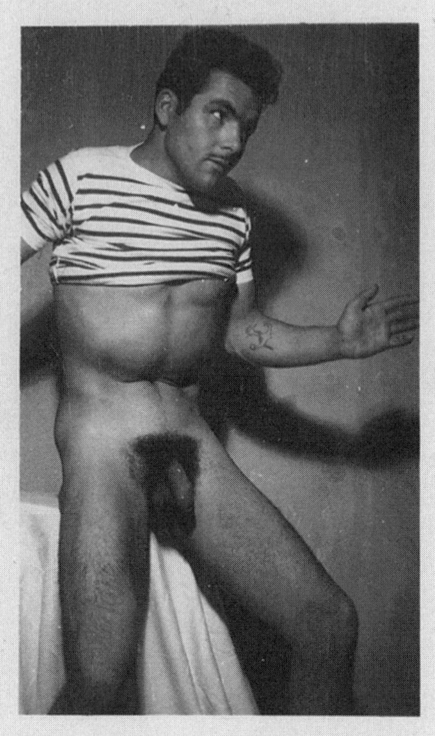

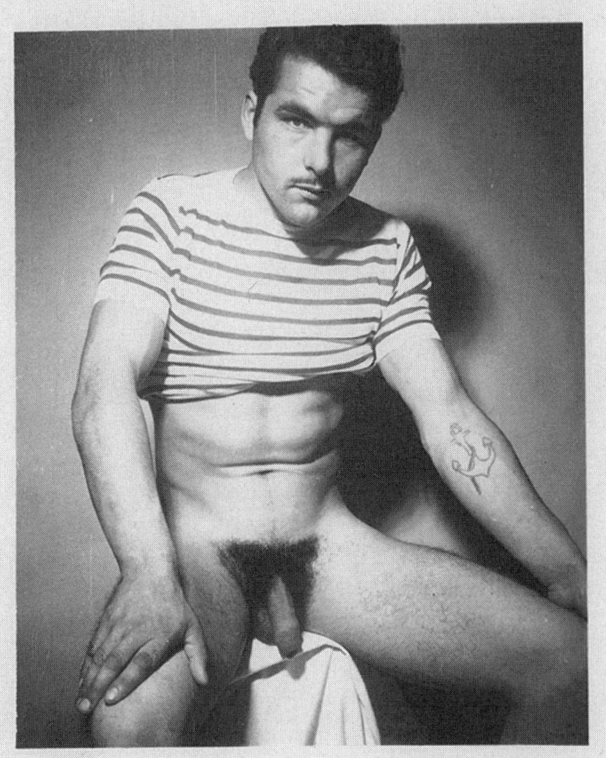

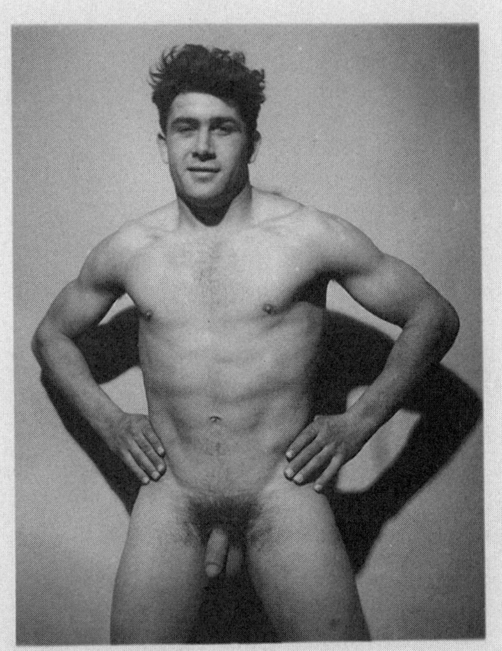

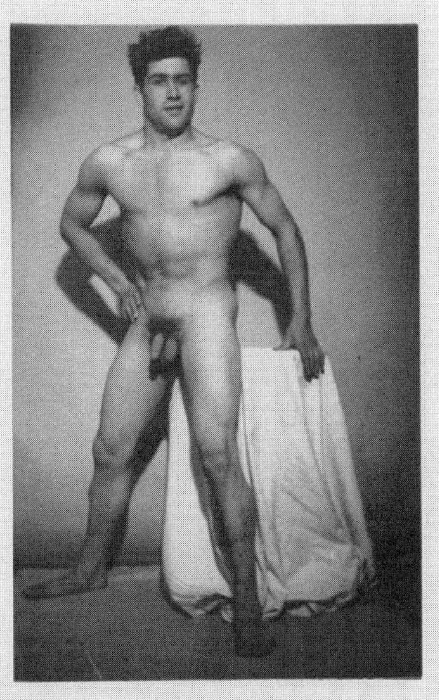

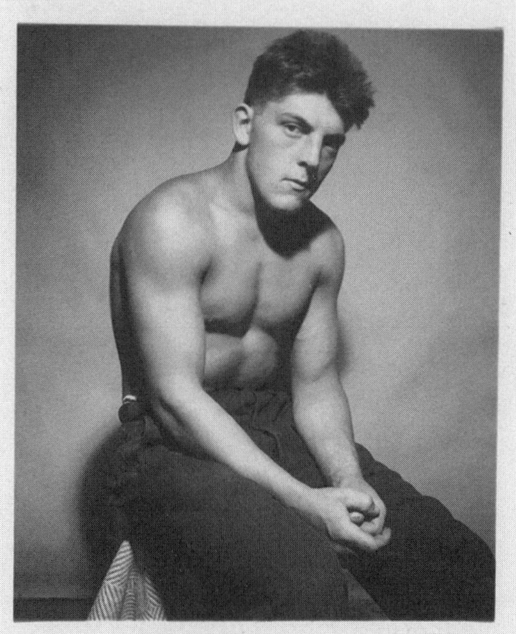

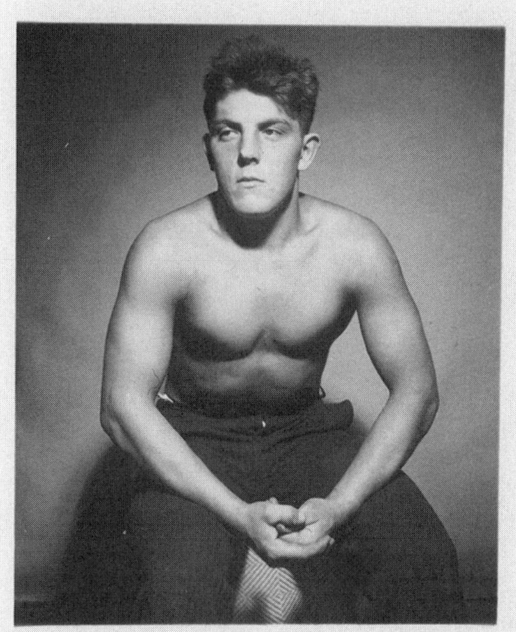

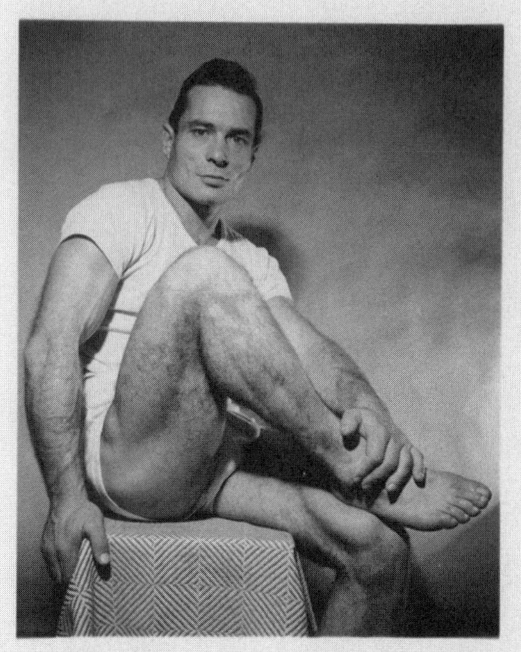

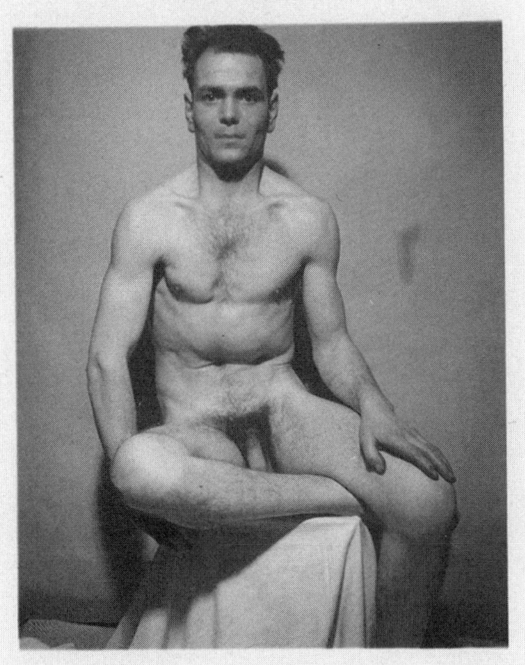

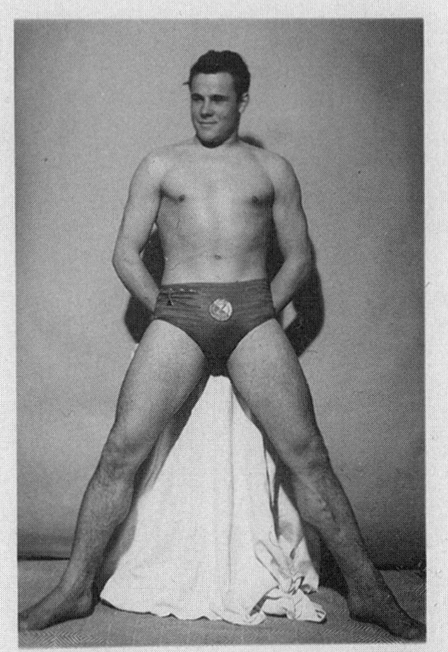

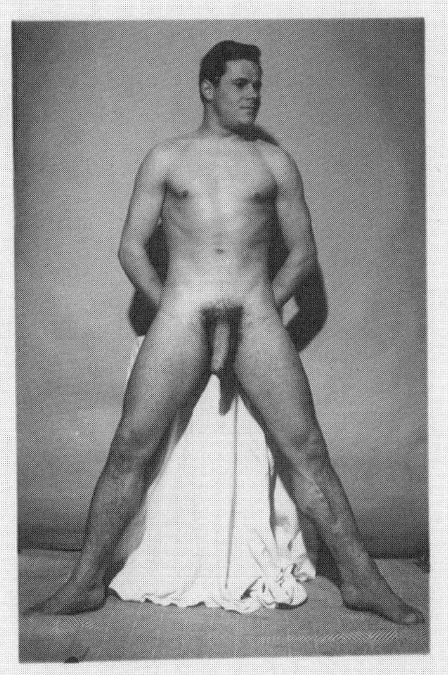

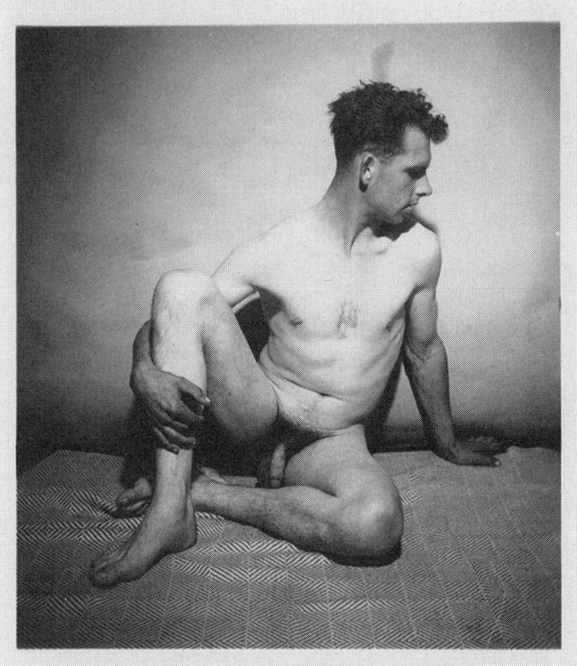

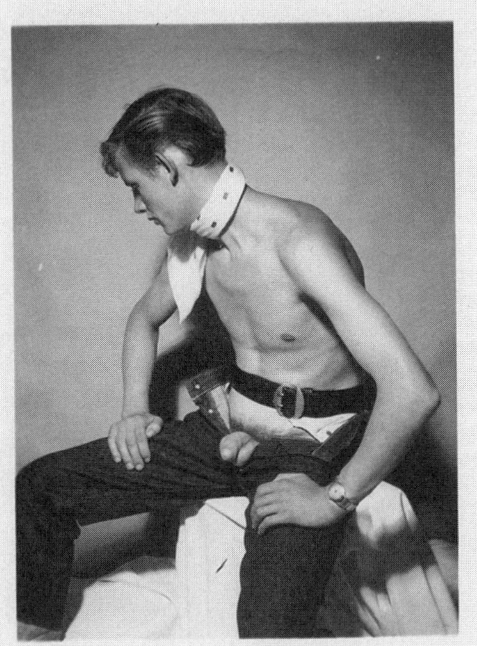

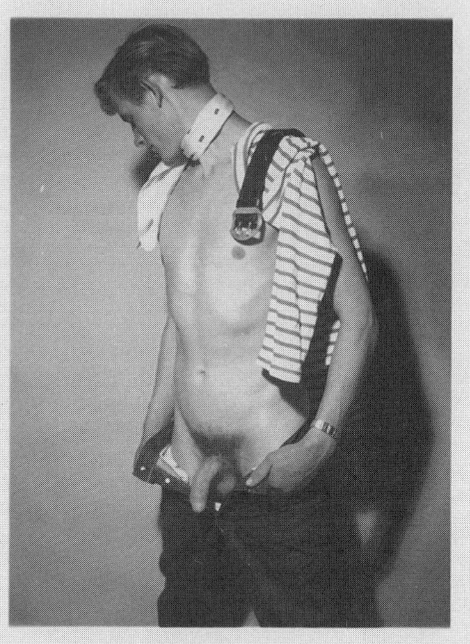

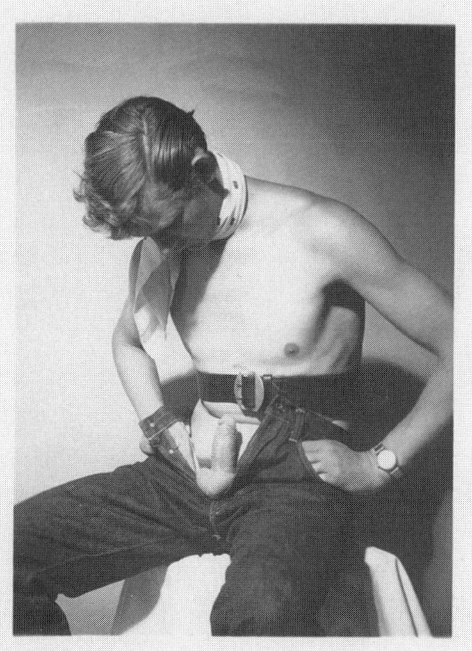

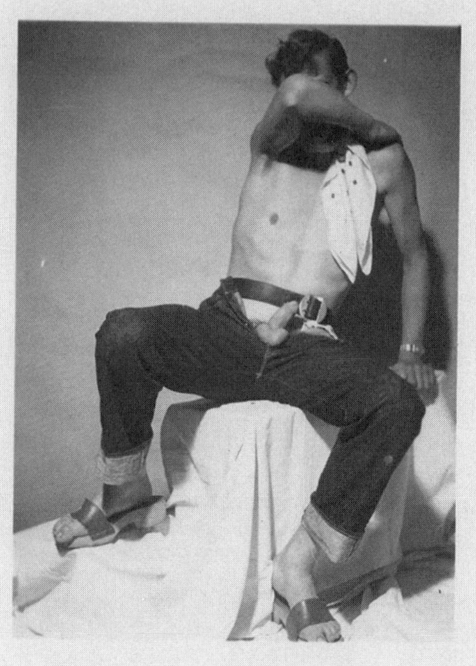

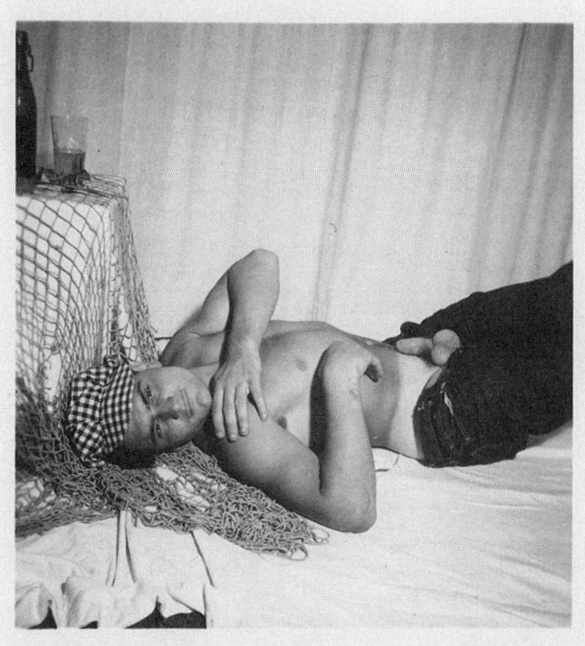

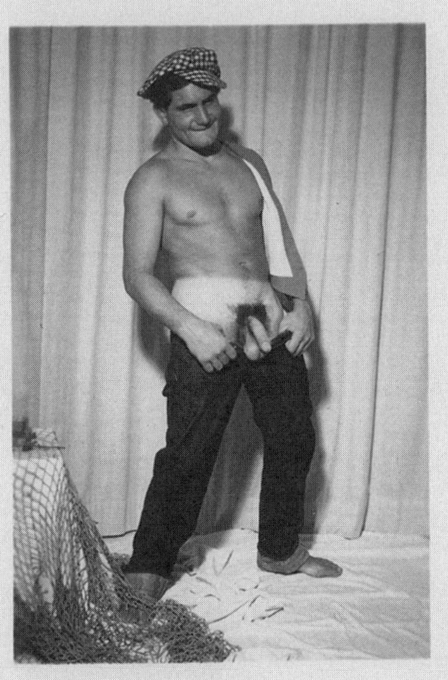

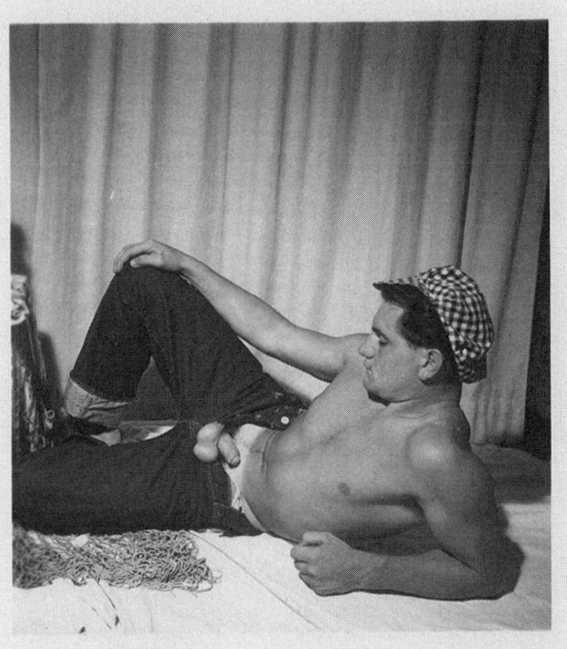

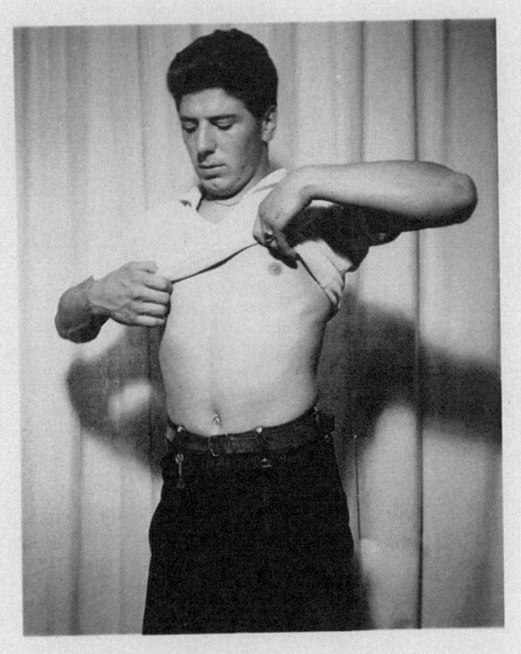

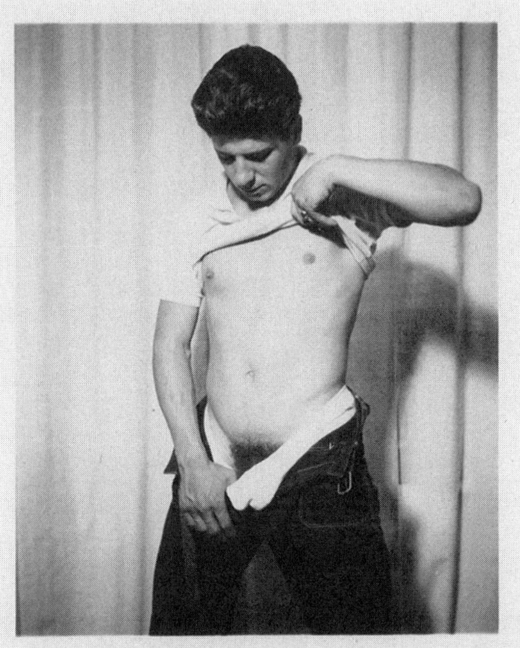

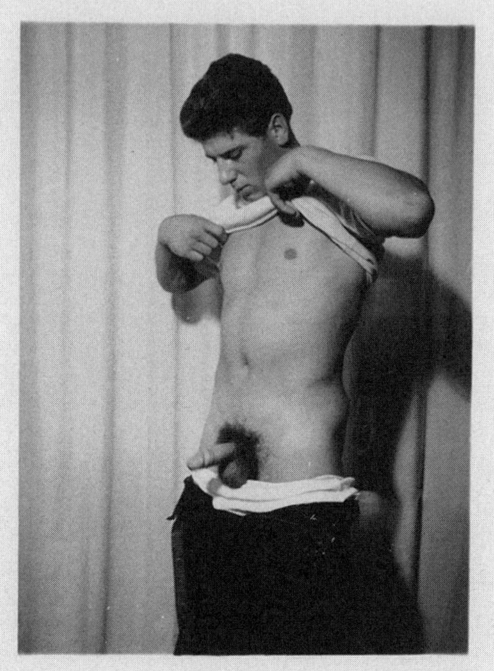

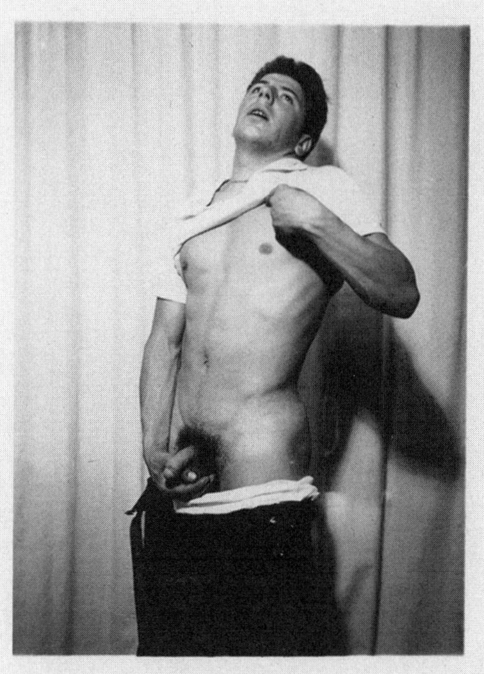

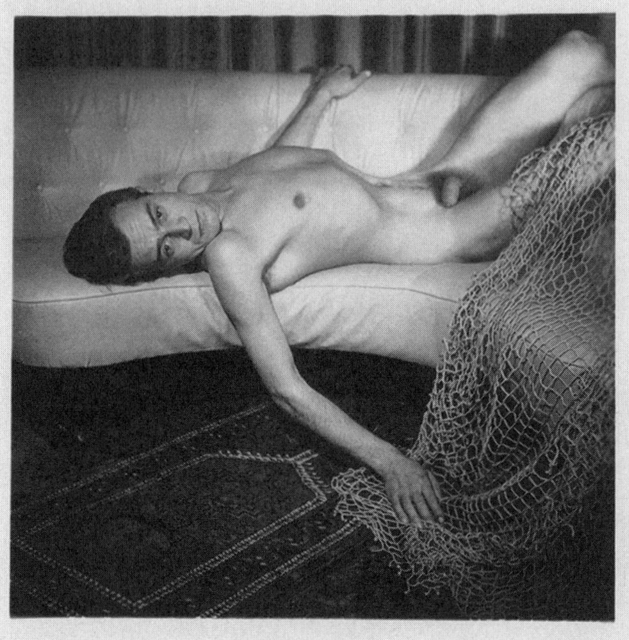

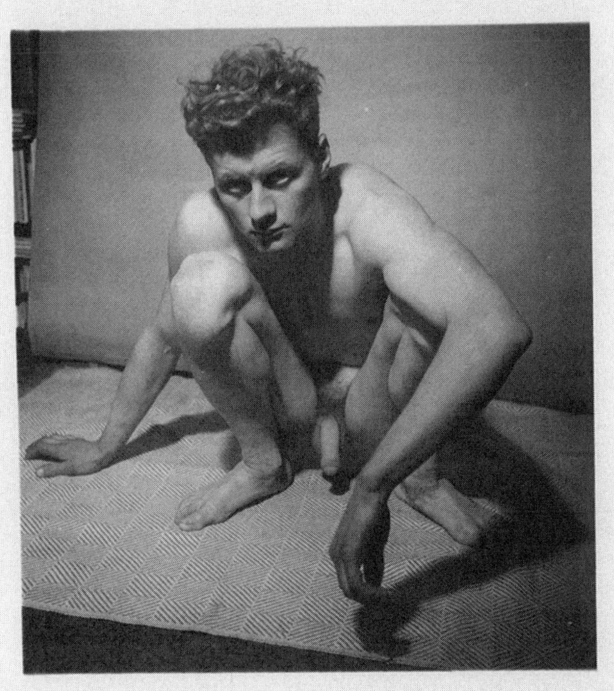

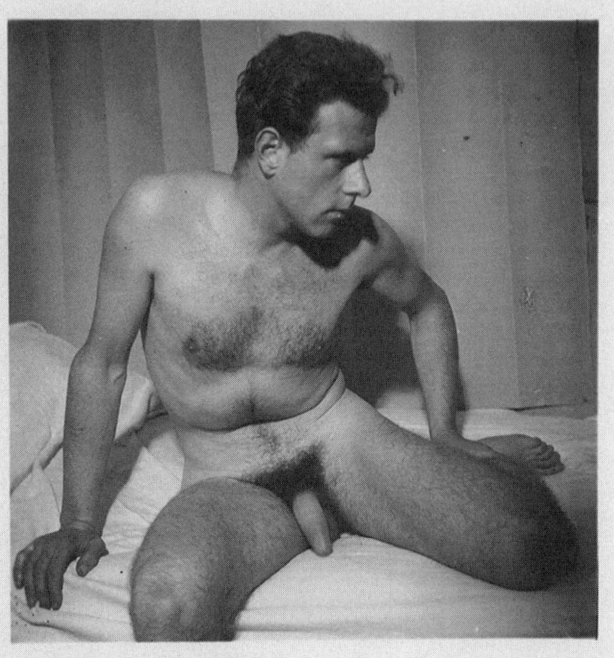

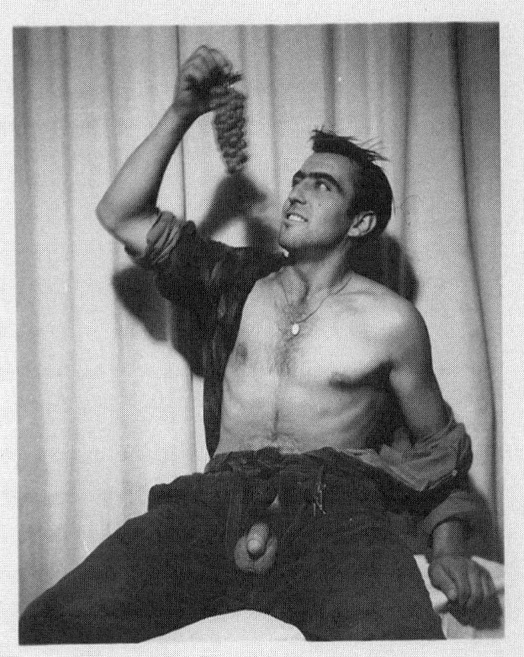

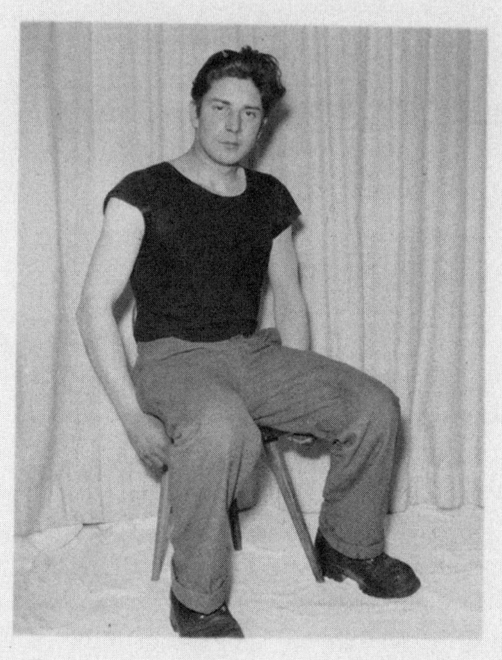

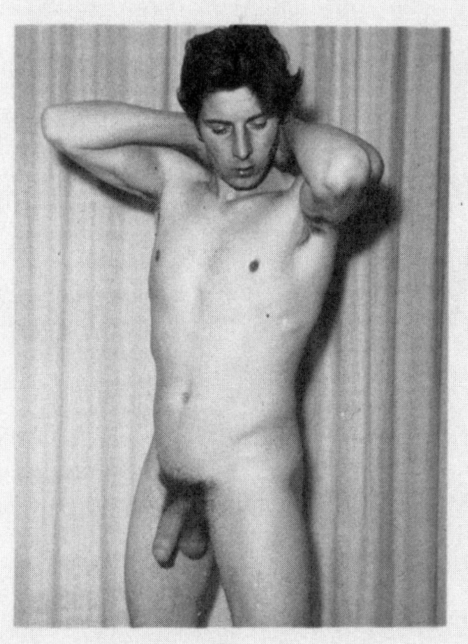

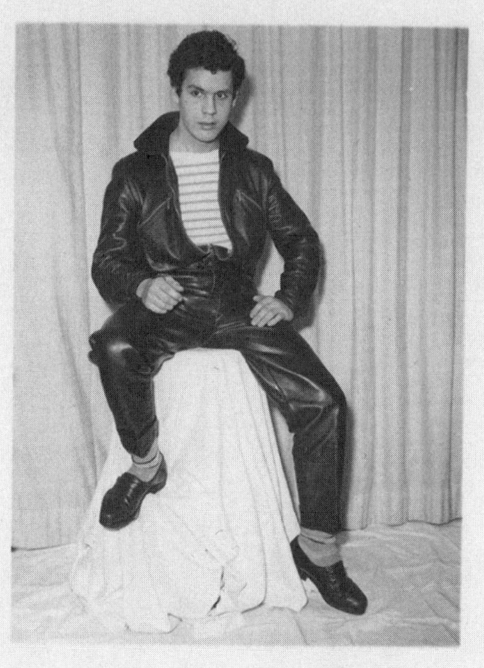

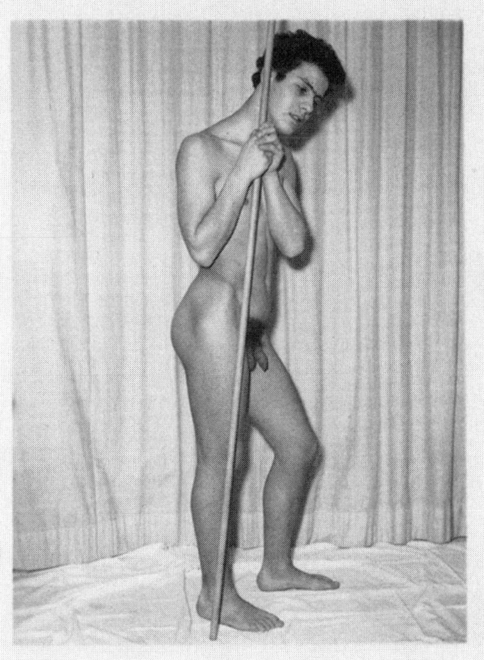

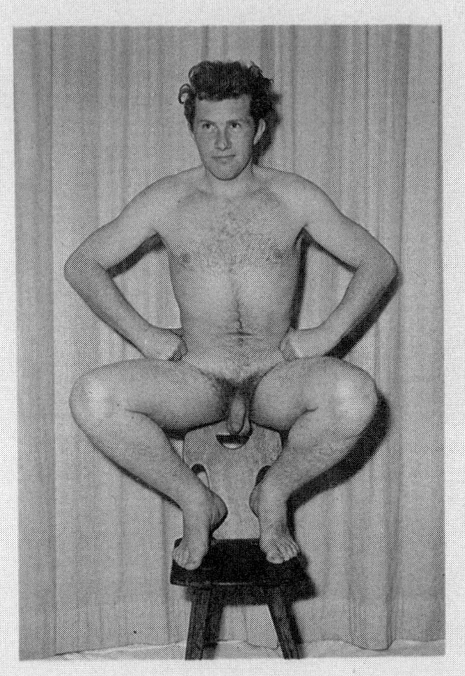

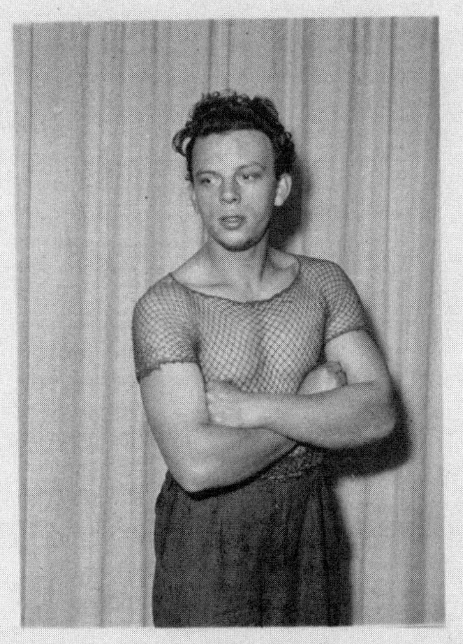

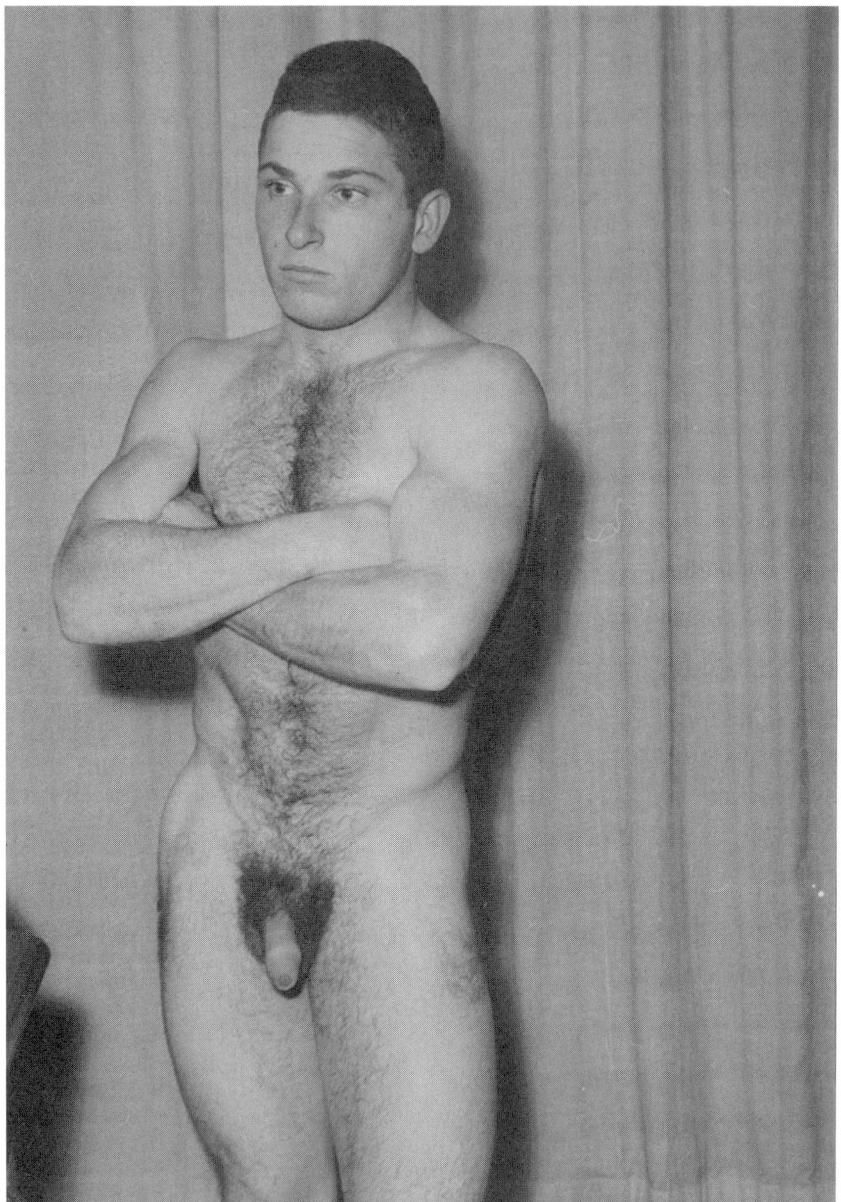

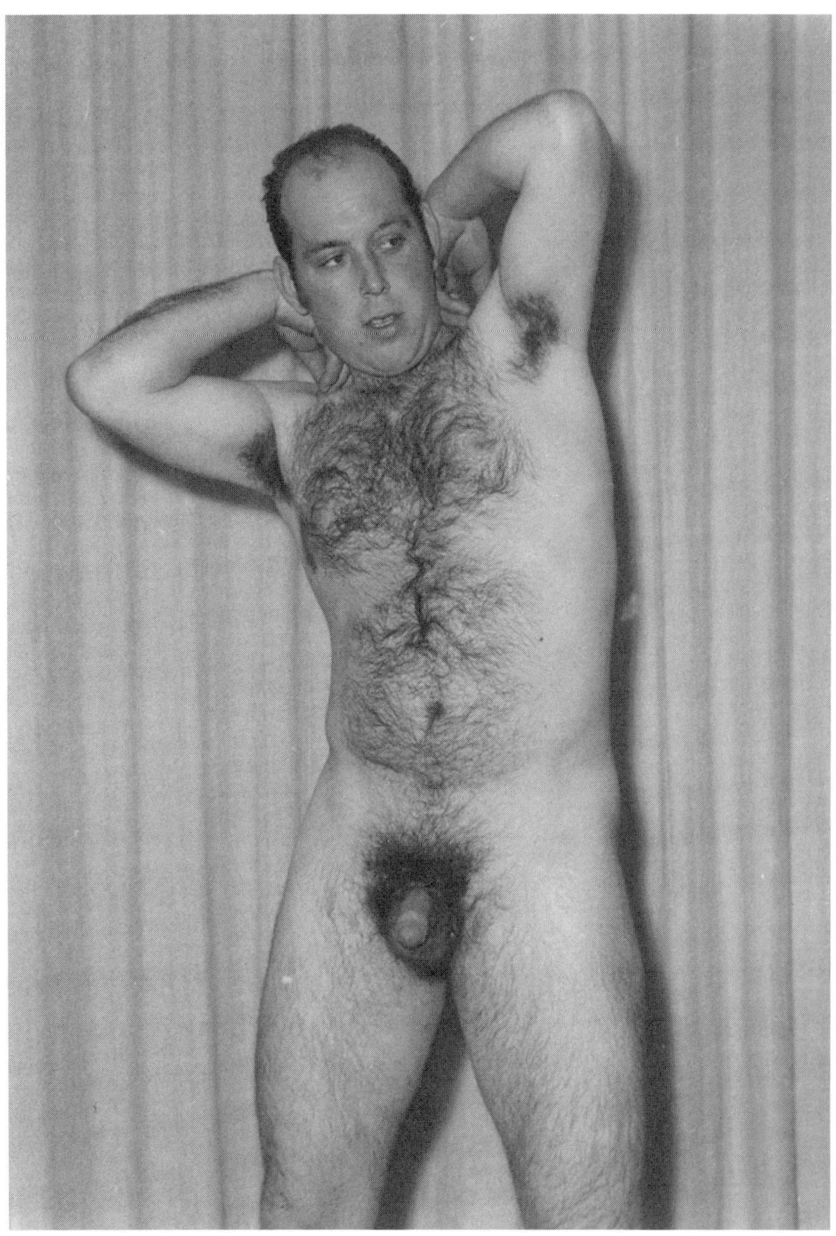

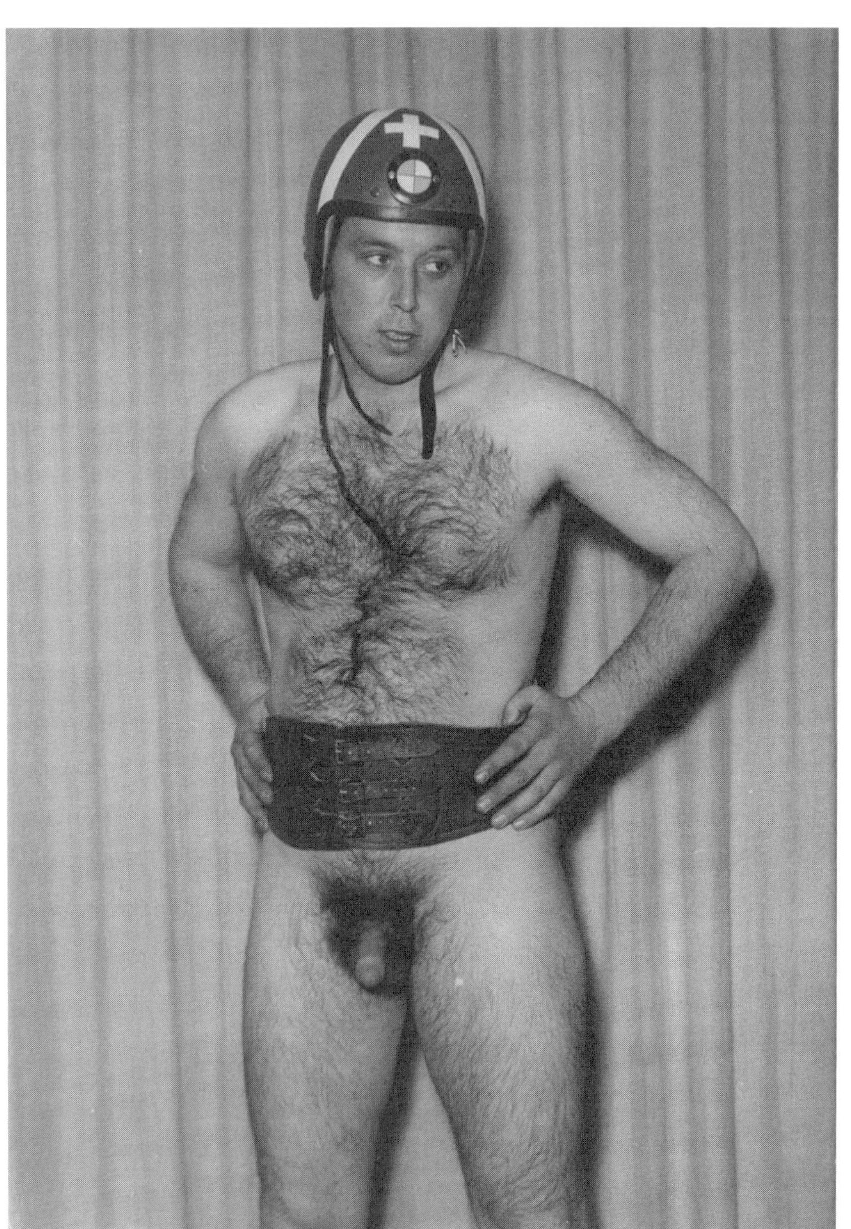

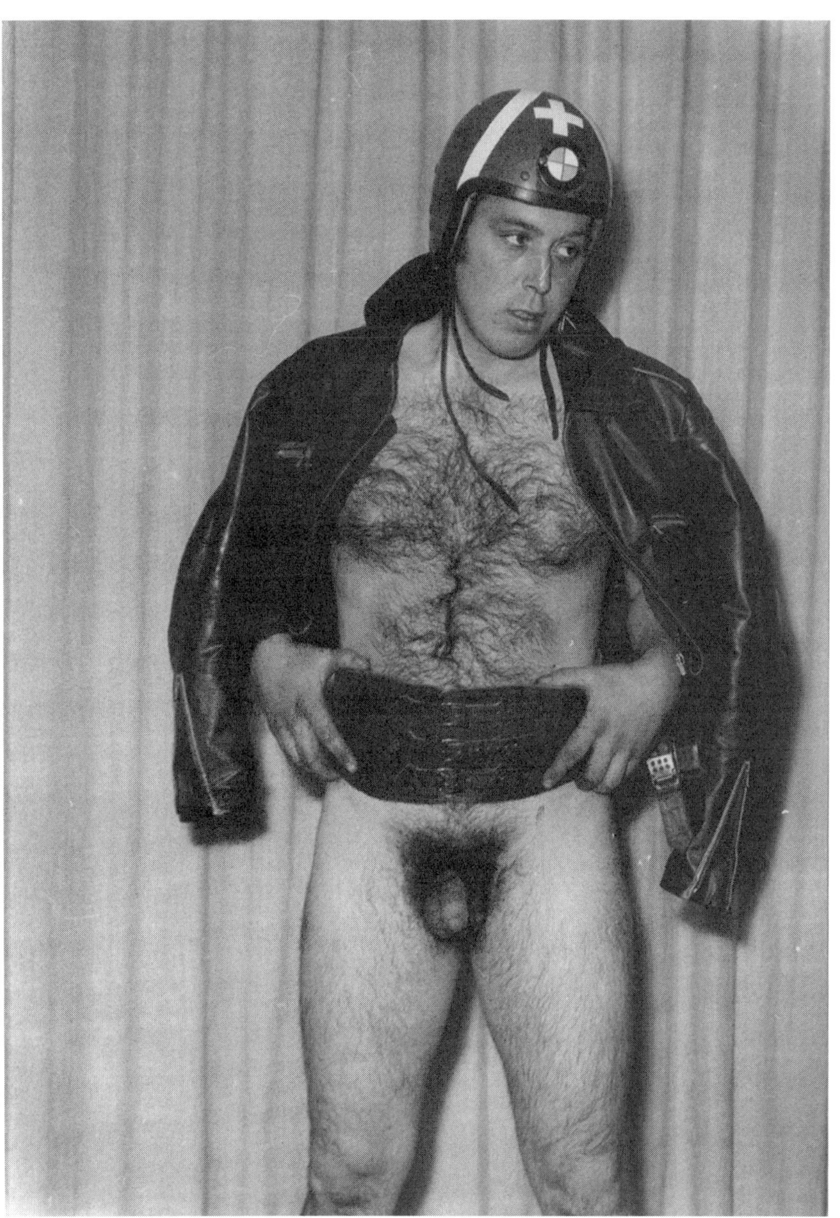

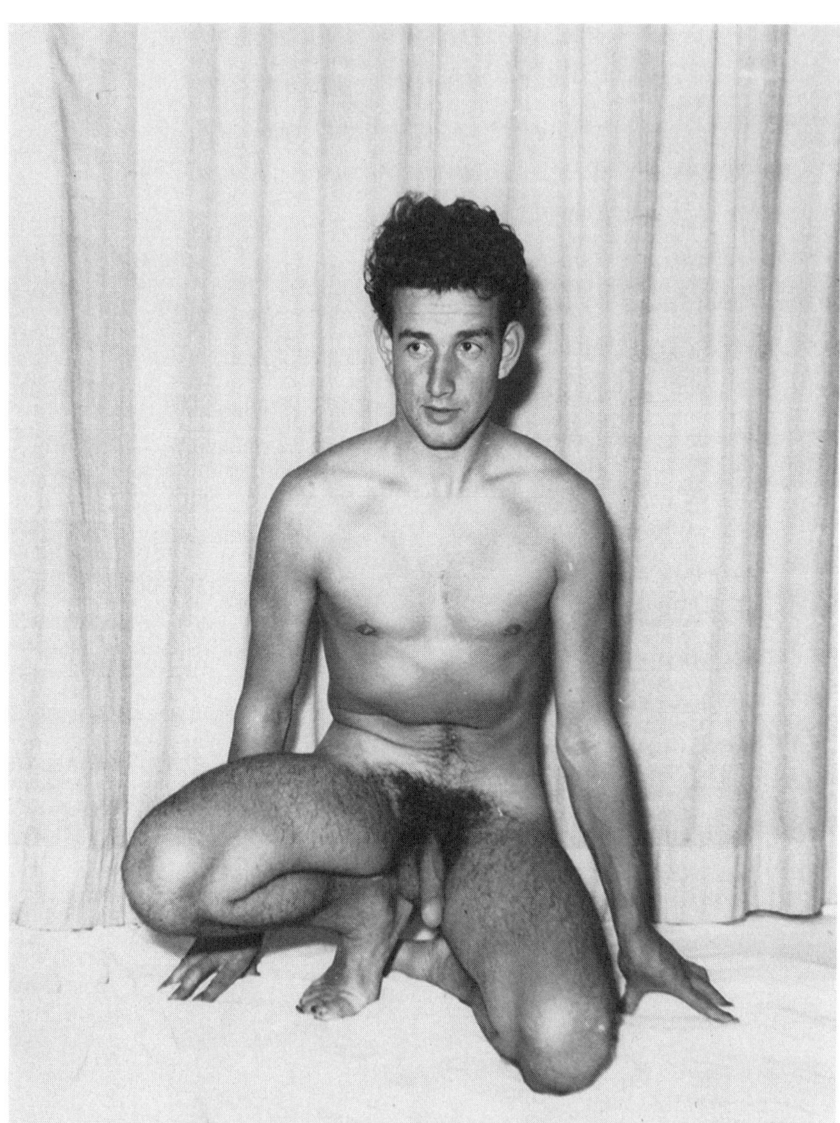

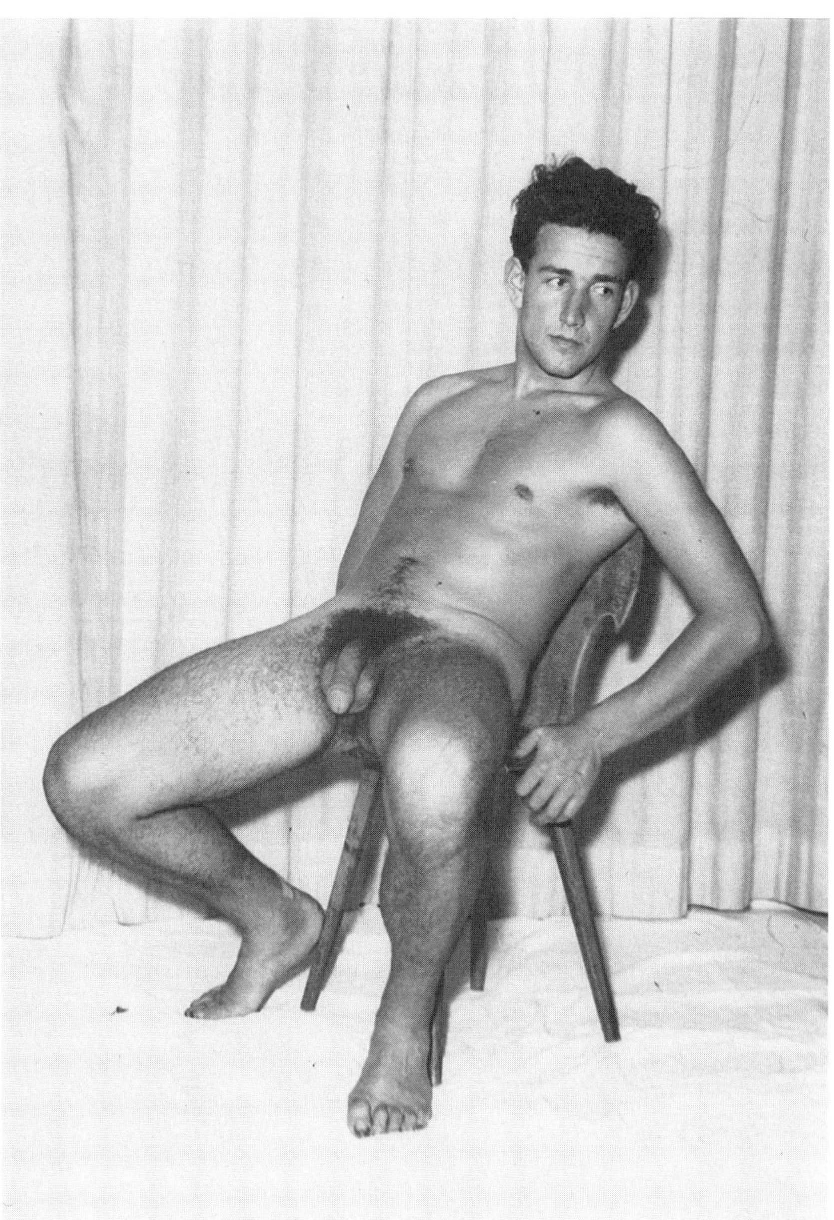

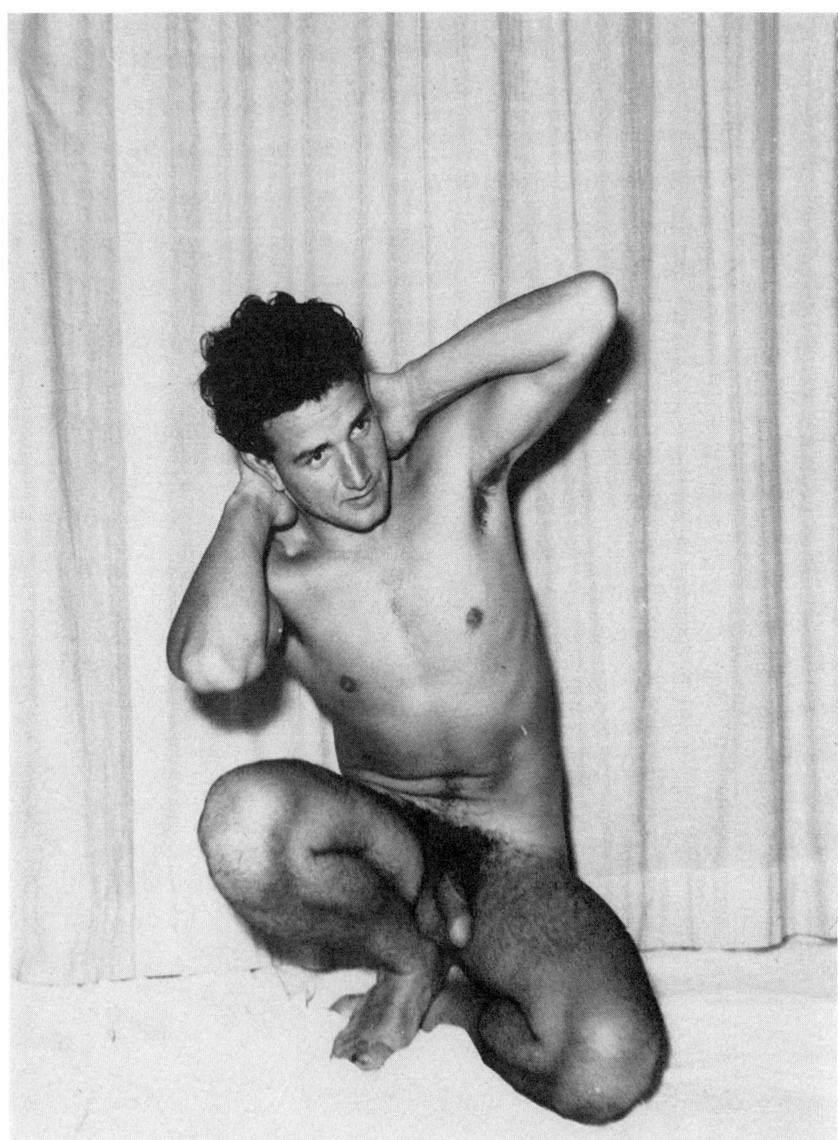

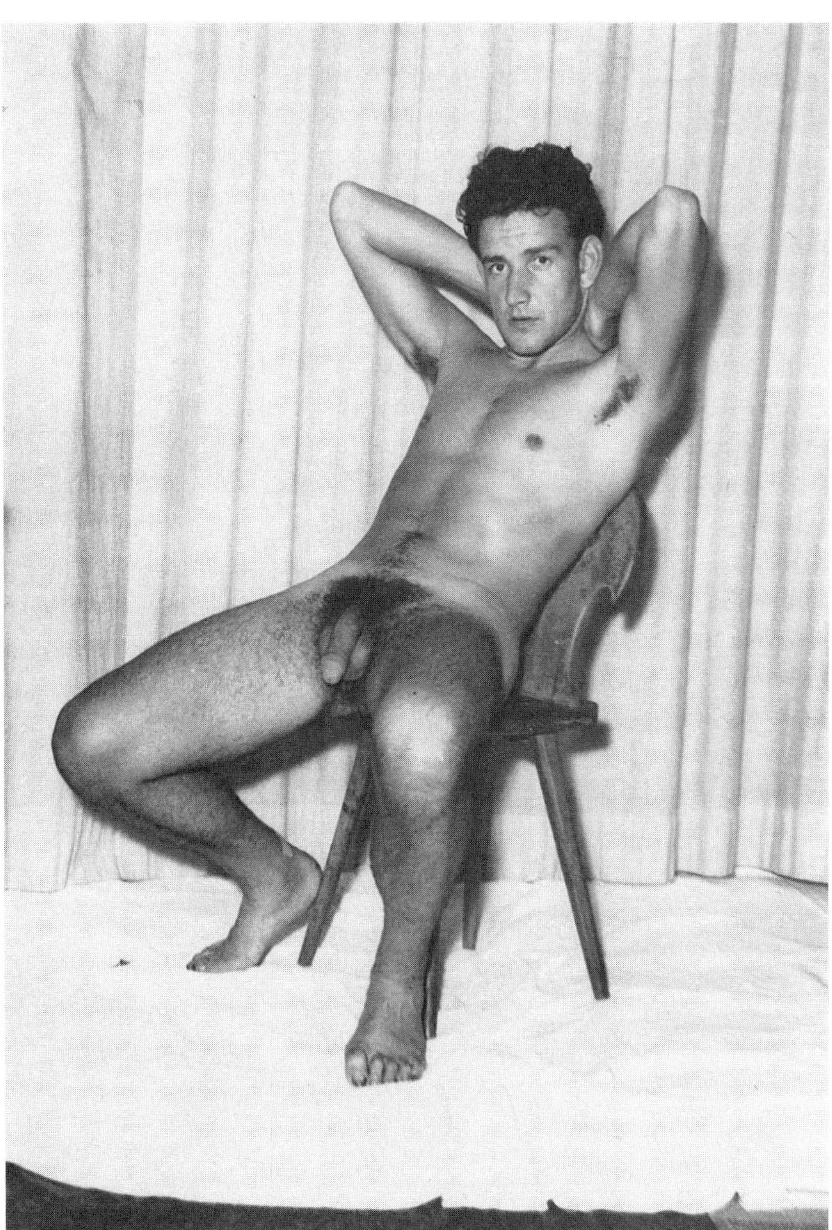

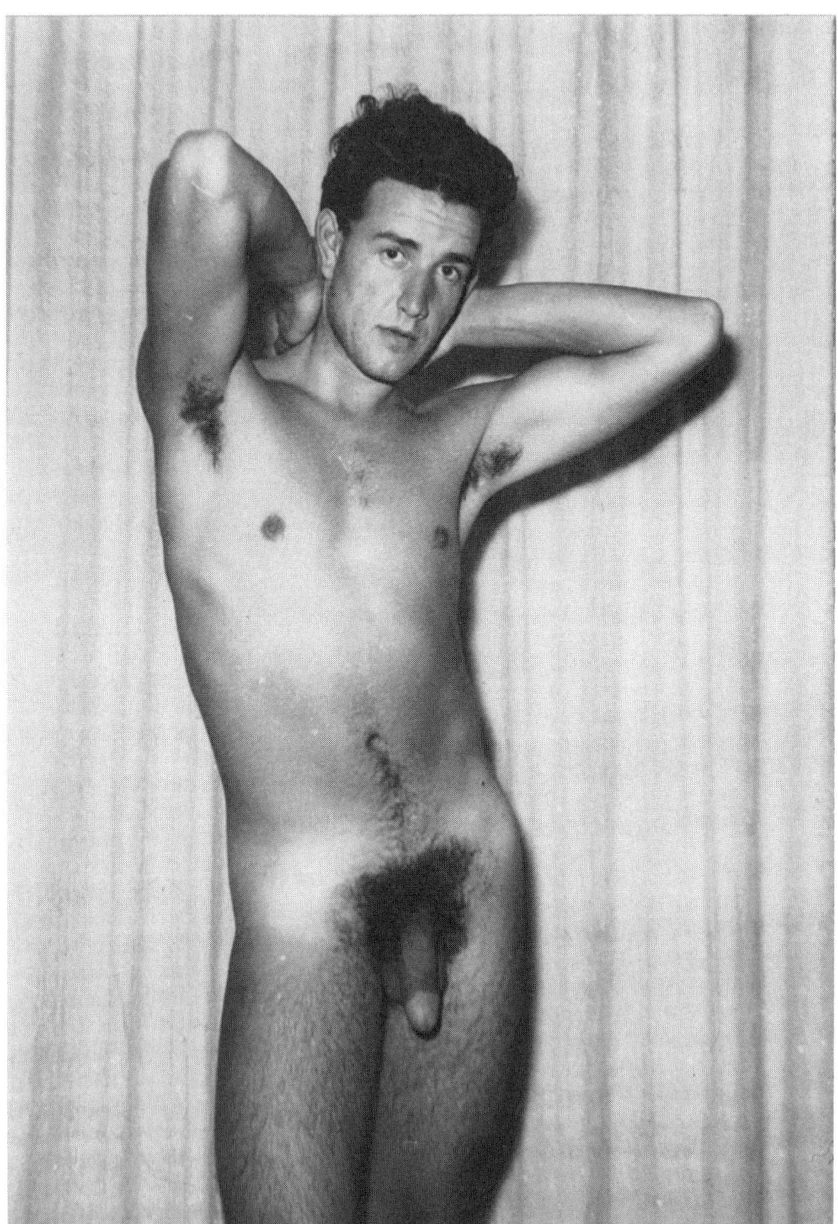

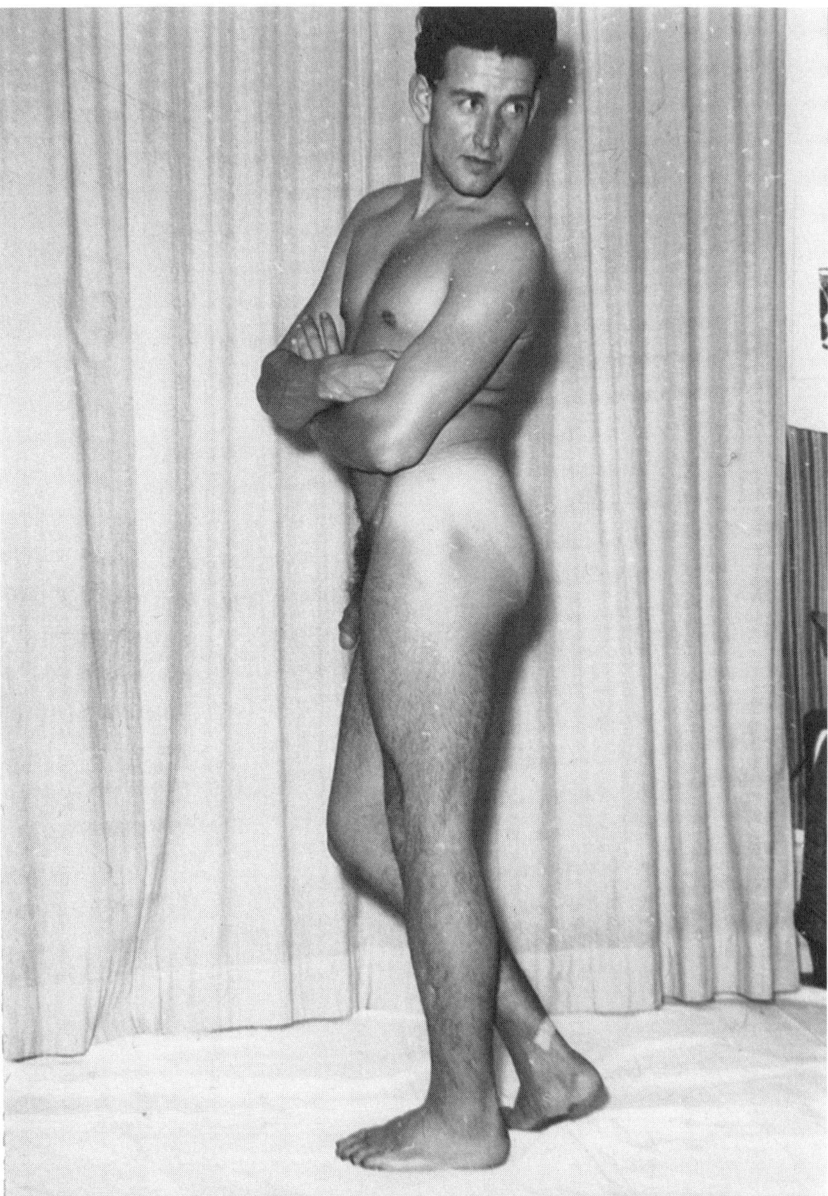

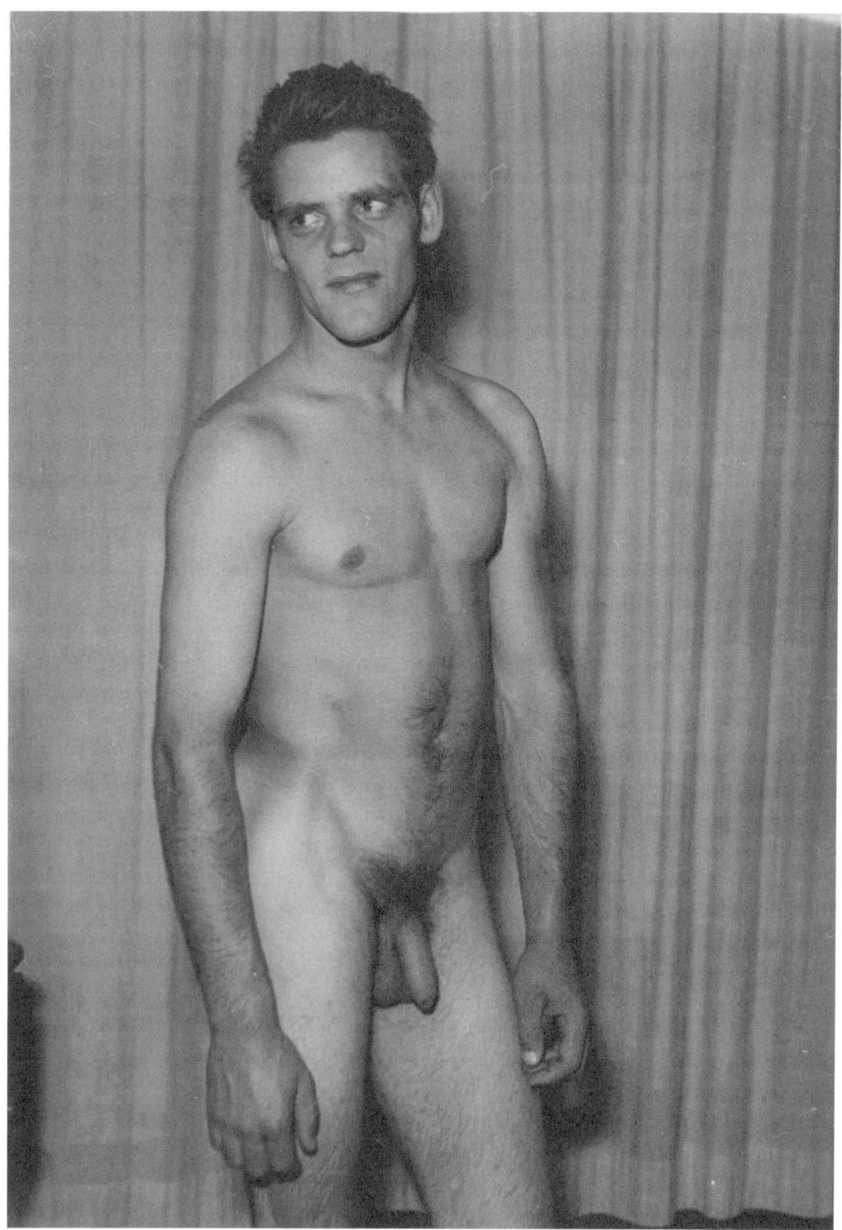

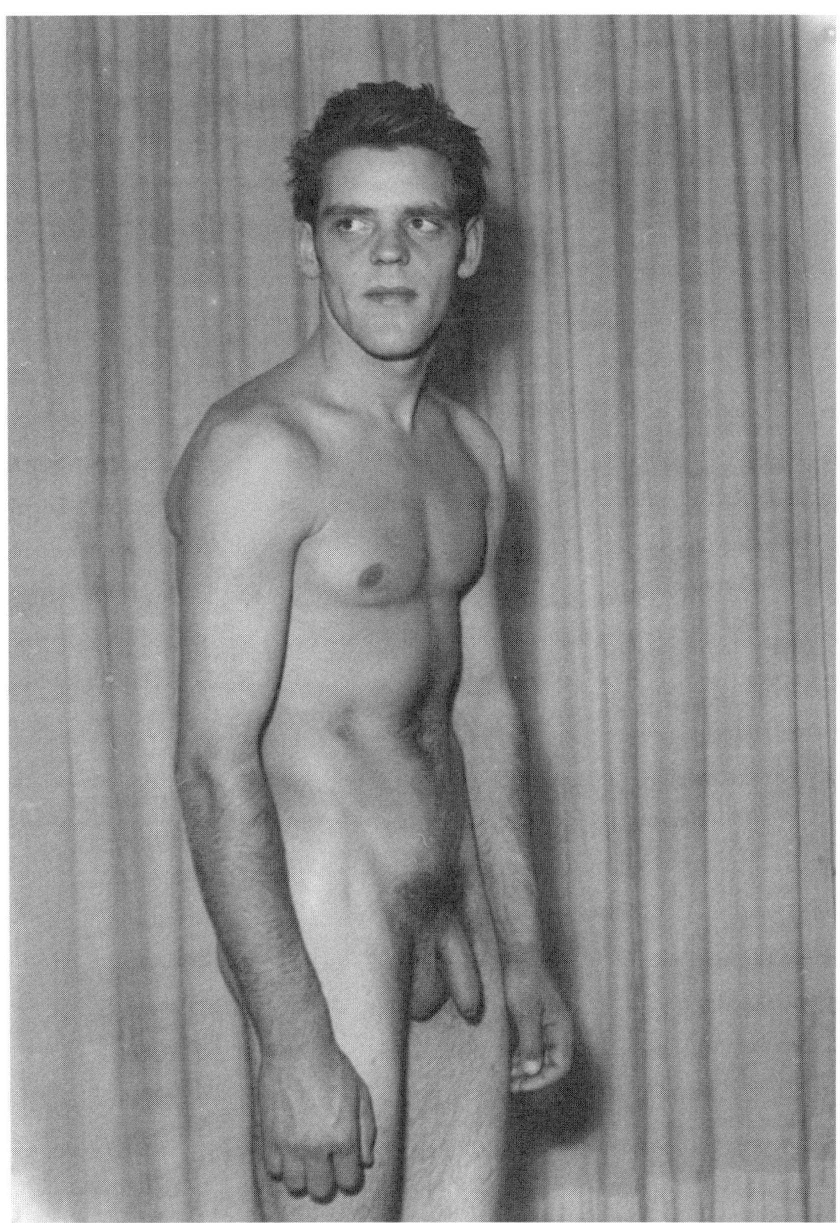

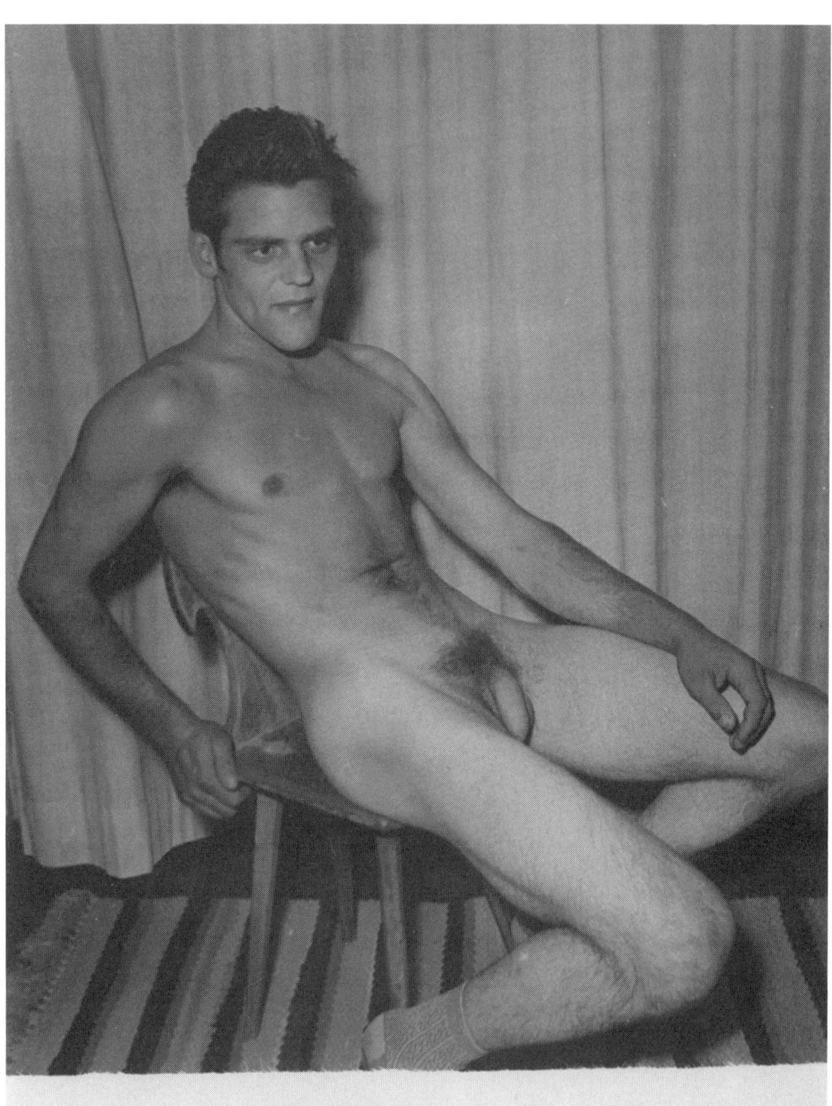

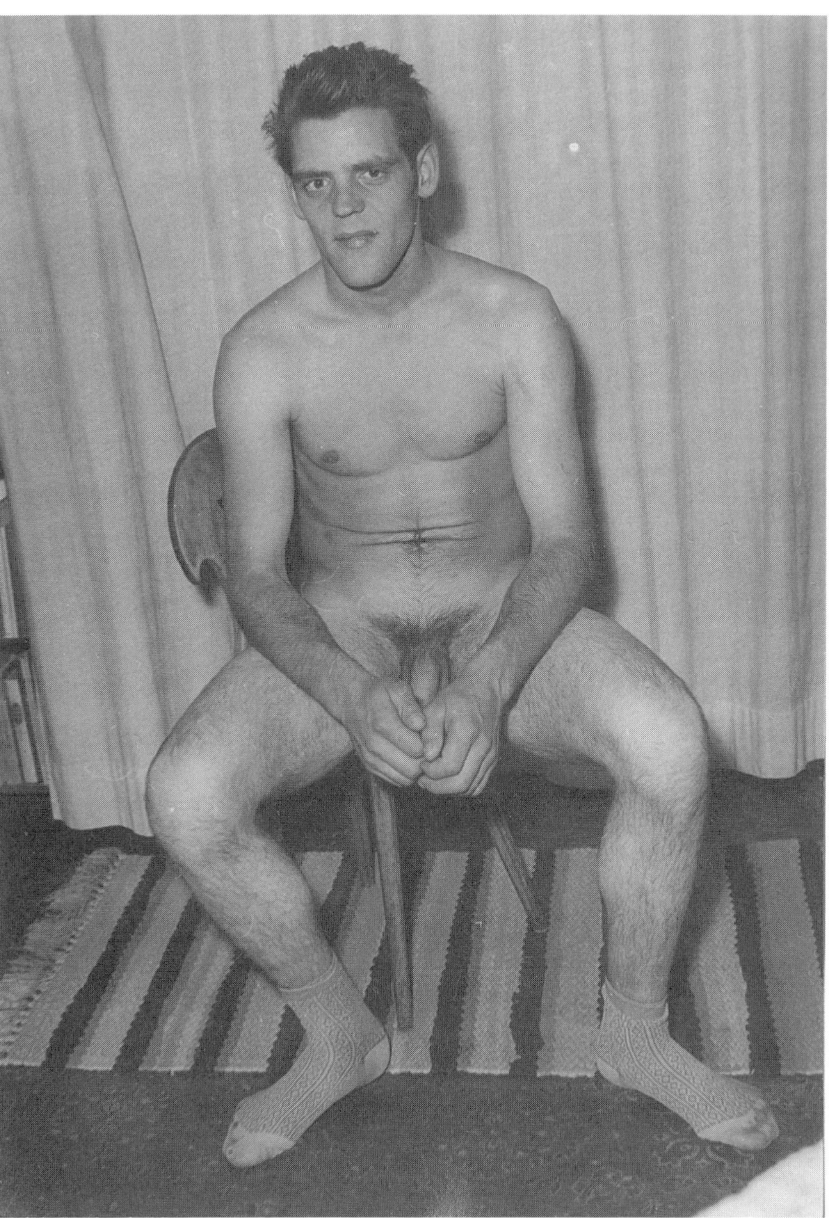

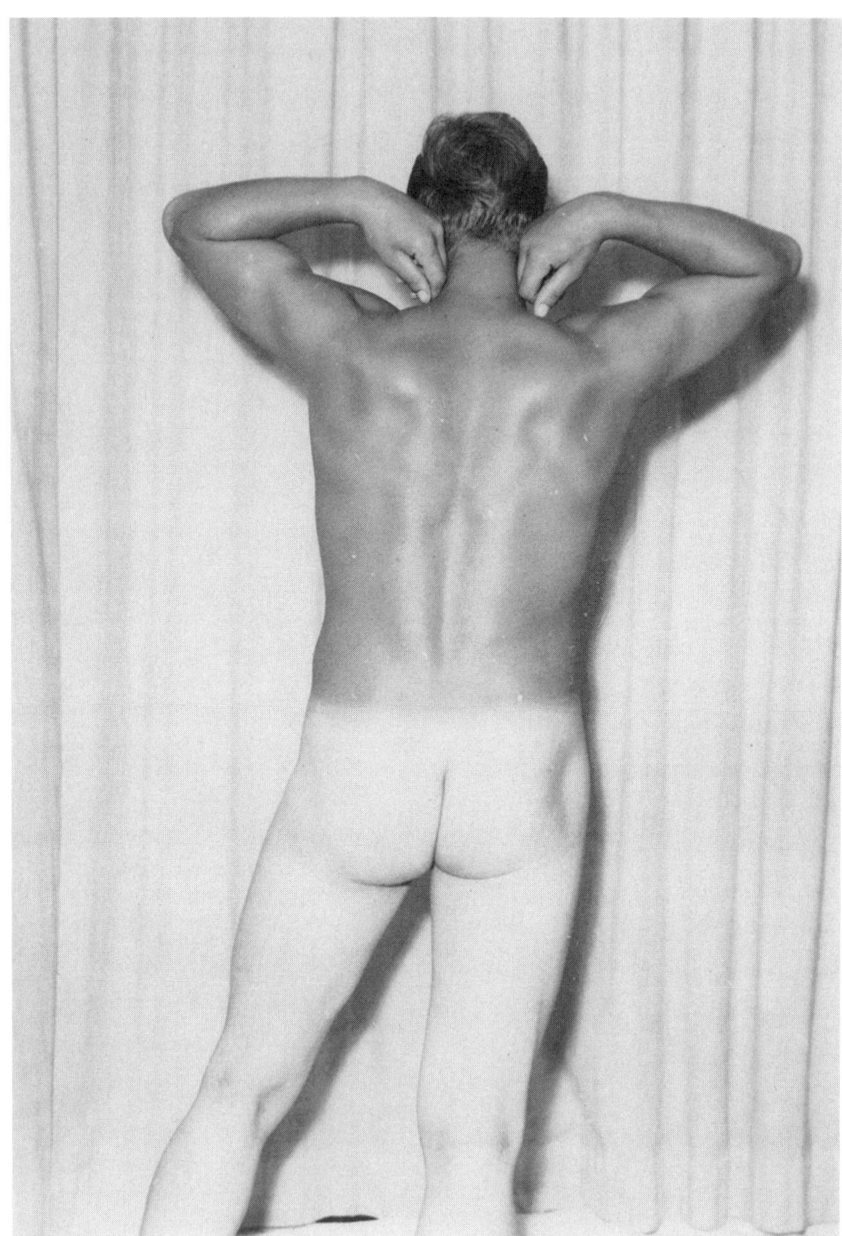

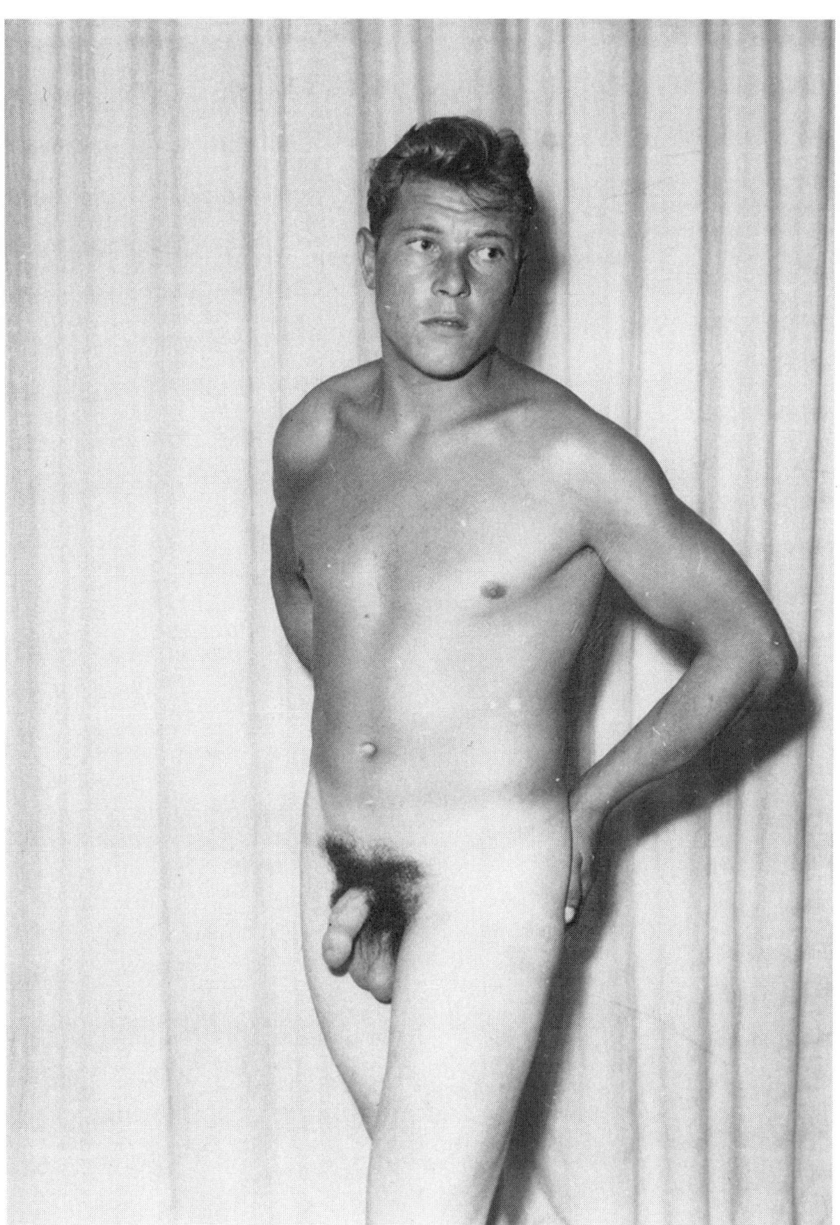

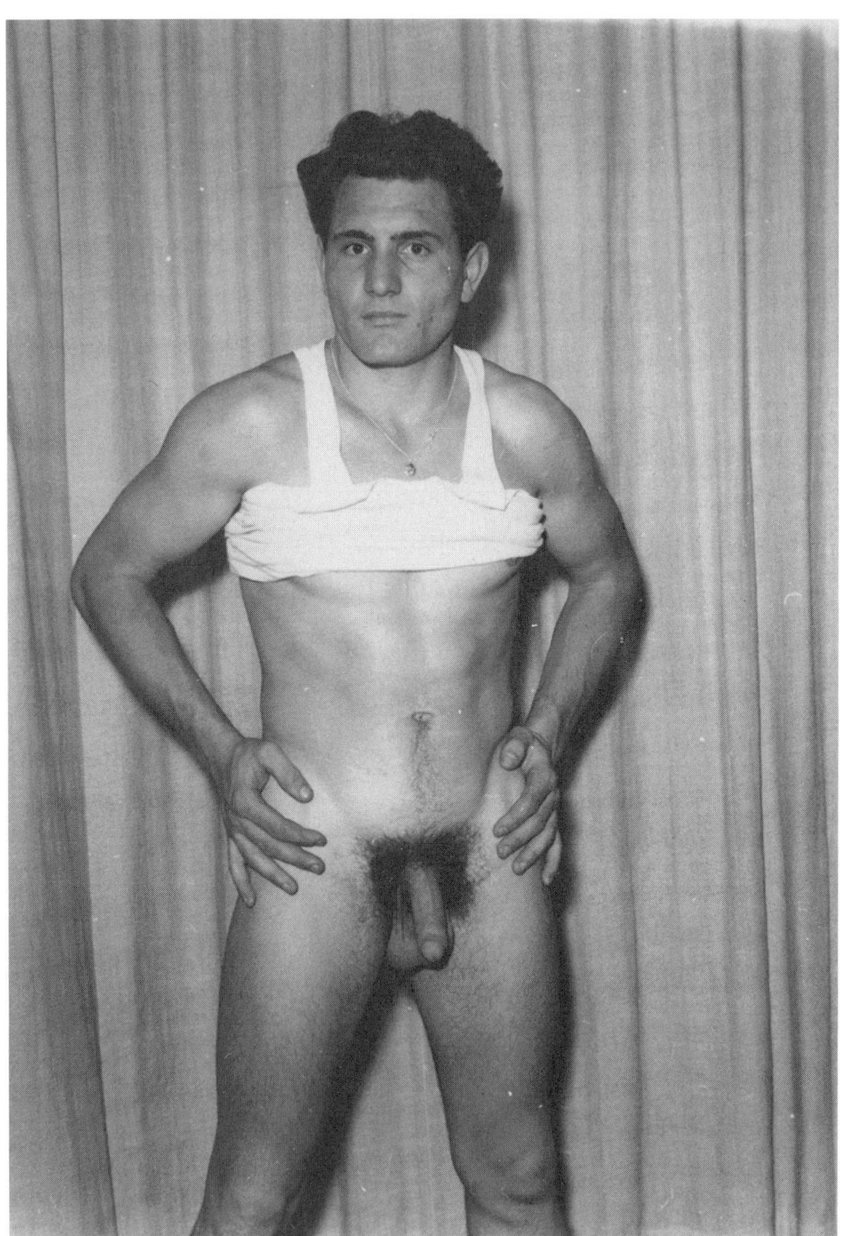

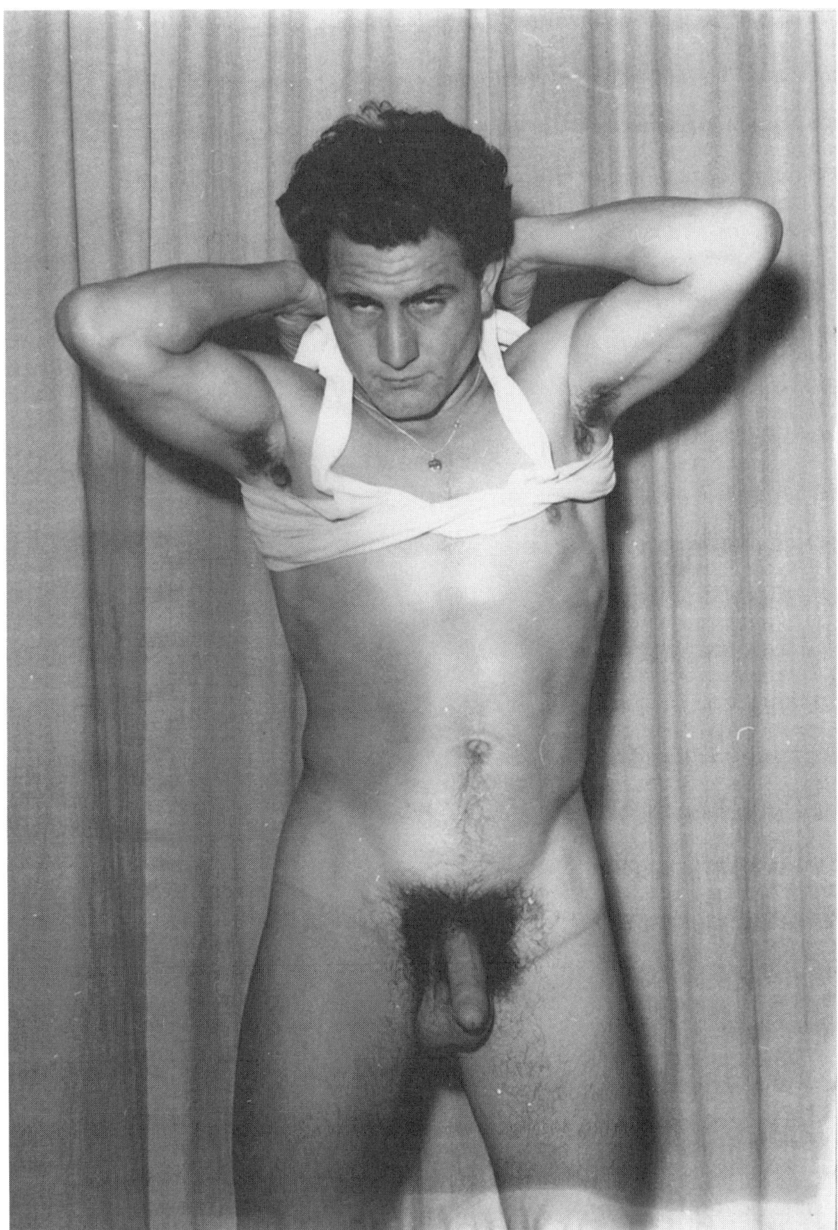

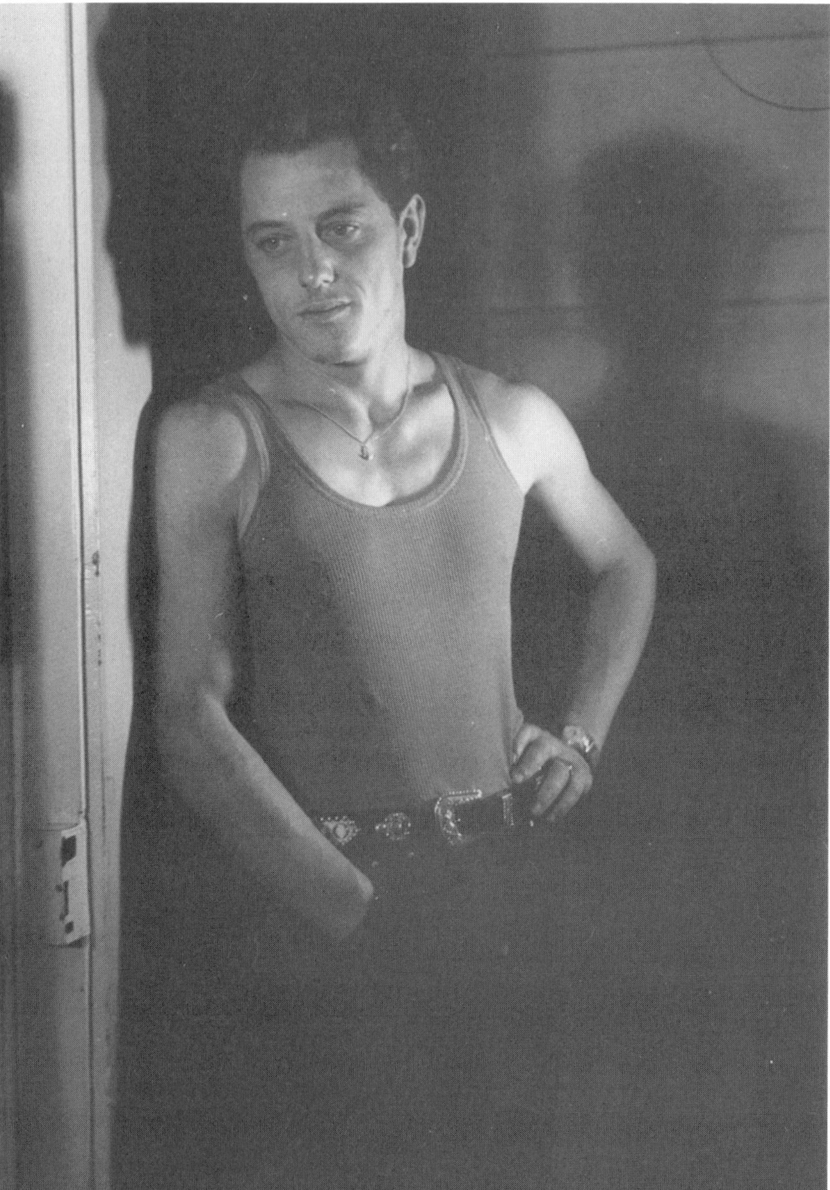

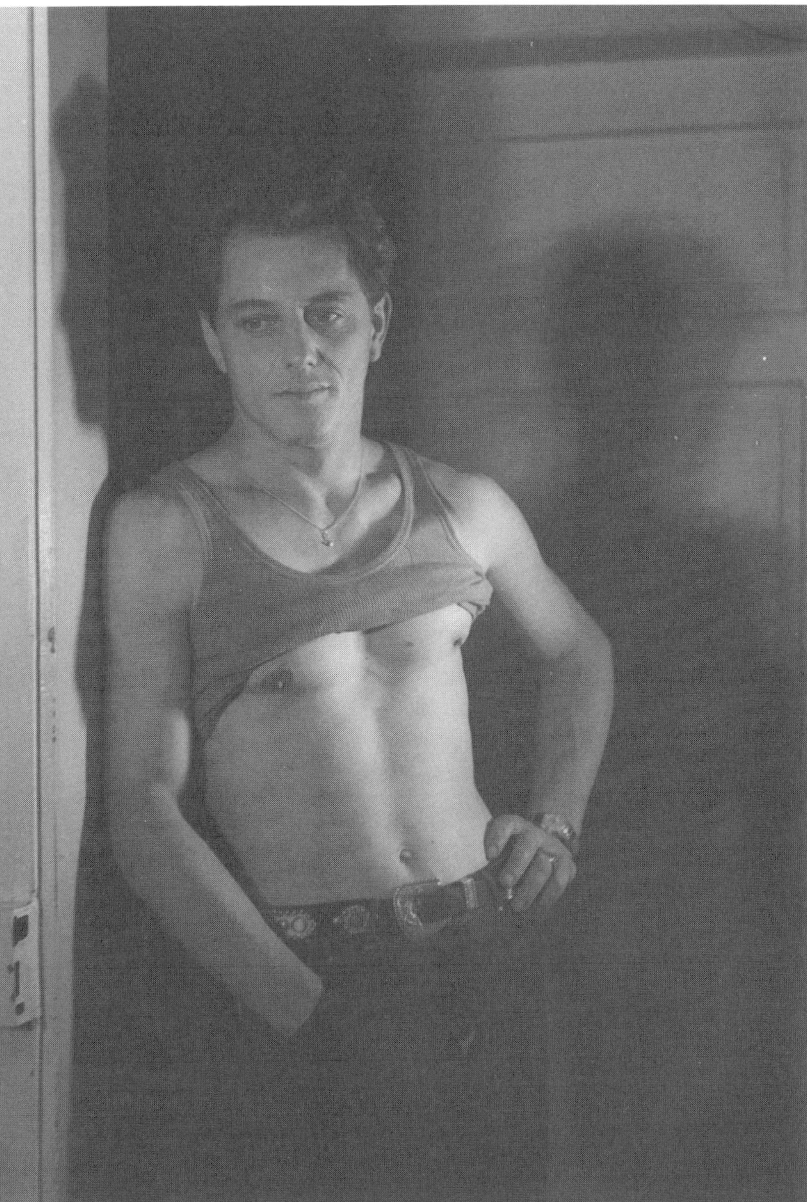

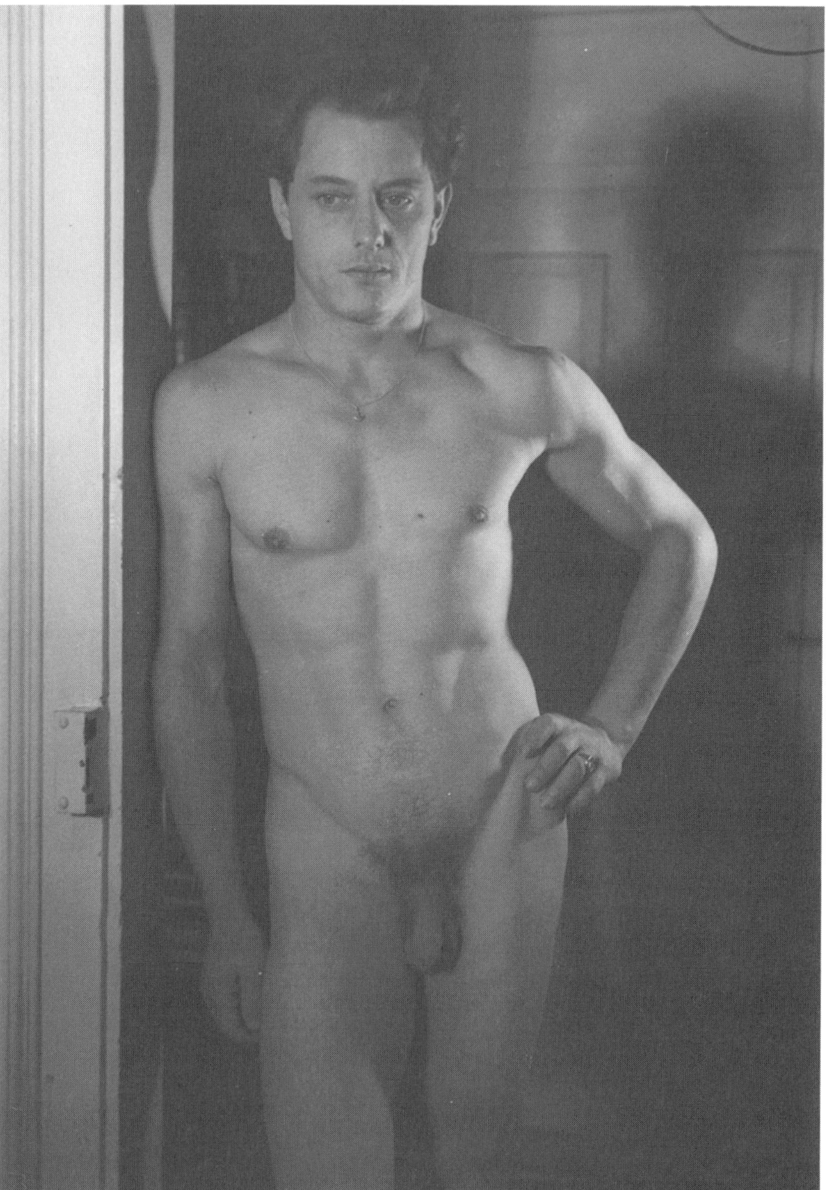

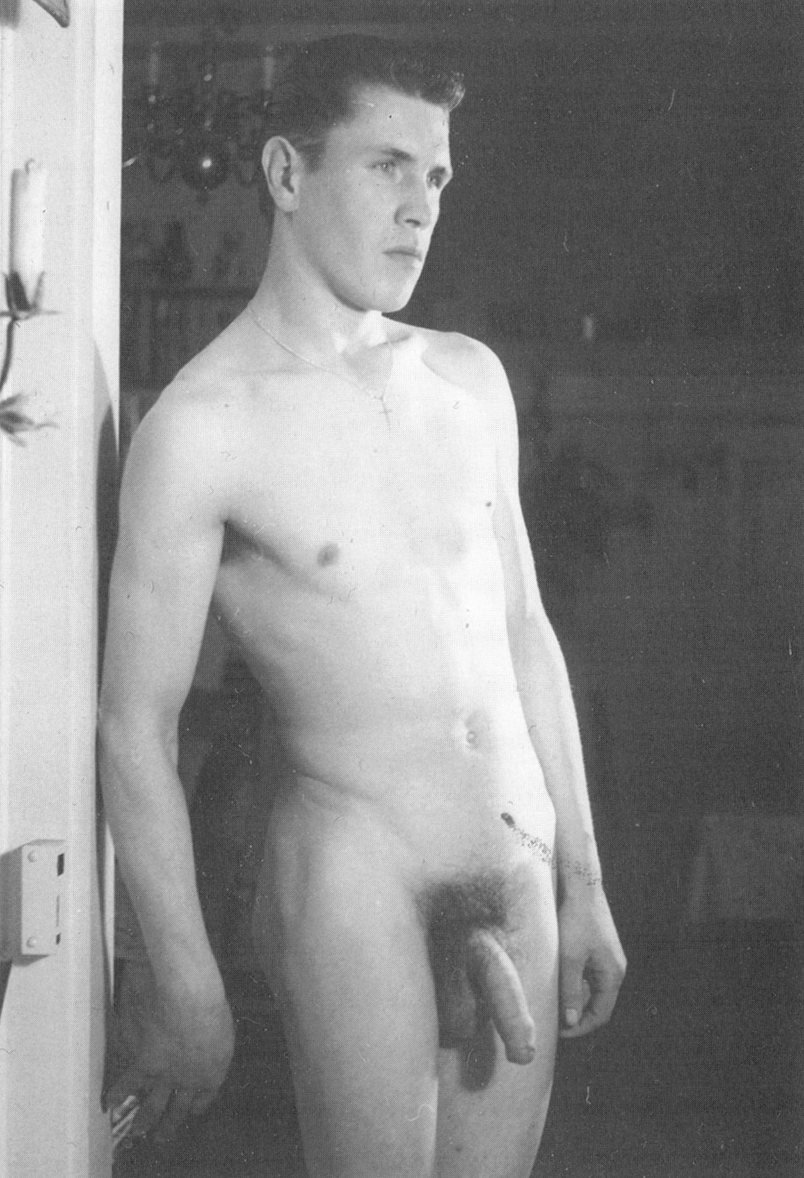

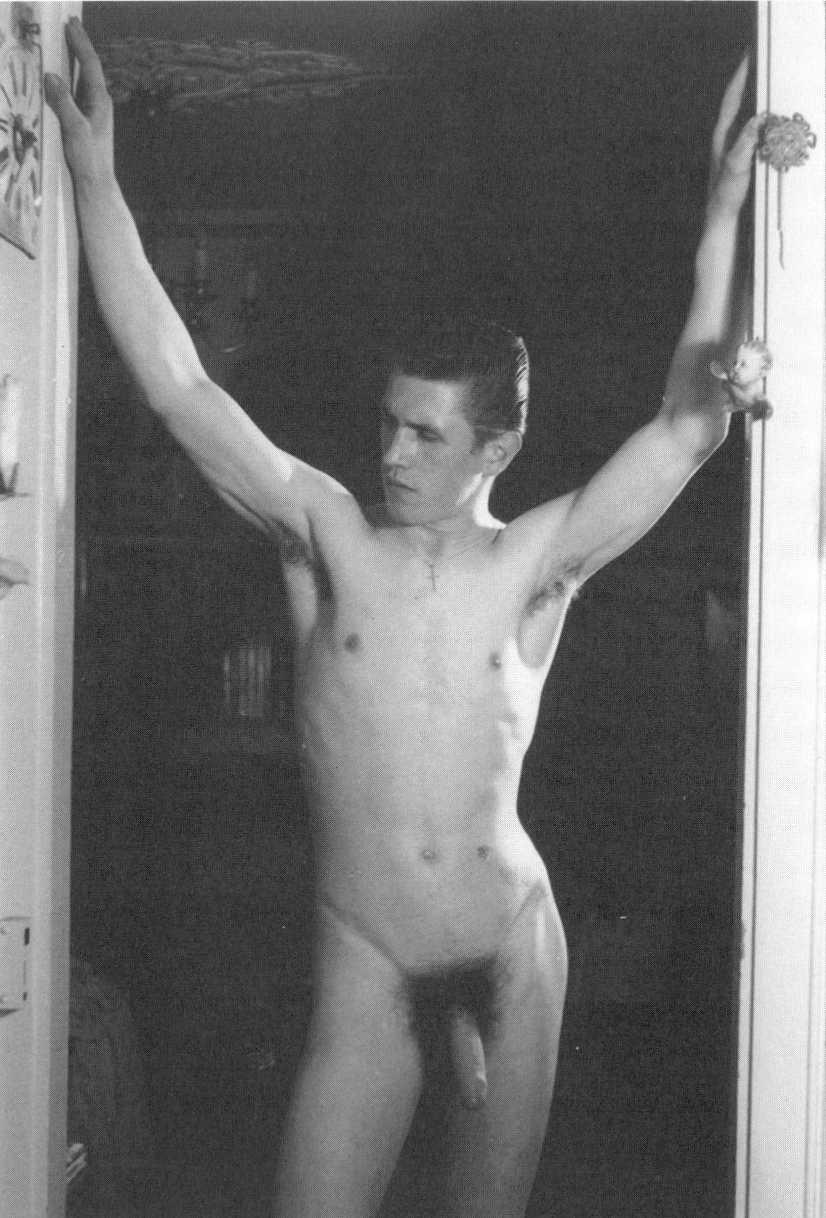

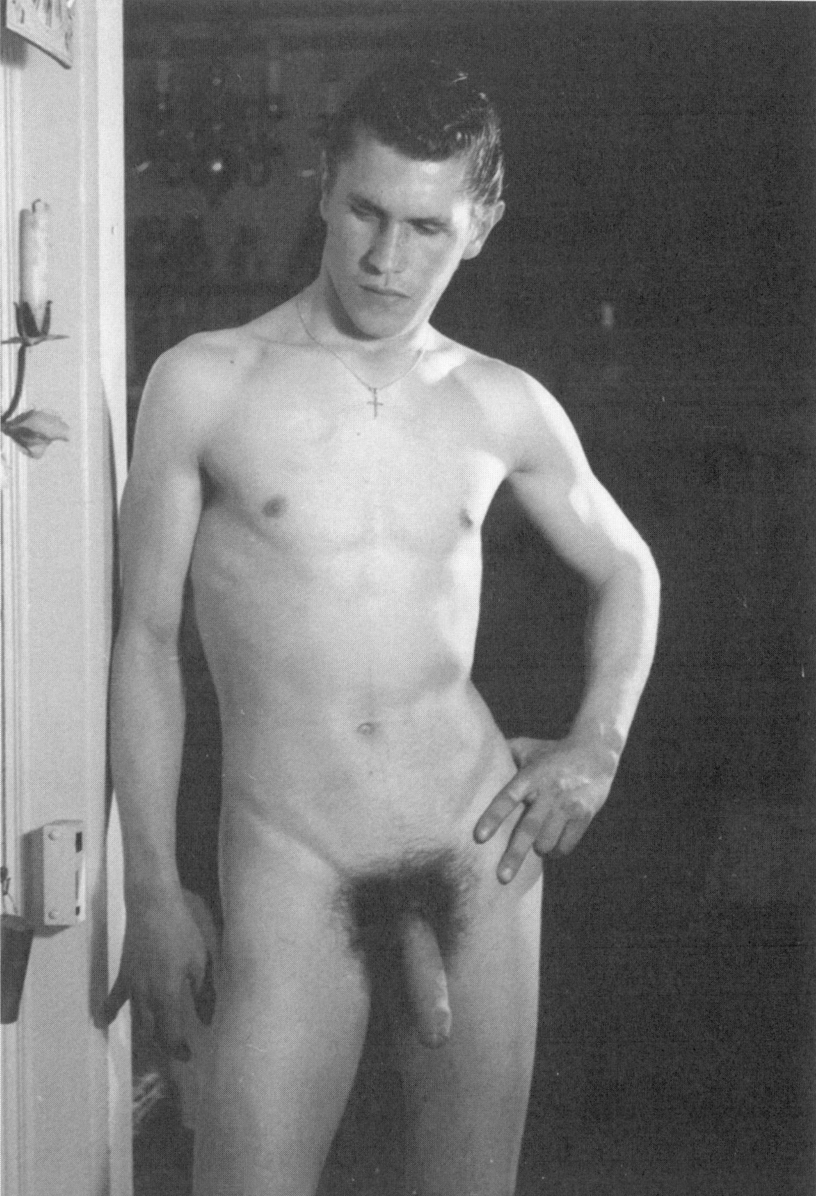

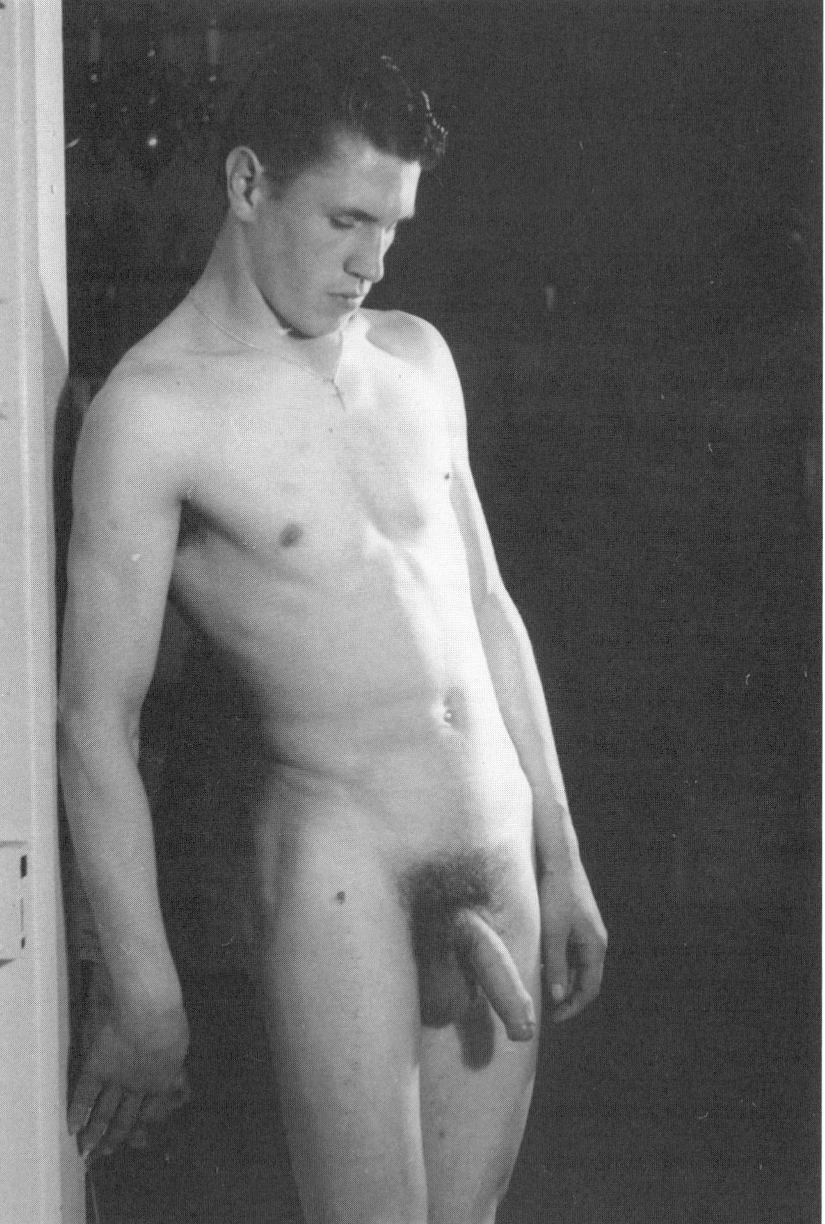

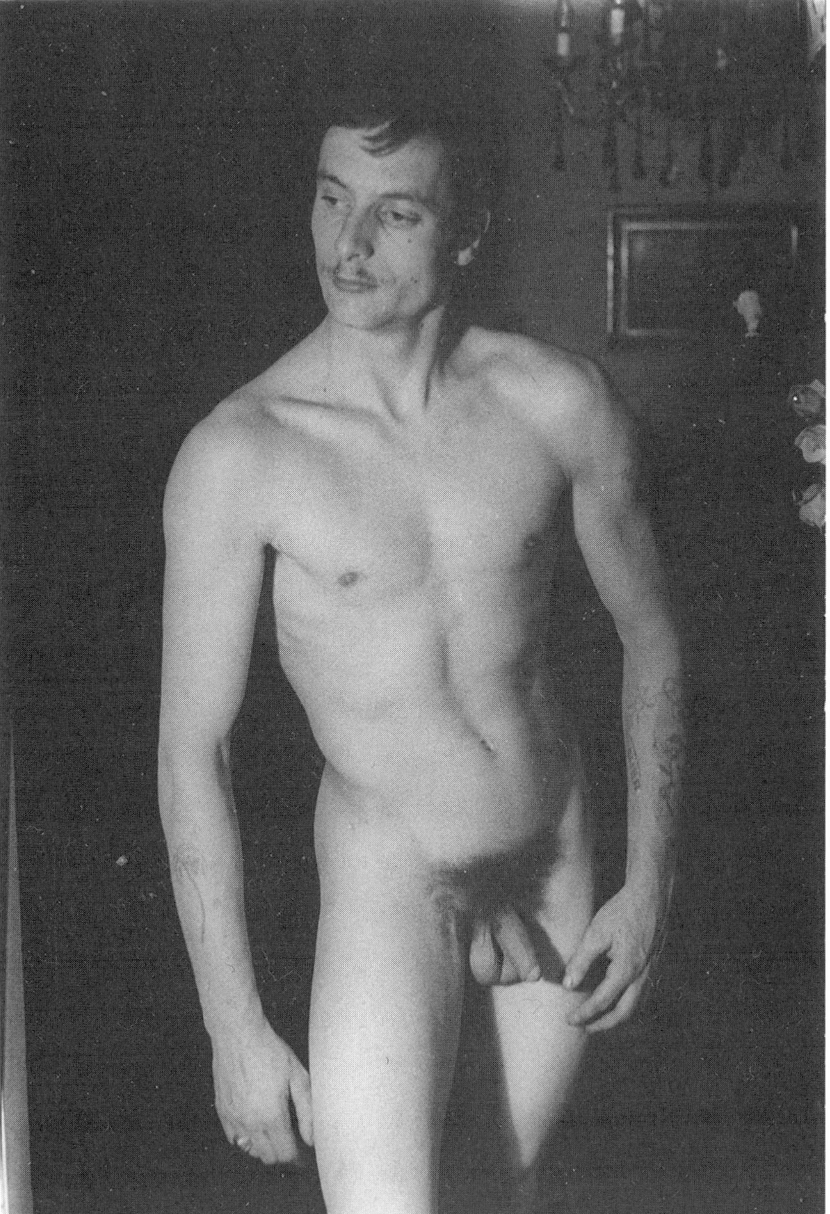

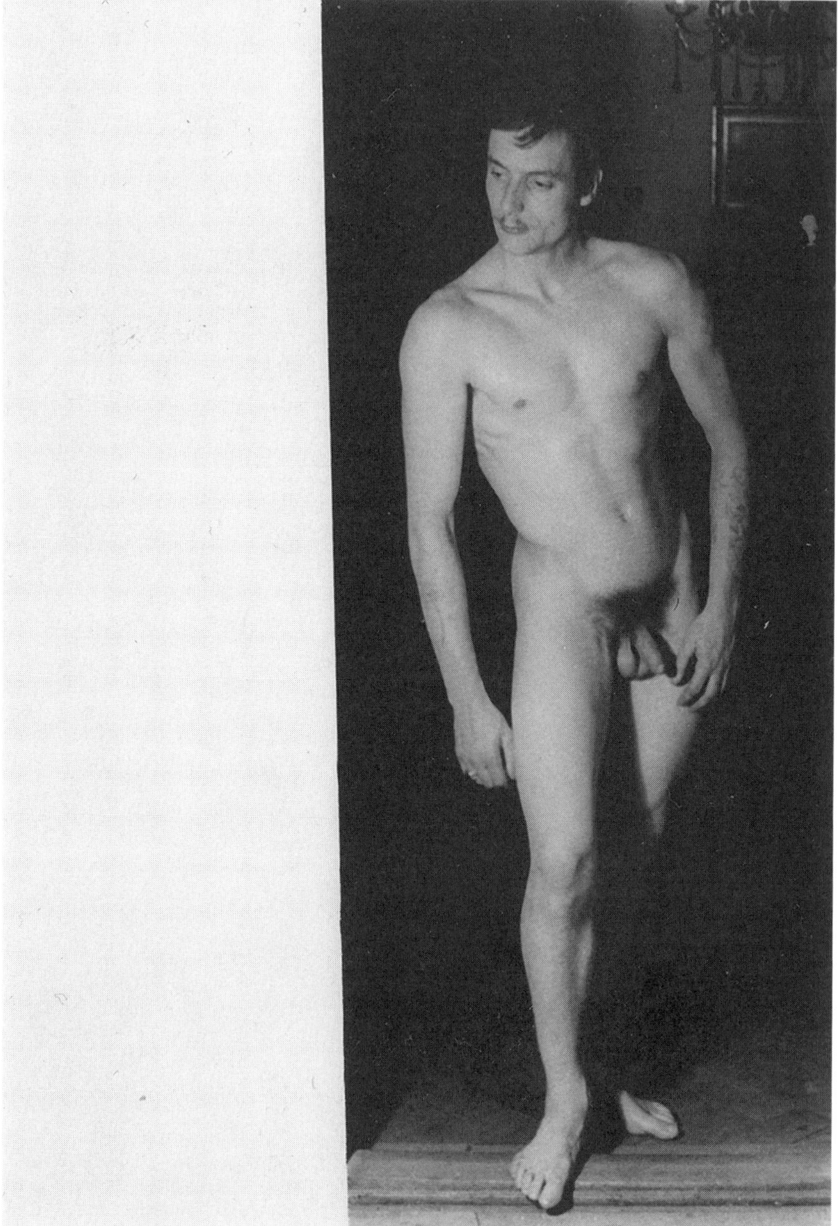

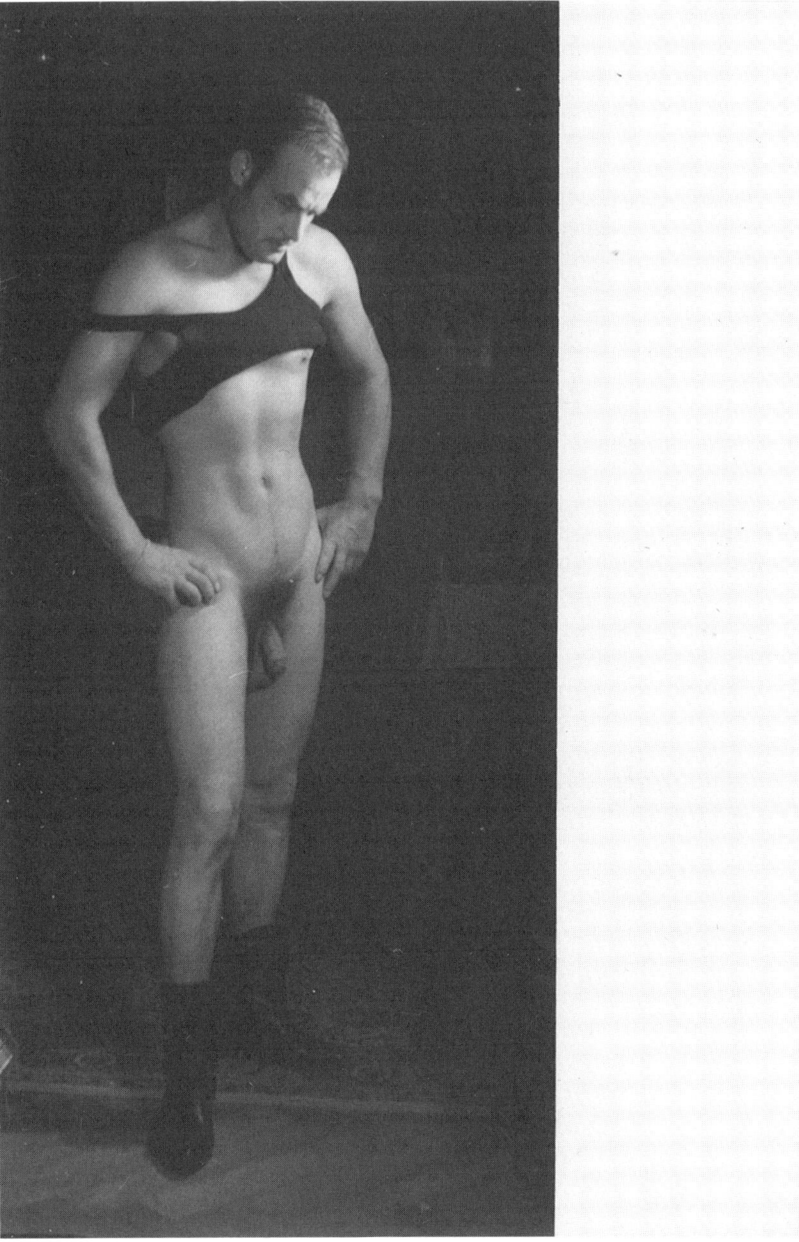

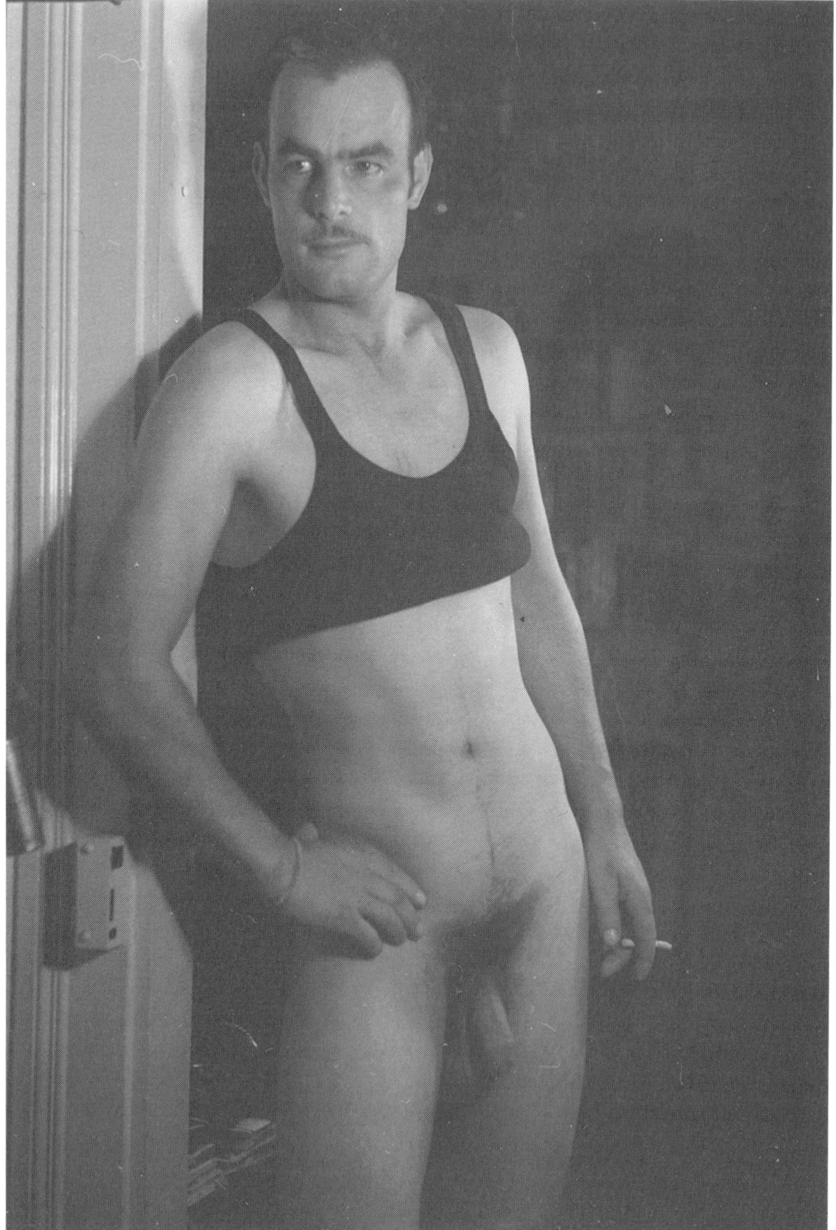

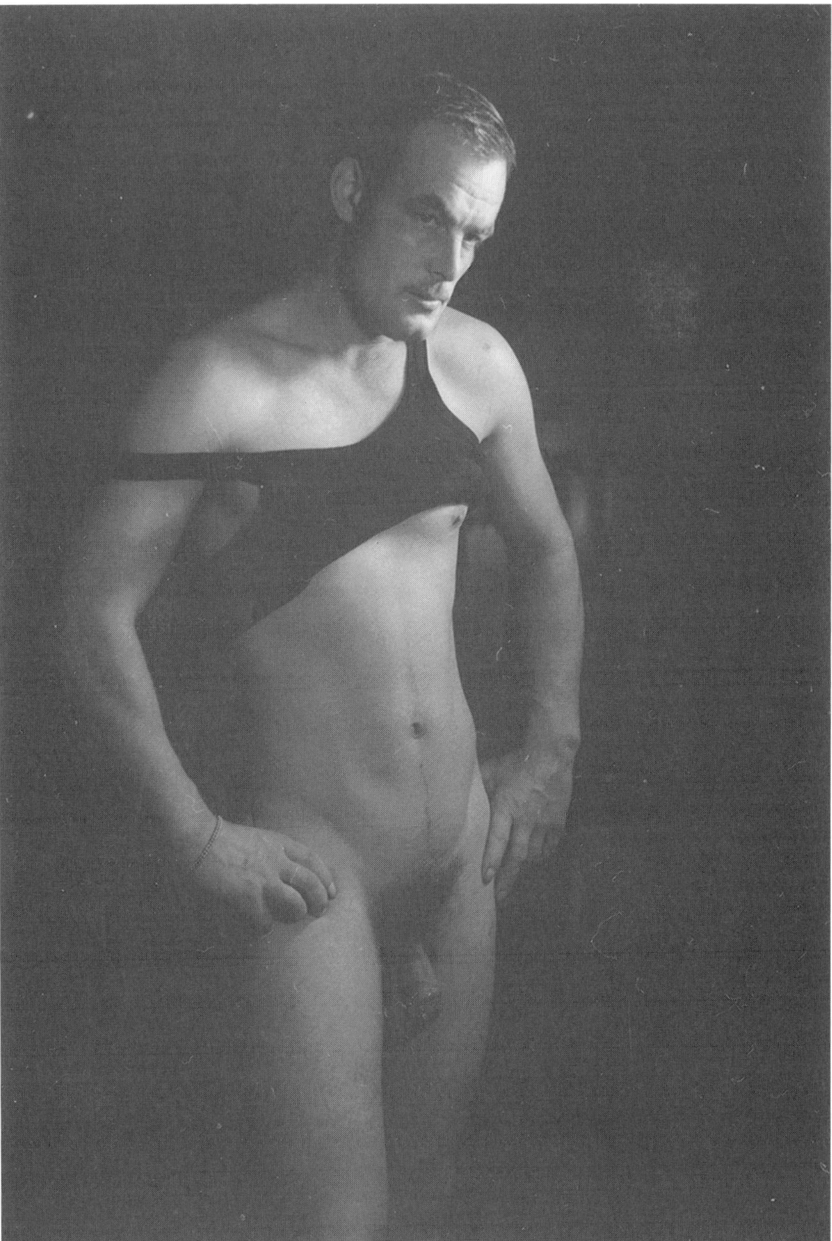

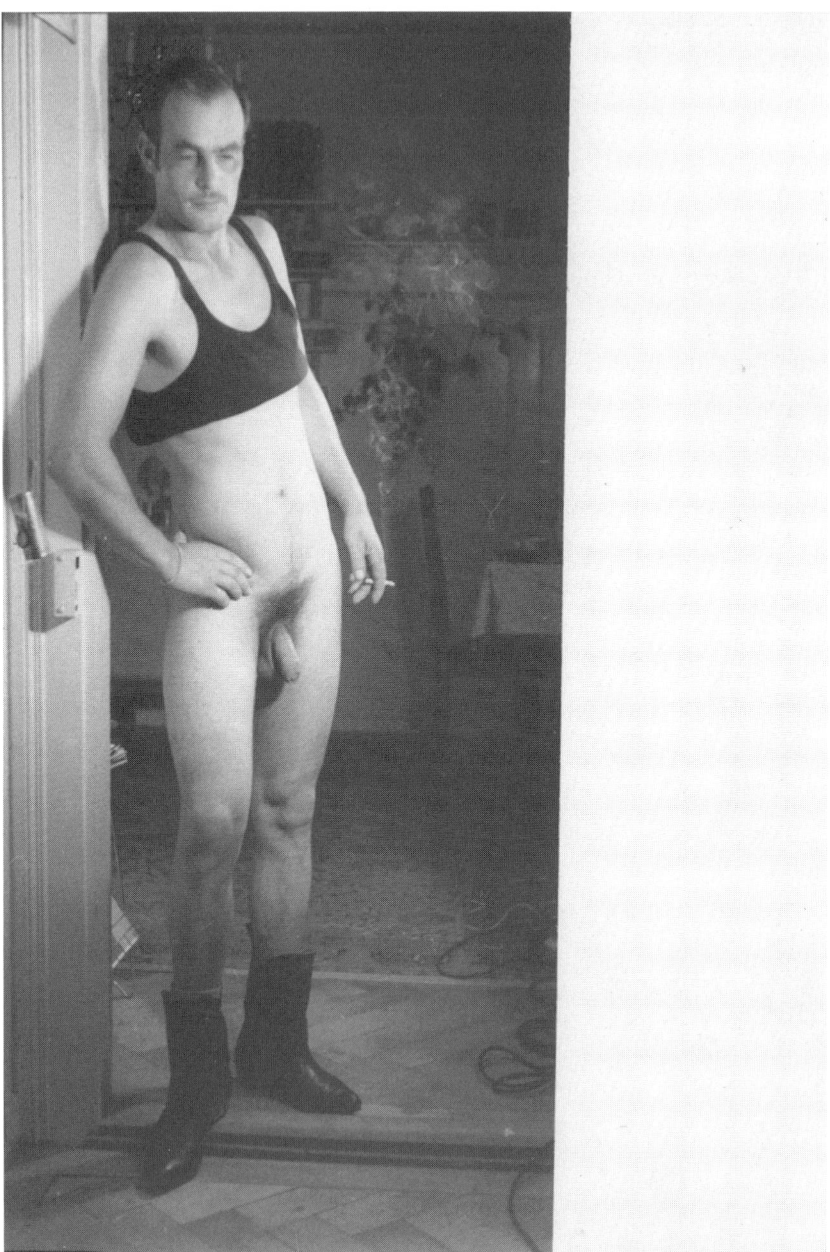

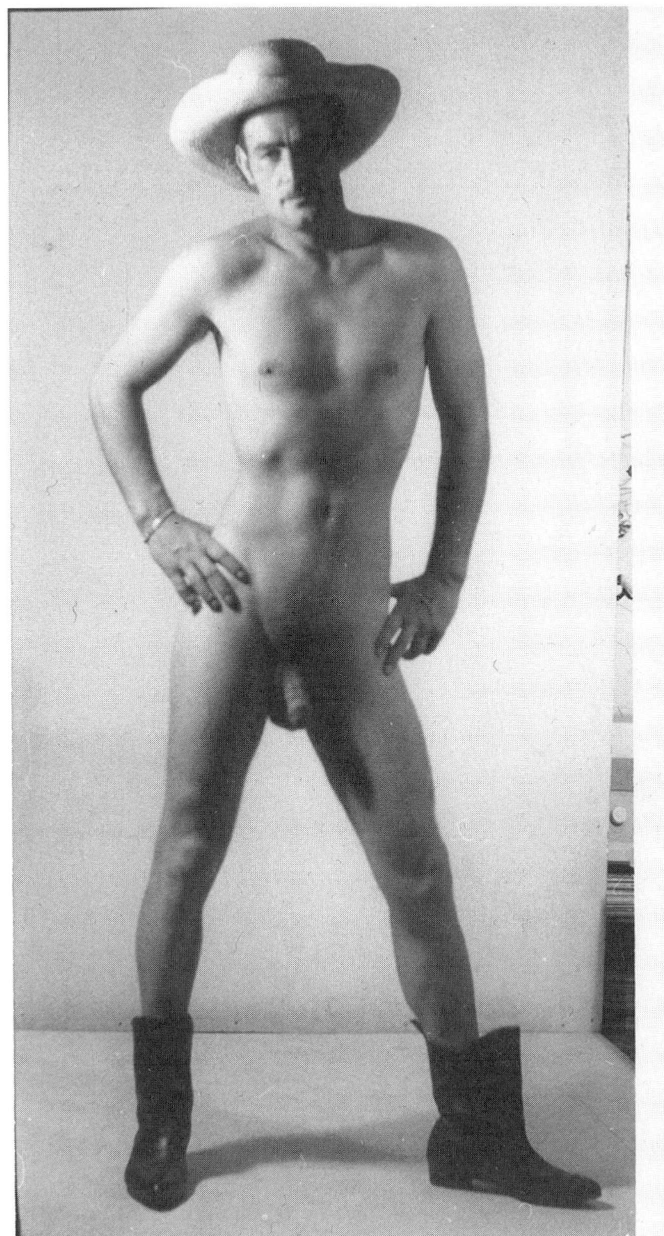

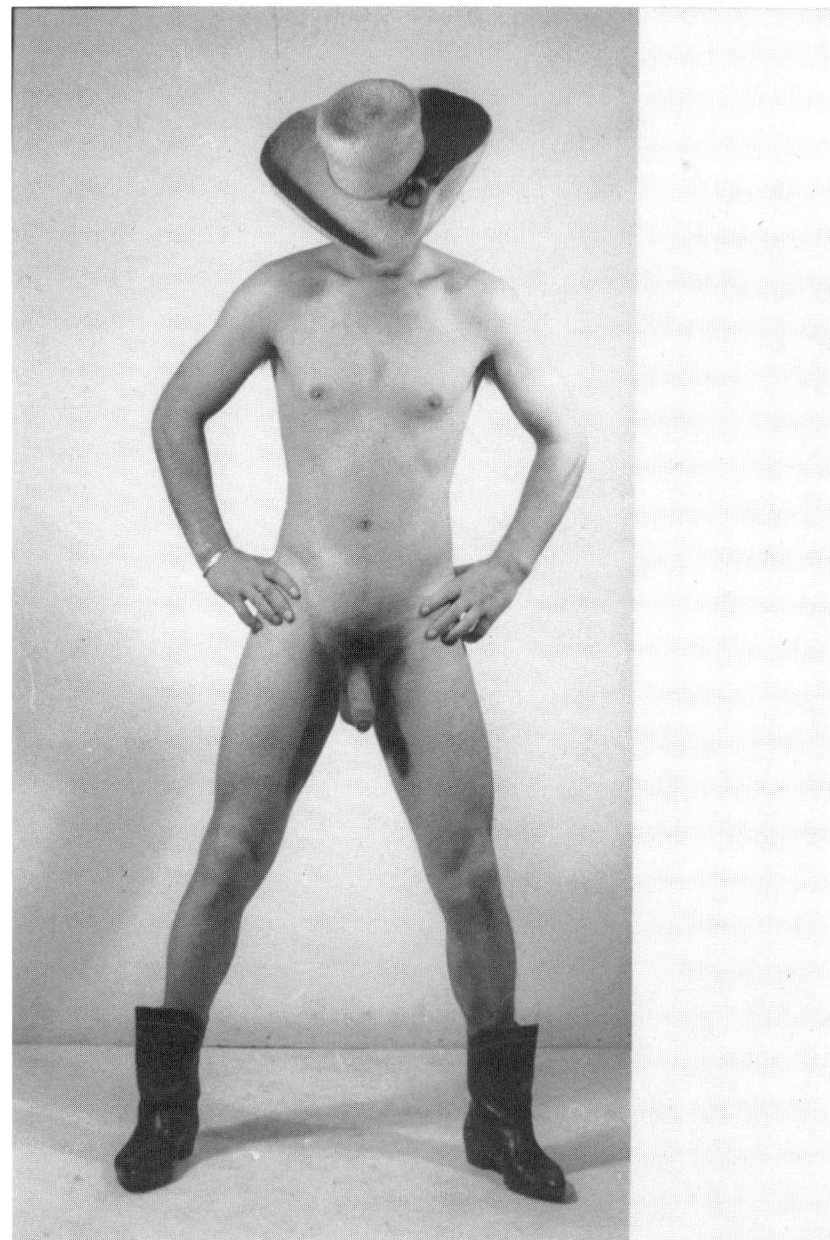

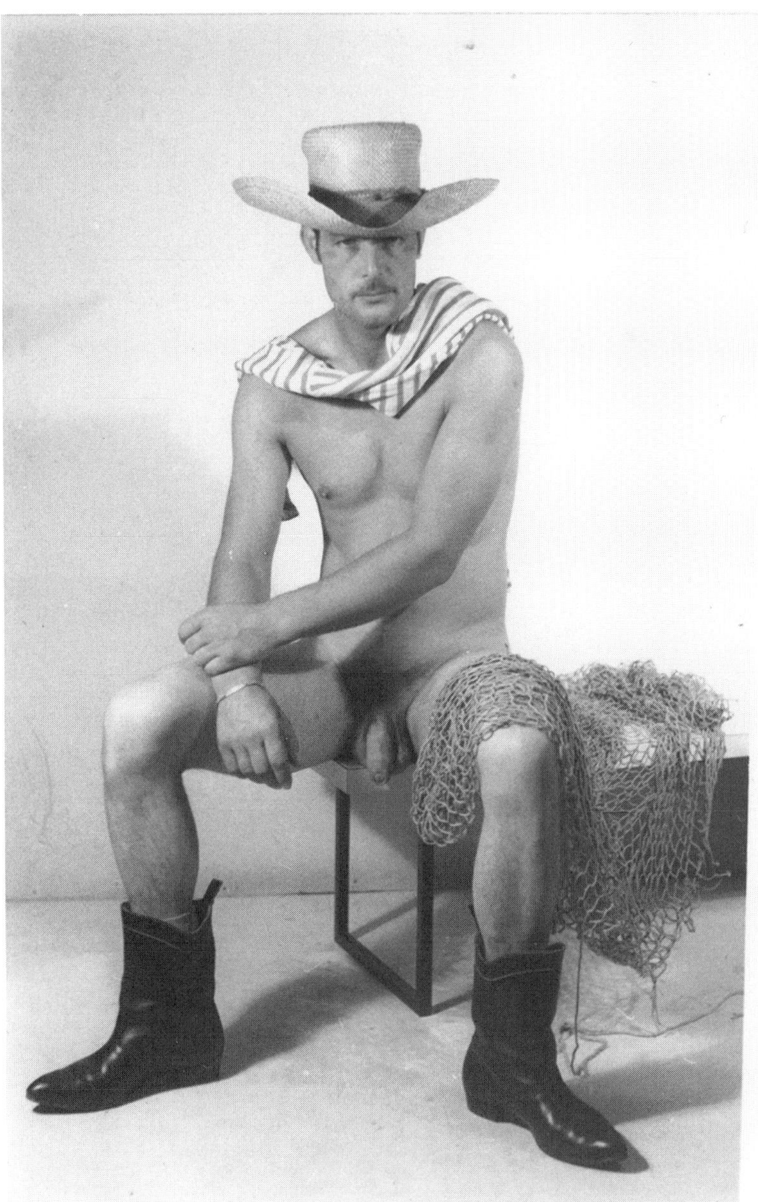

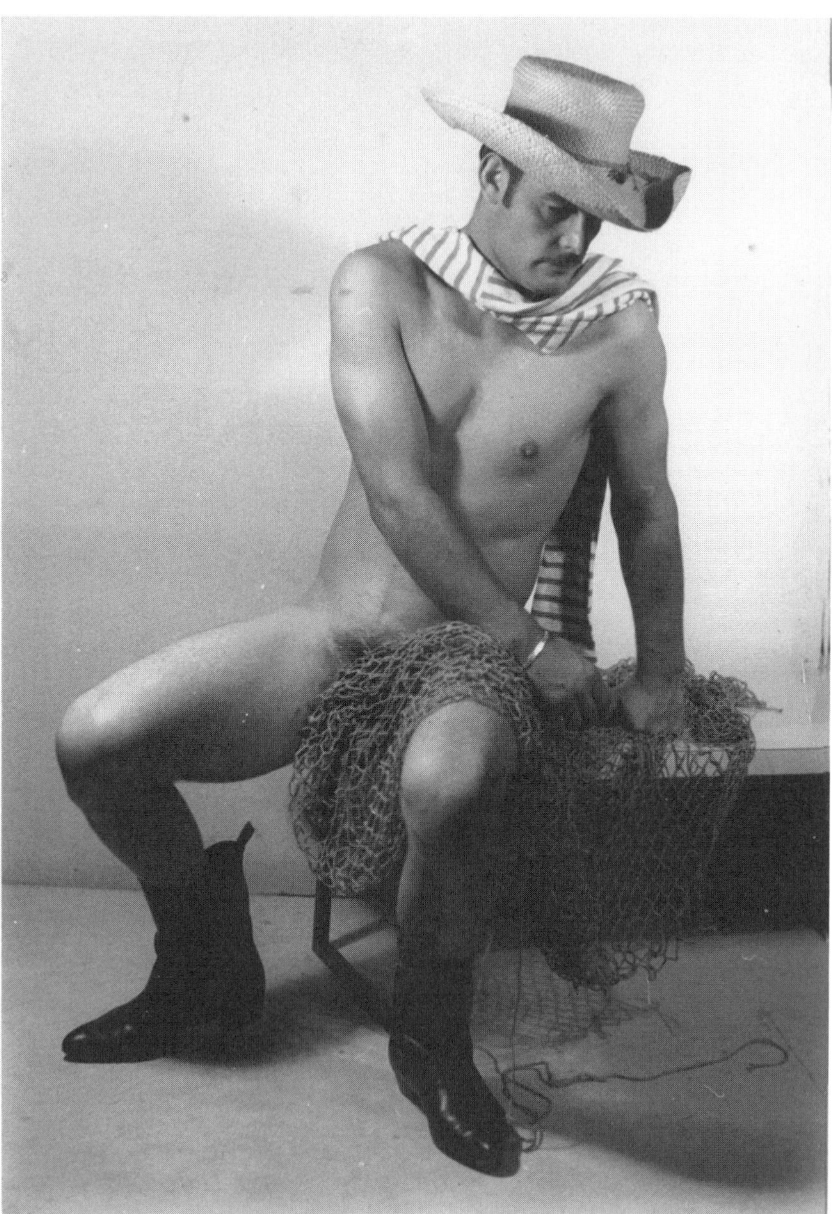

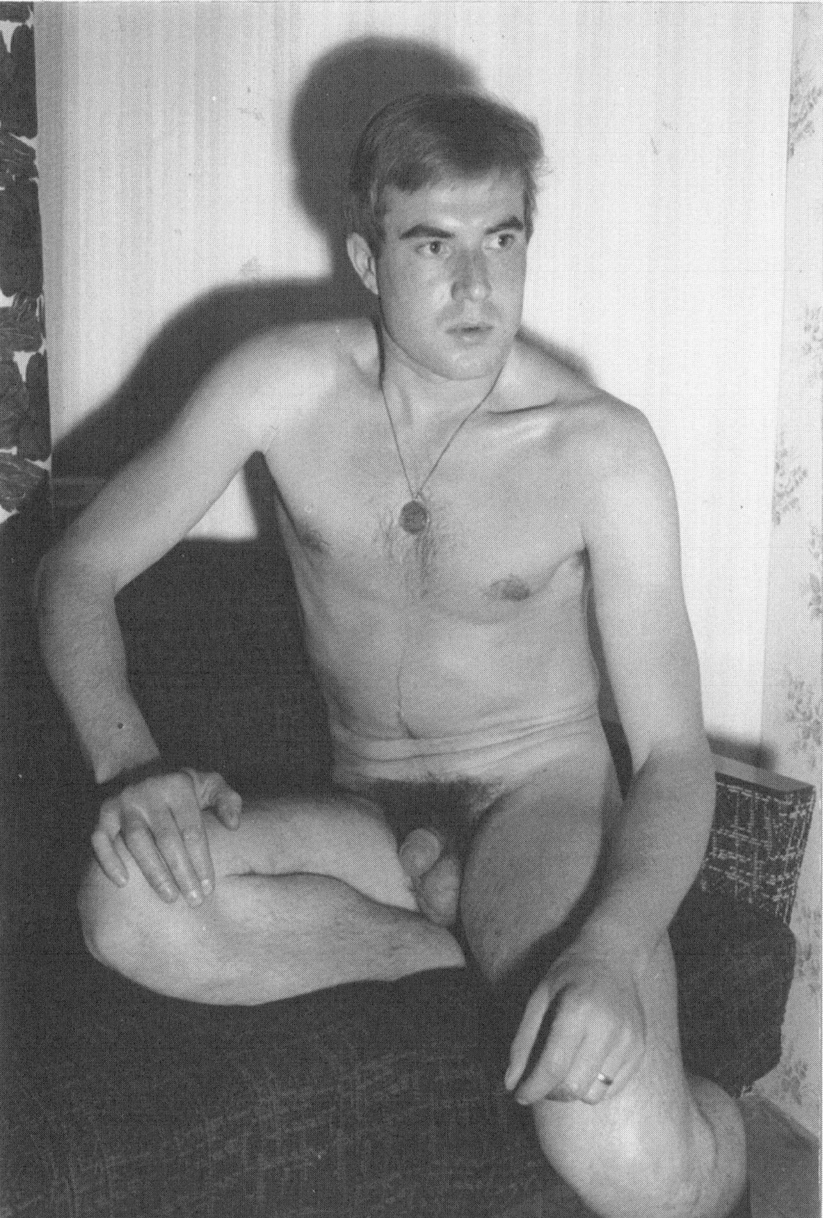

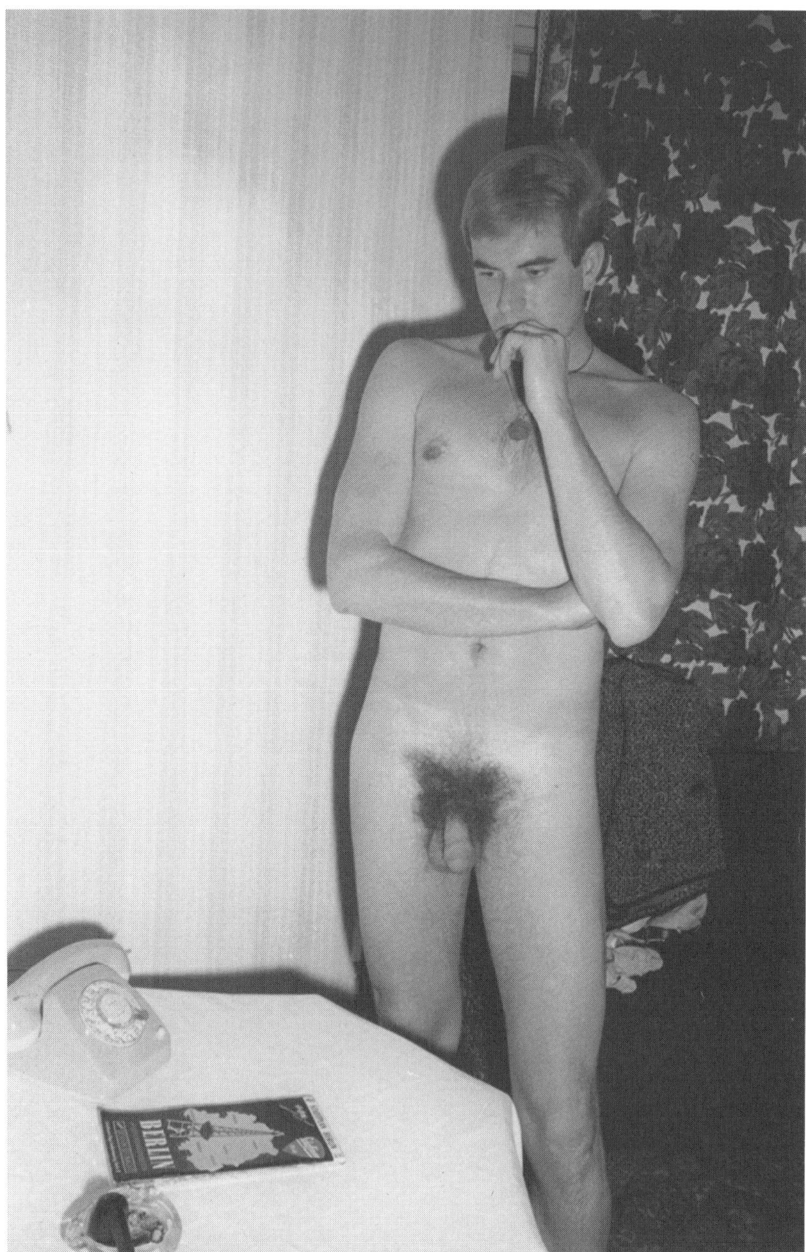
BERLIN

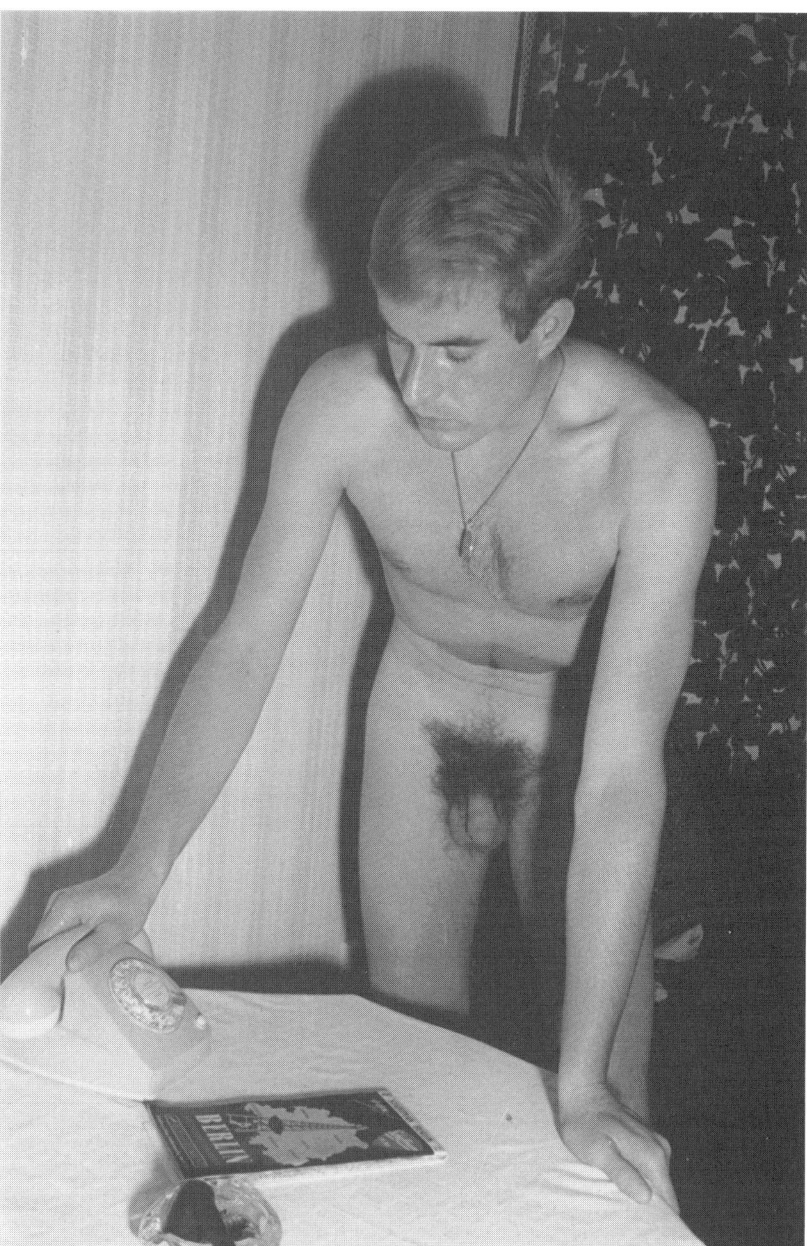
BERLIN

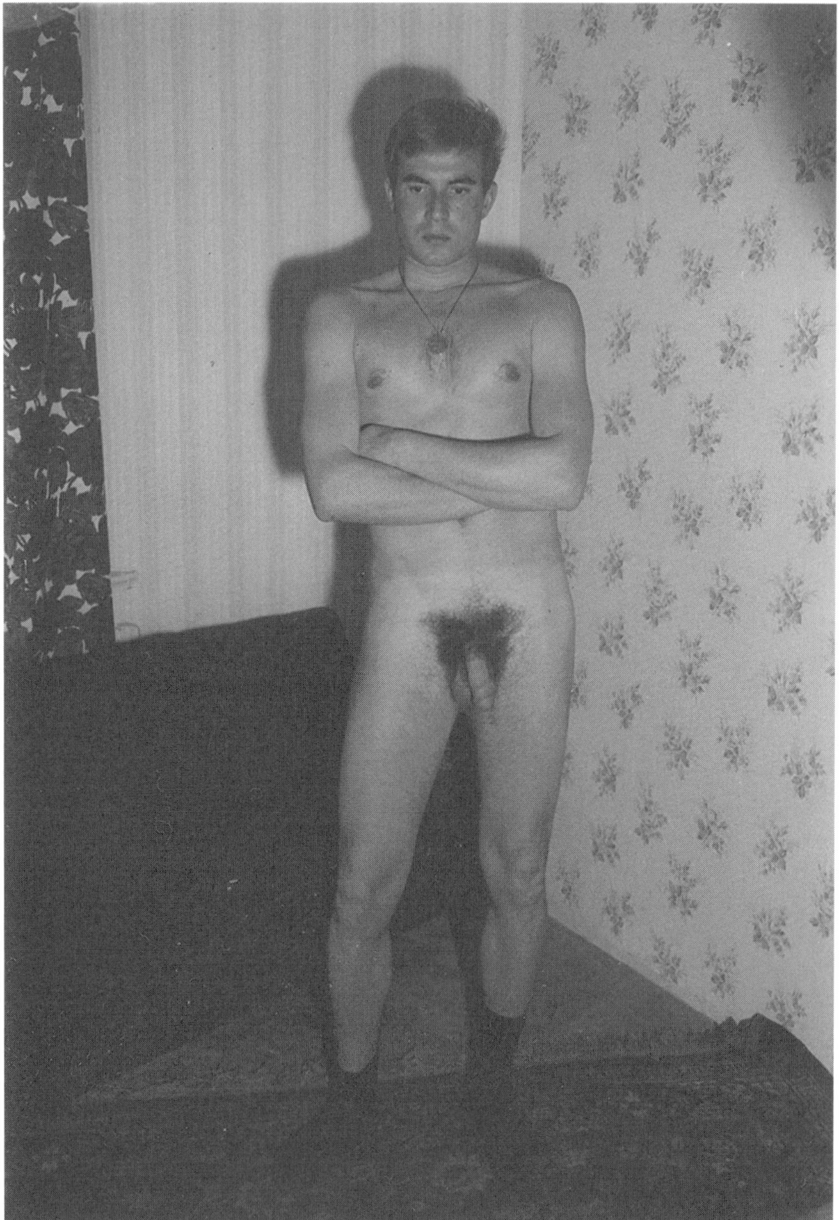

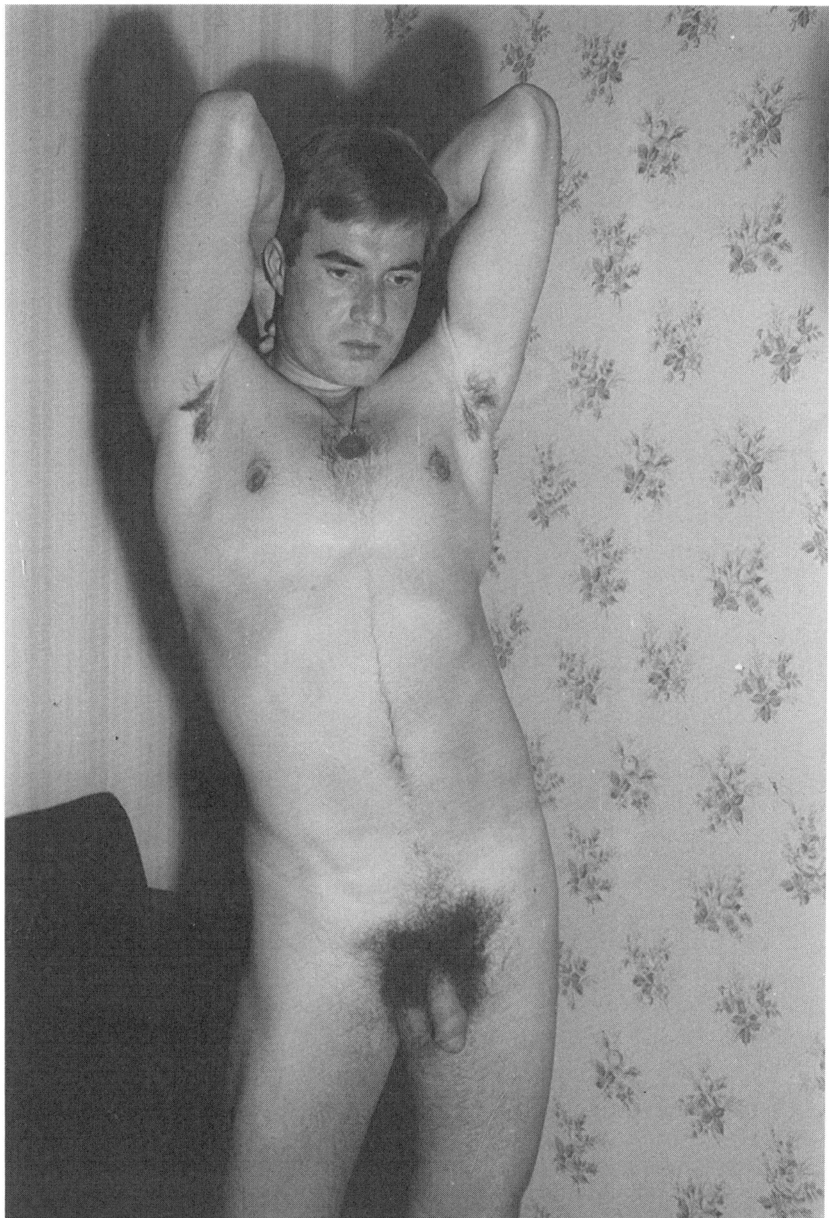

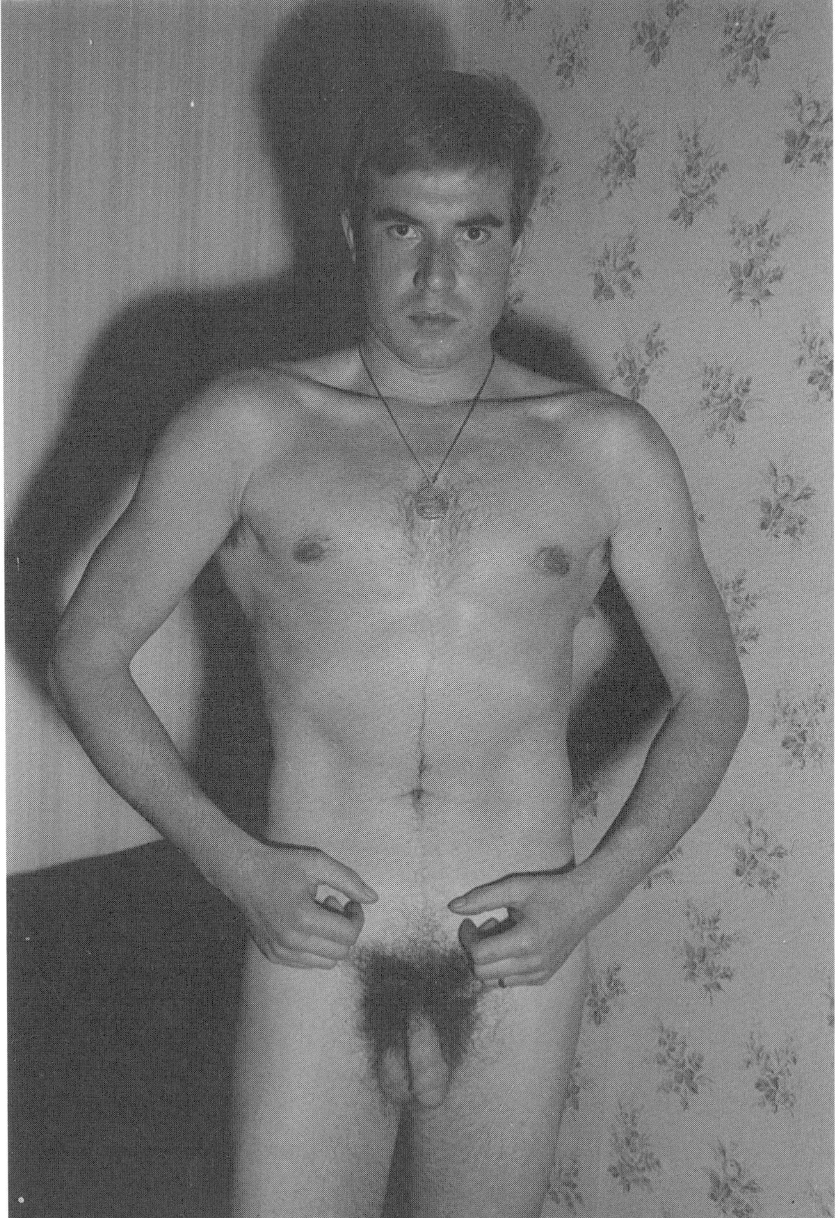

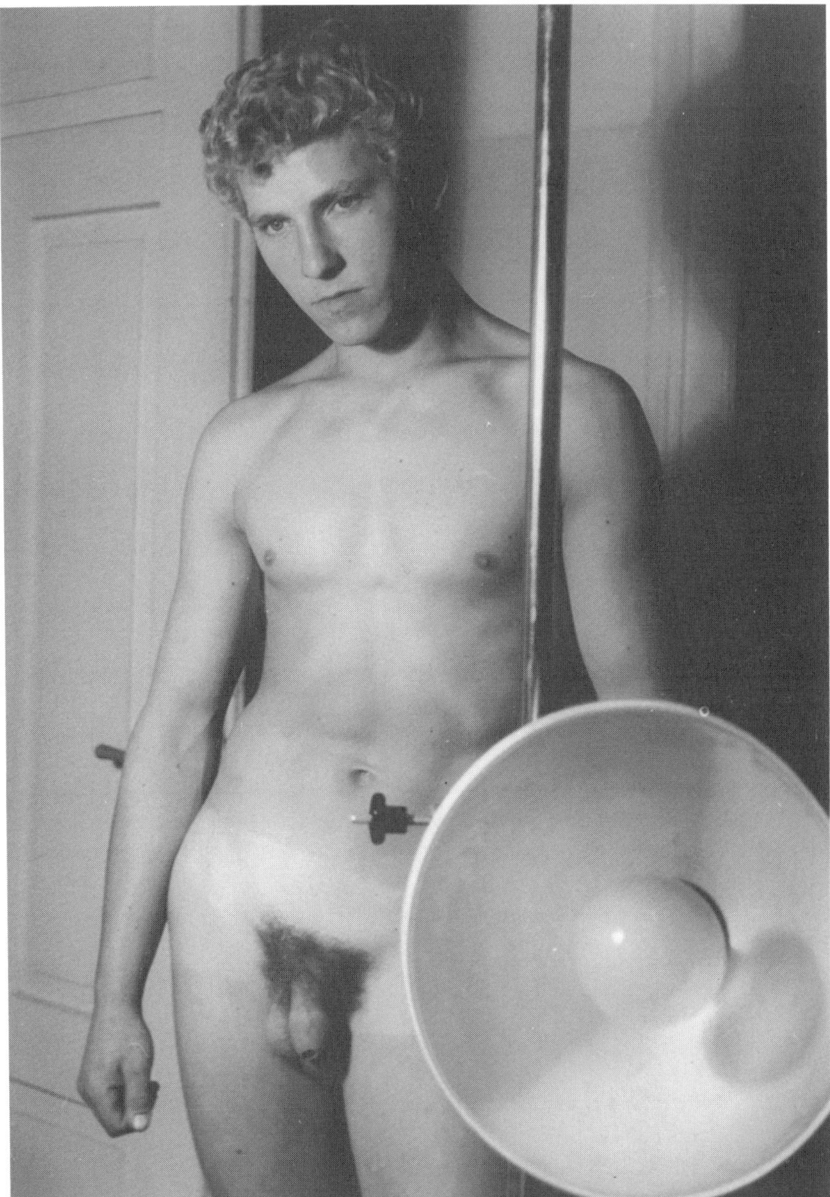

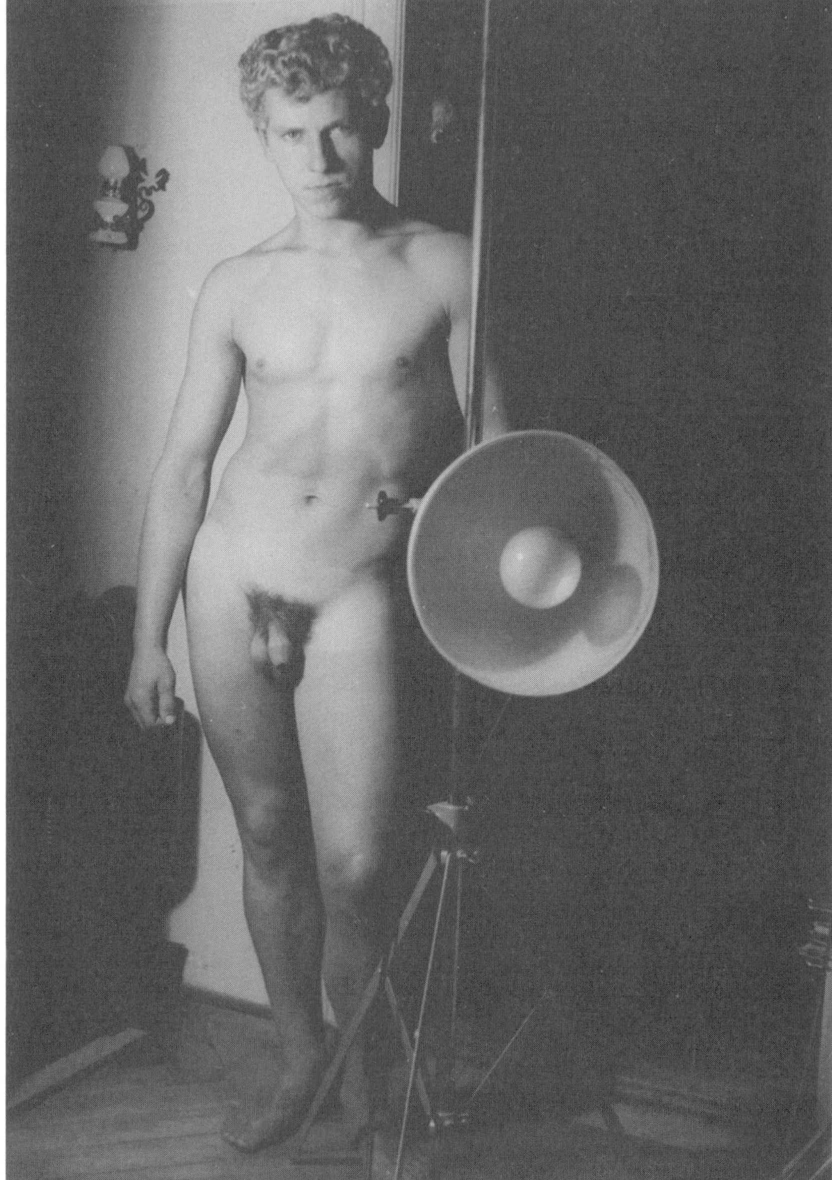

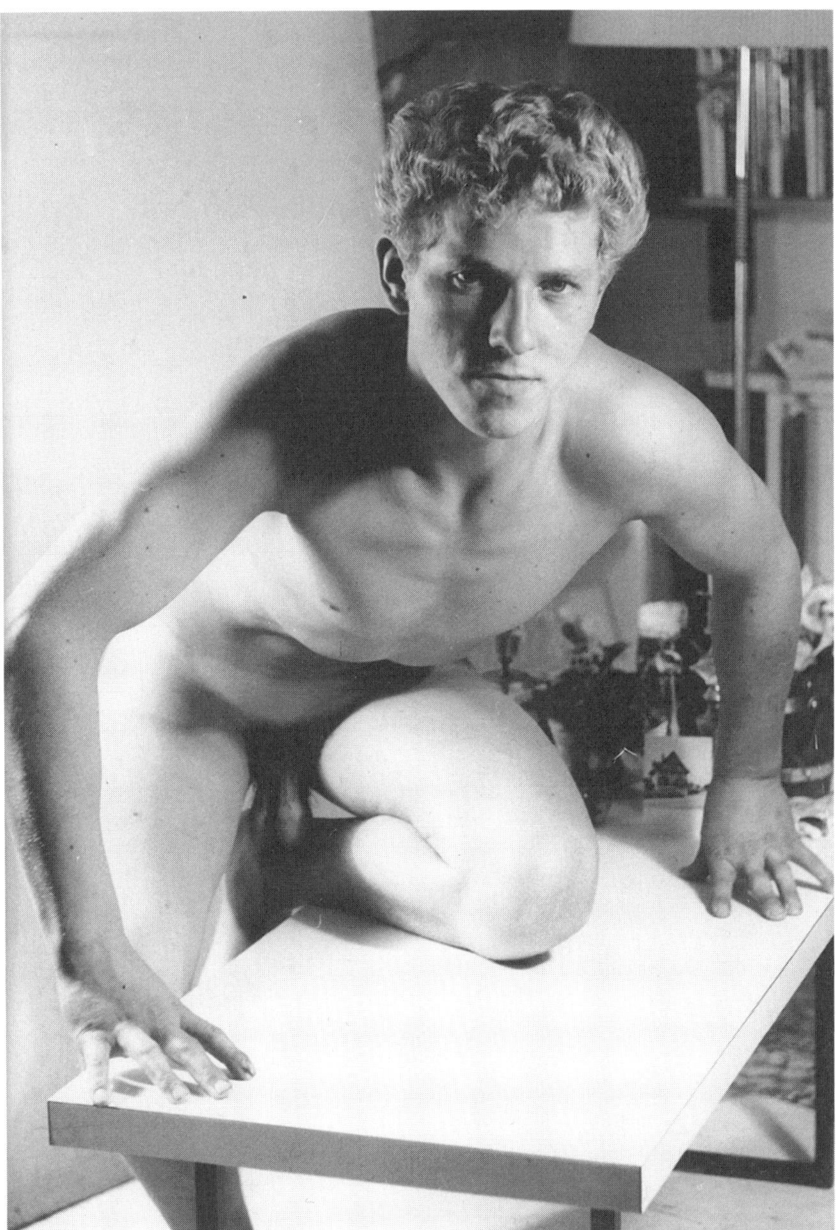

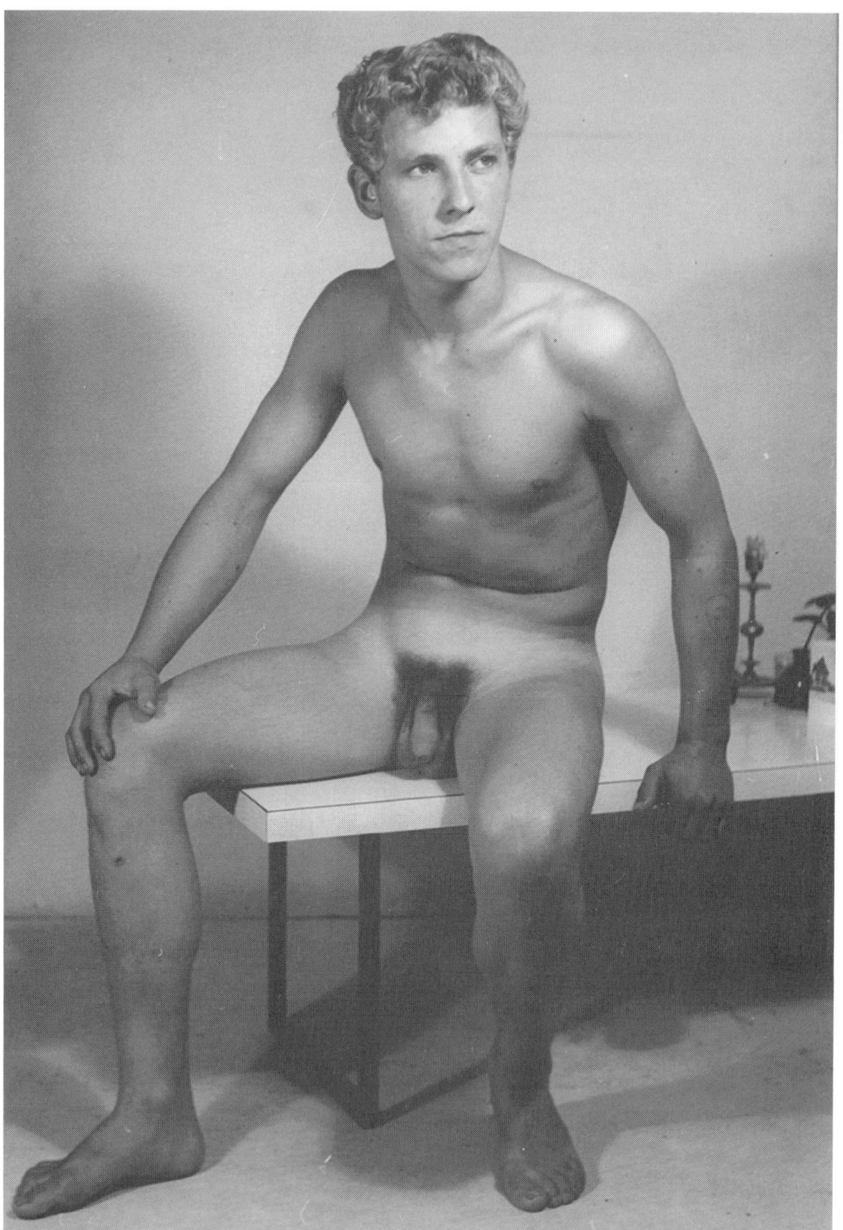

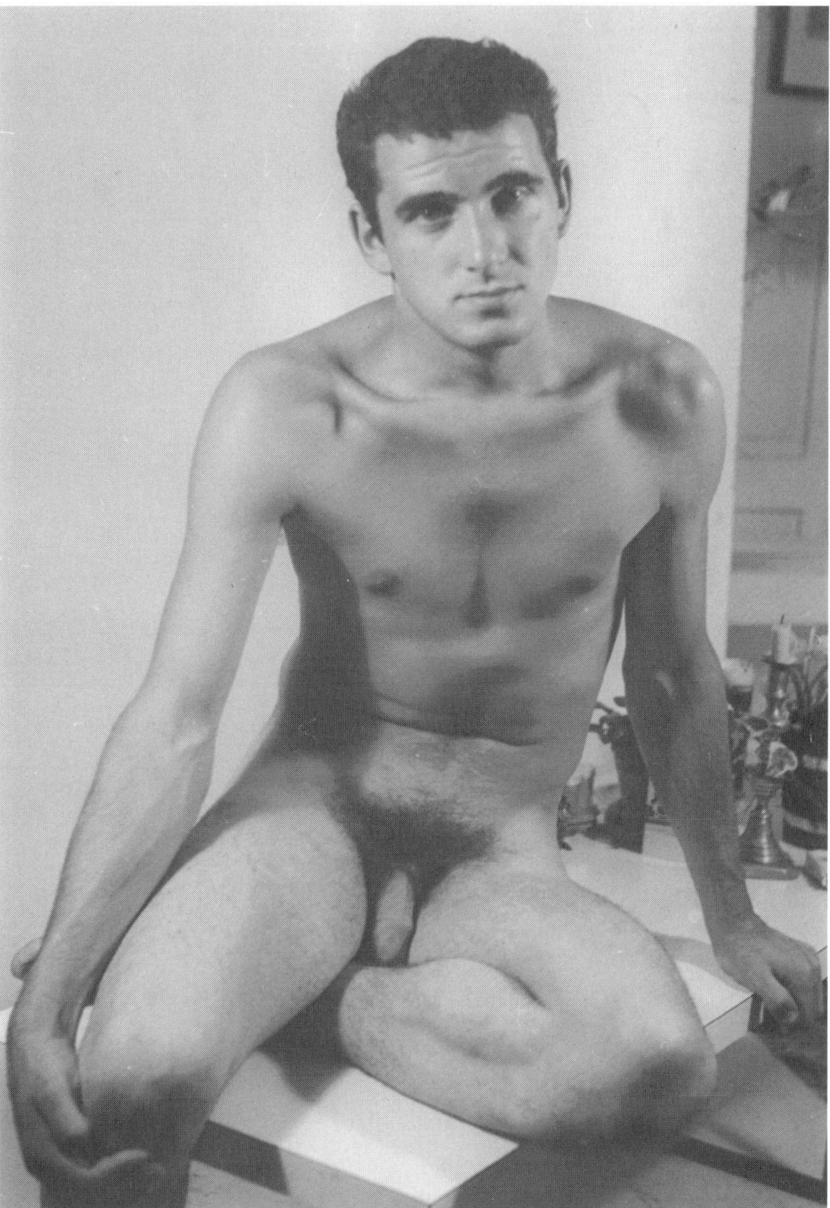

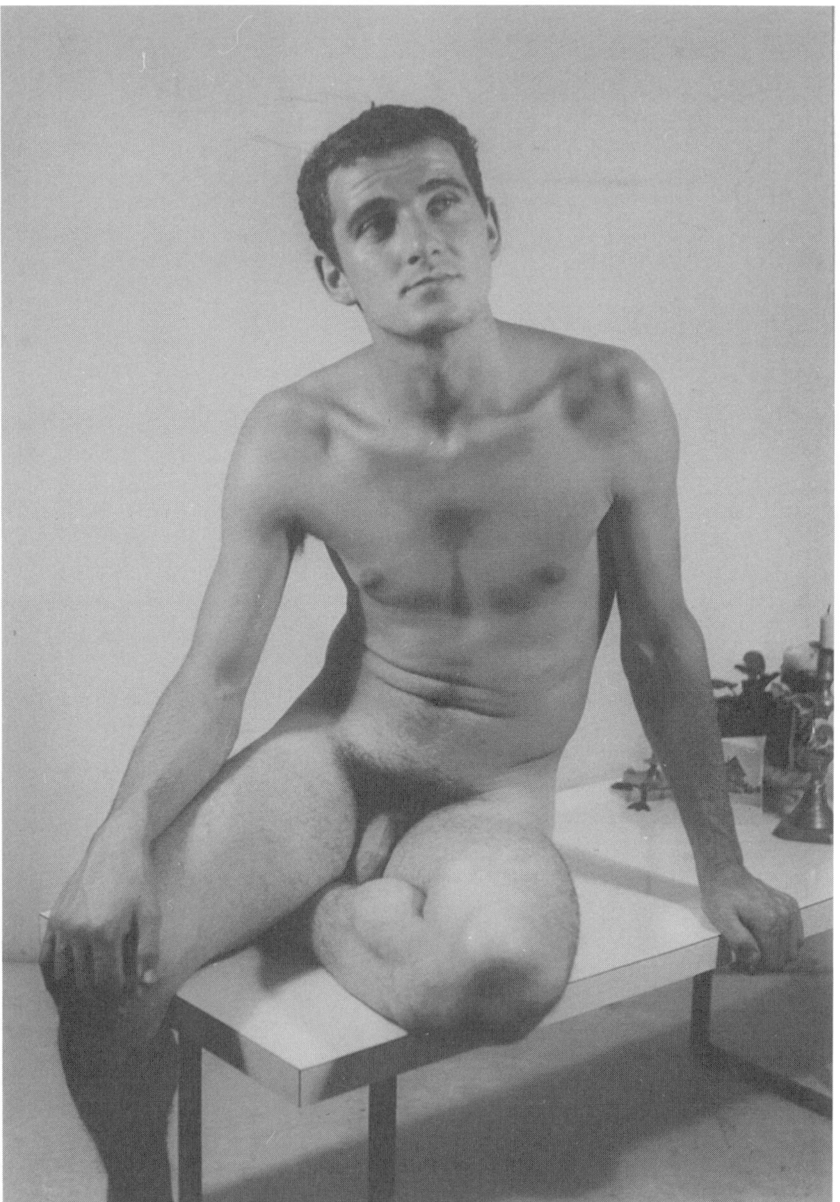

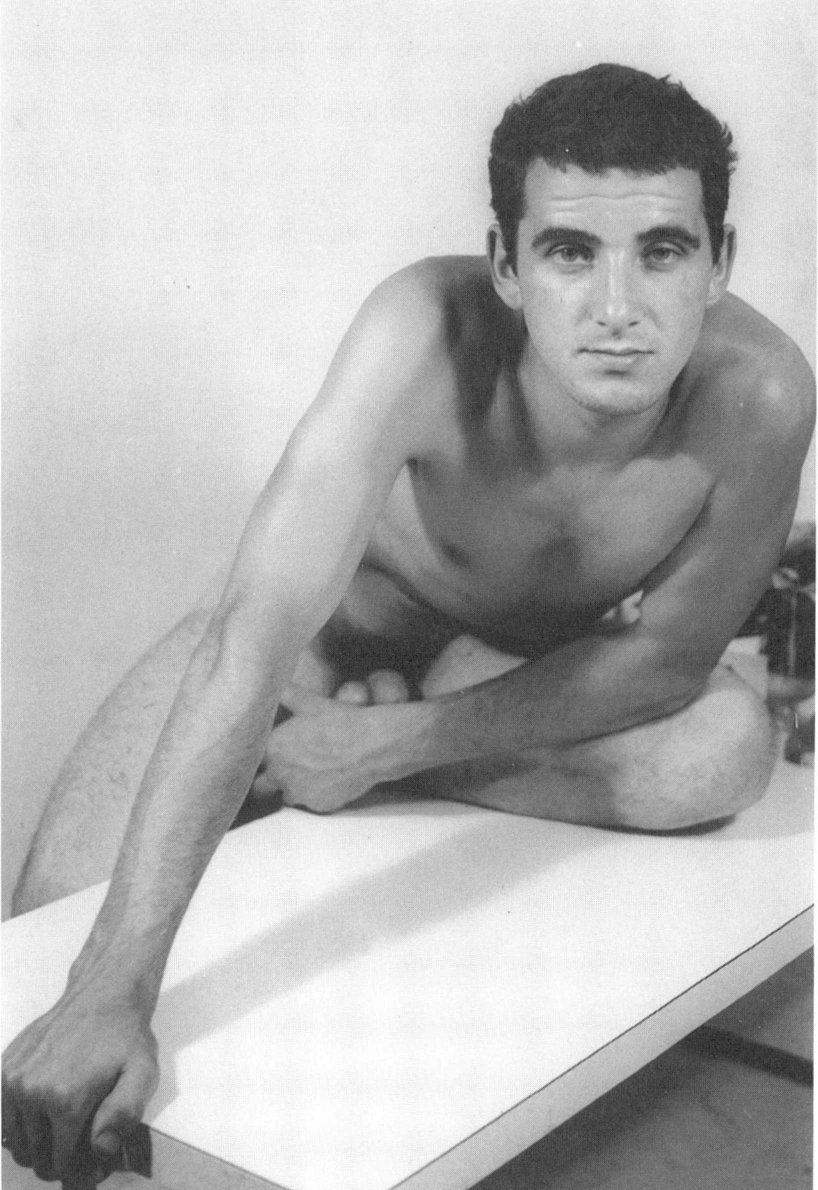

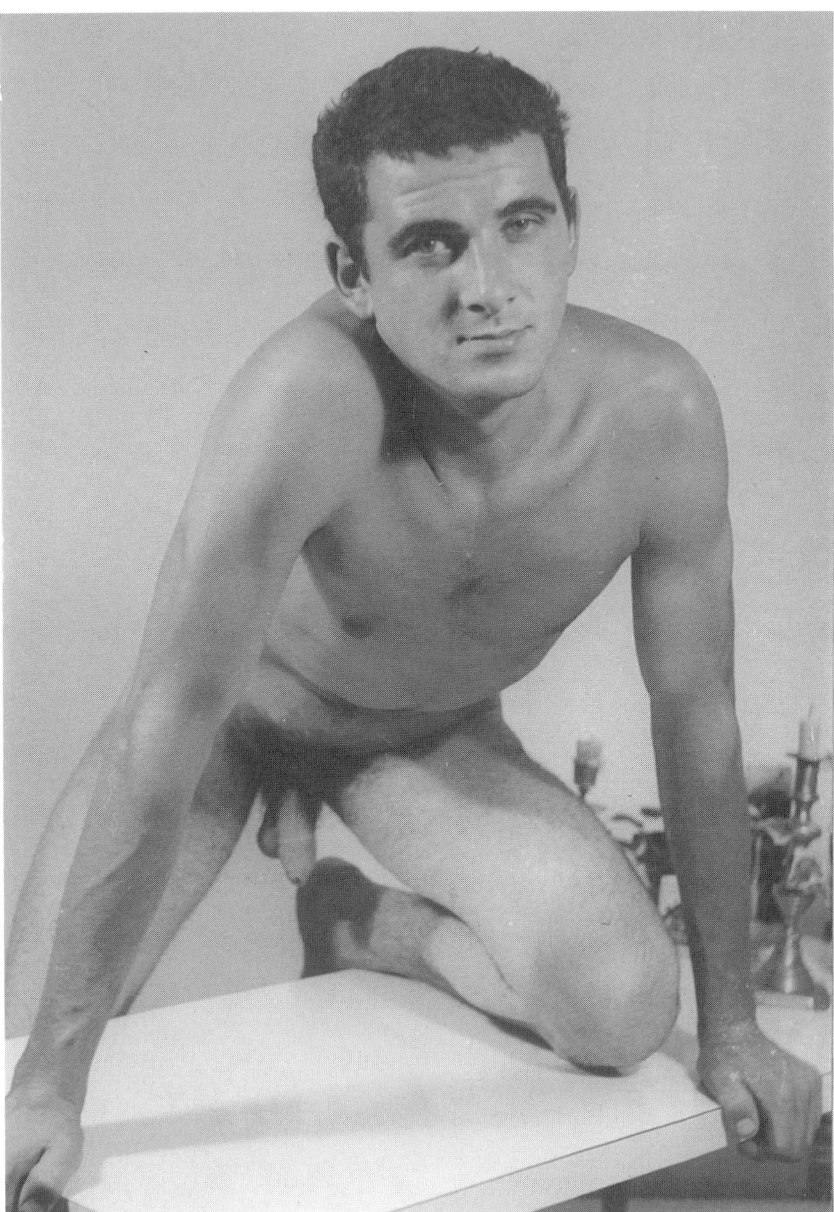

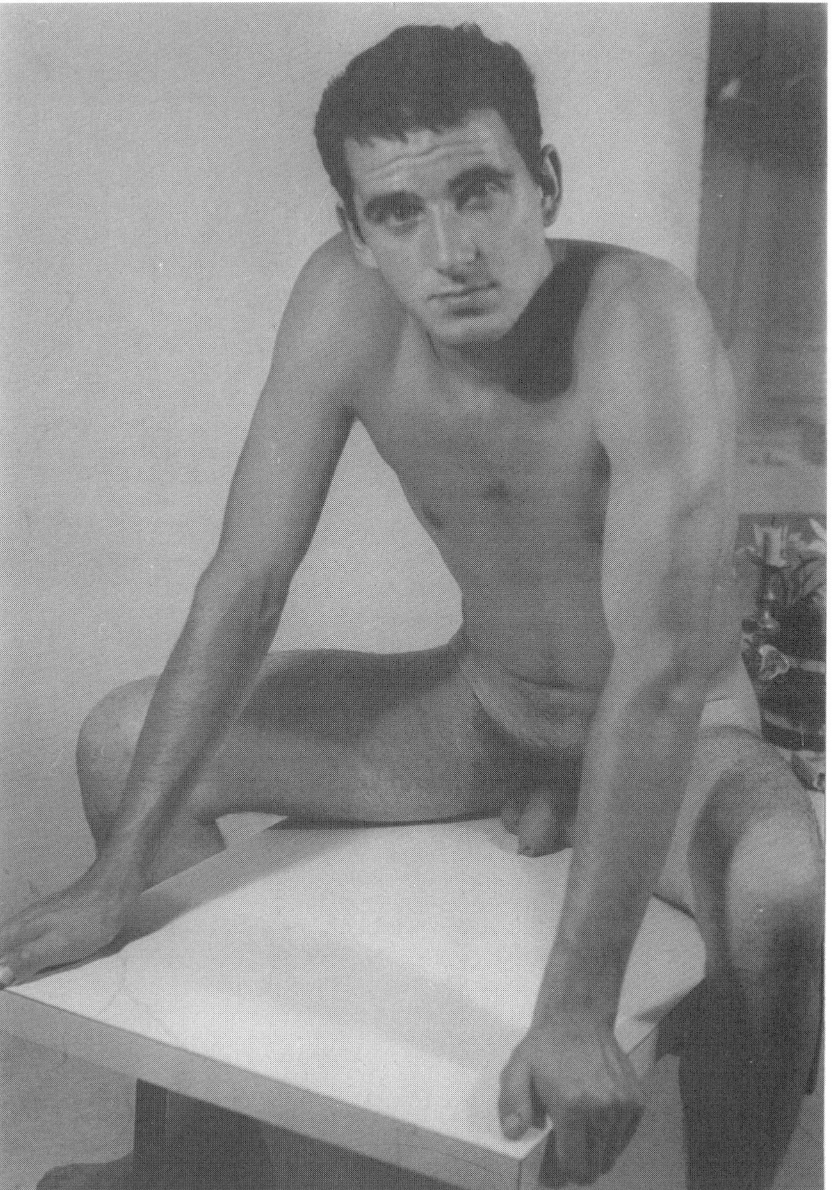

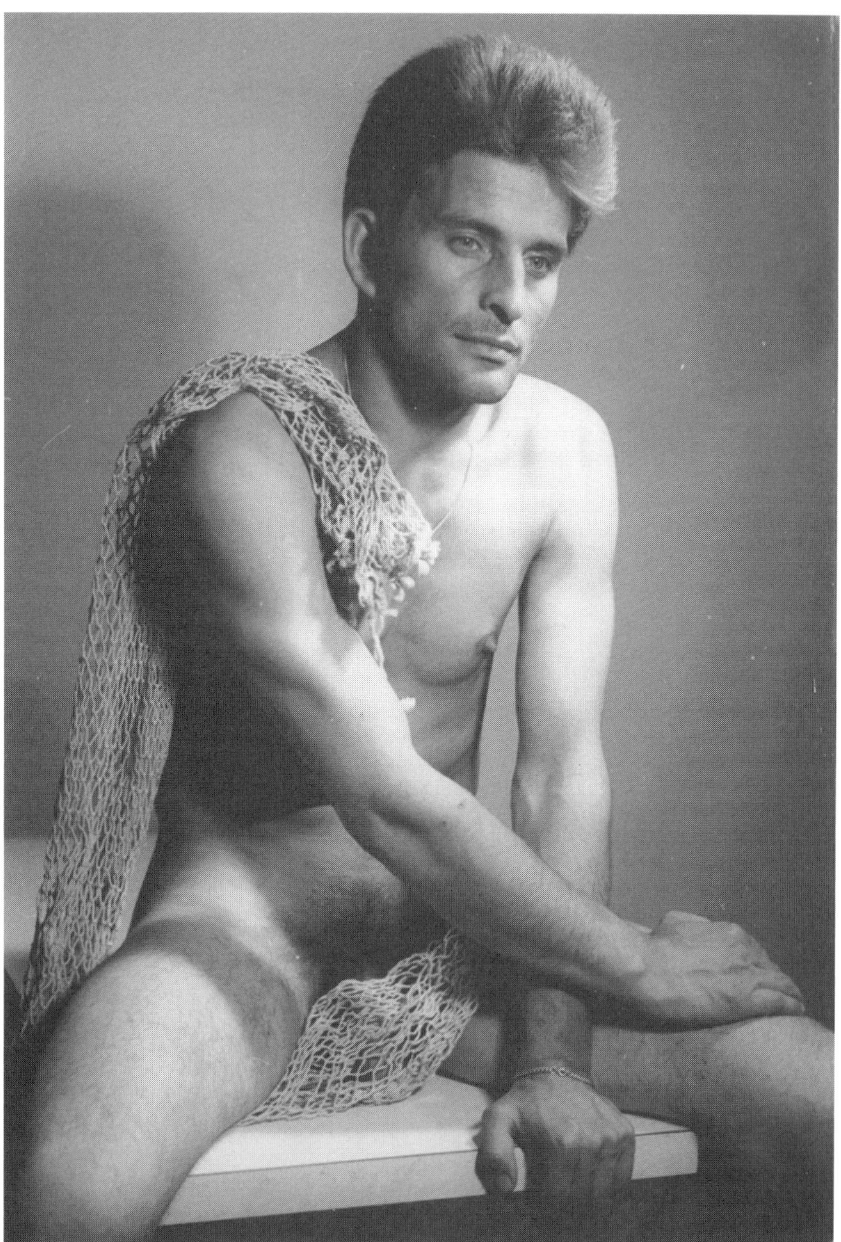

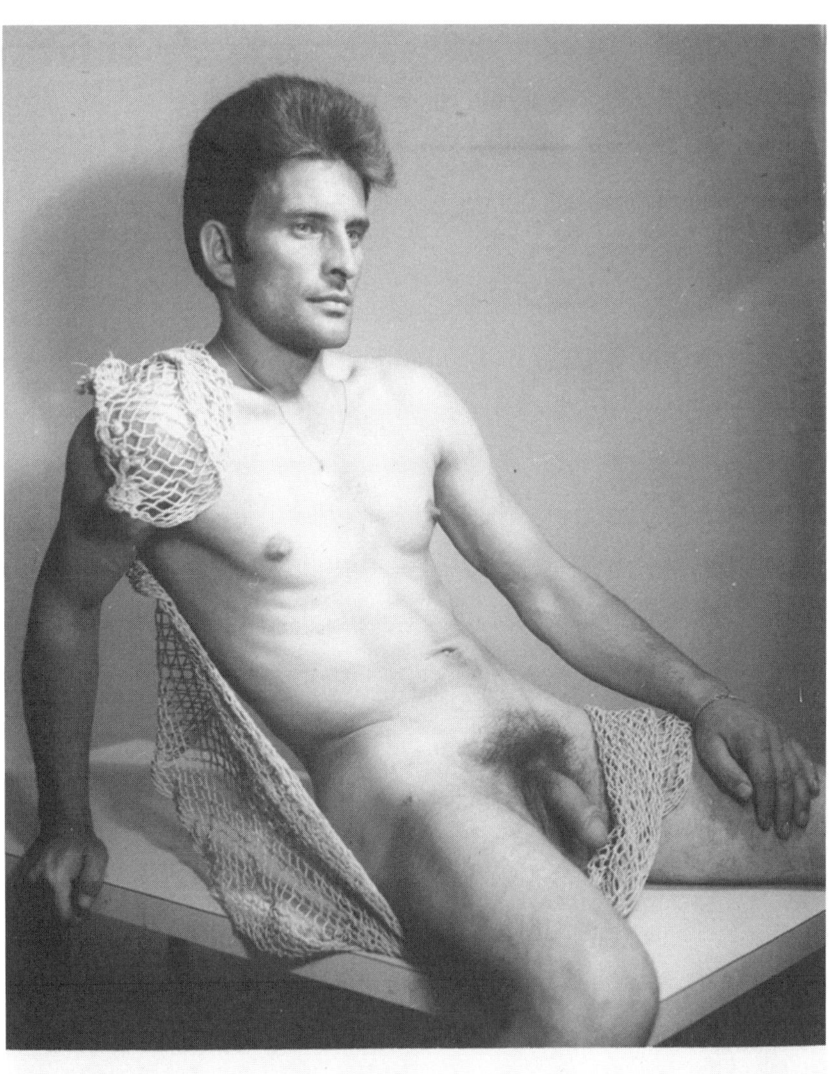

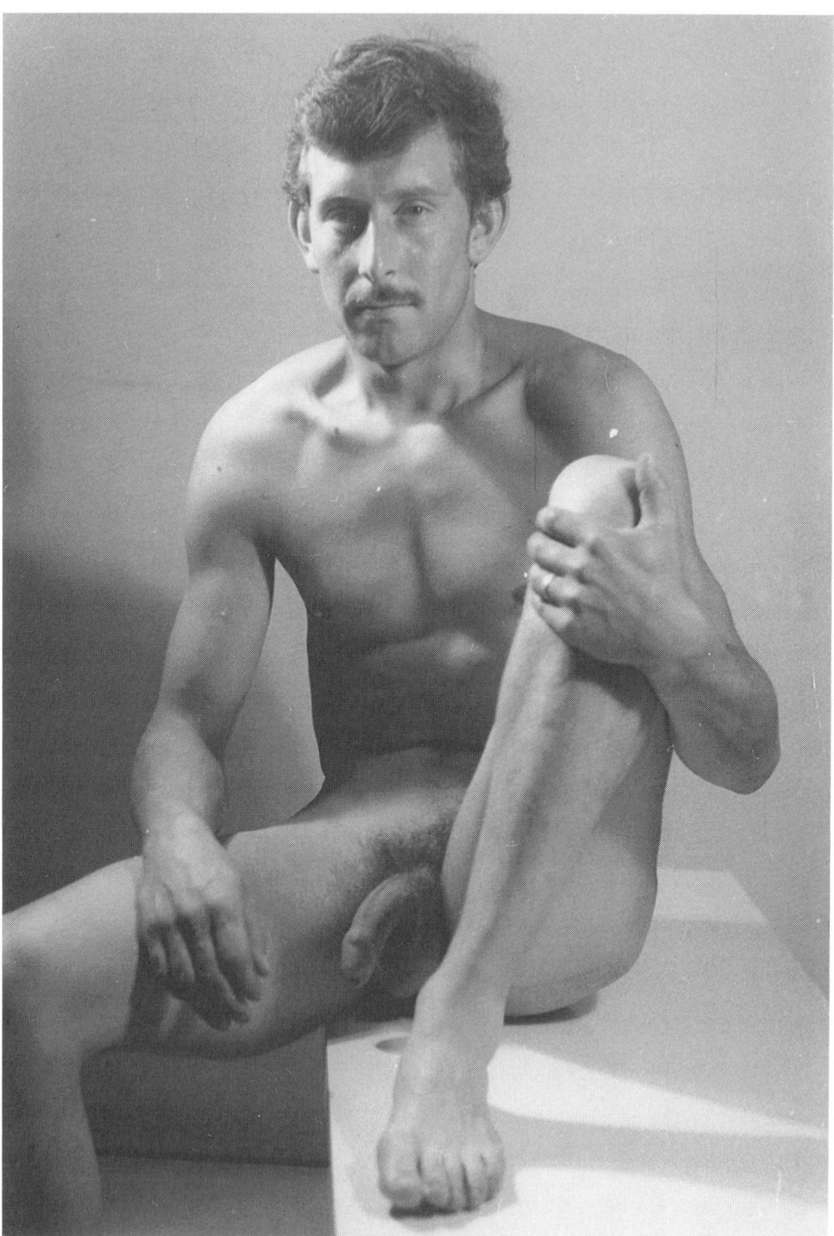

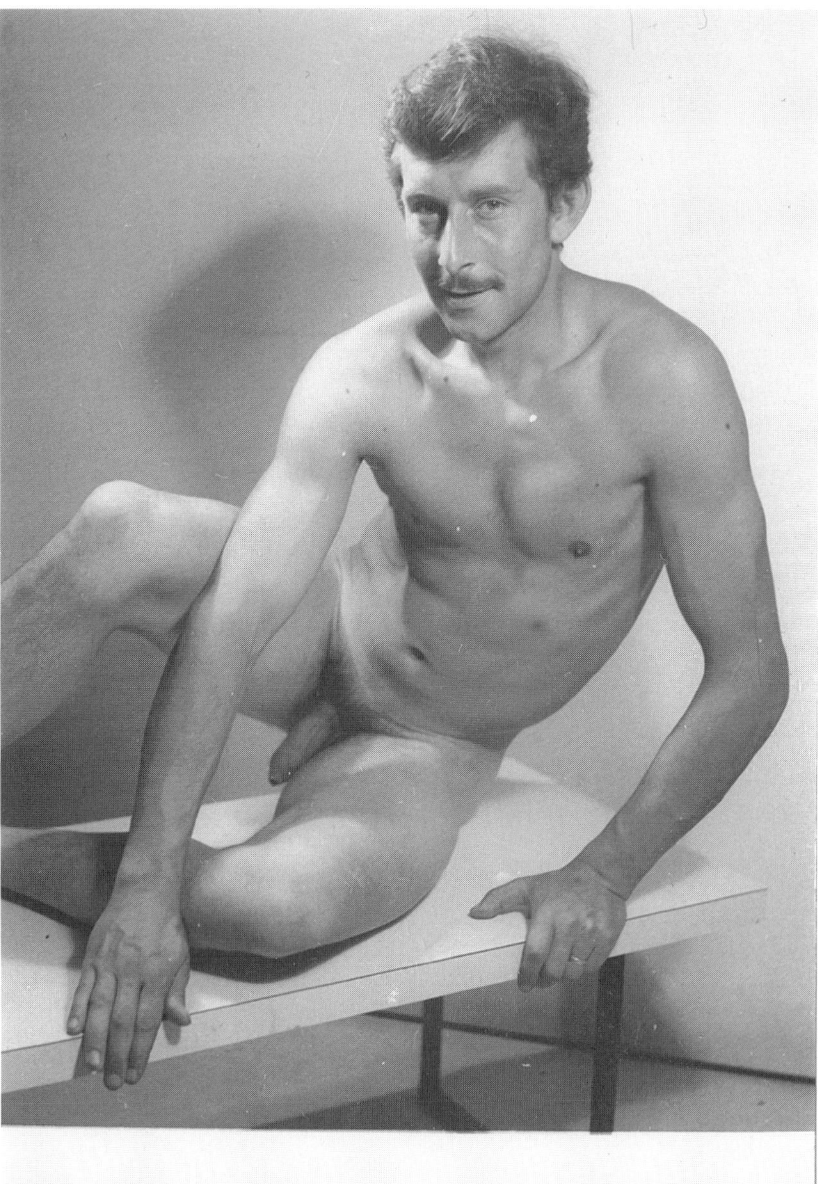

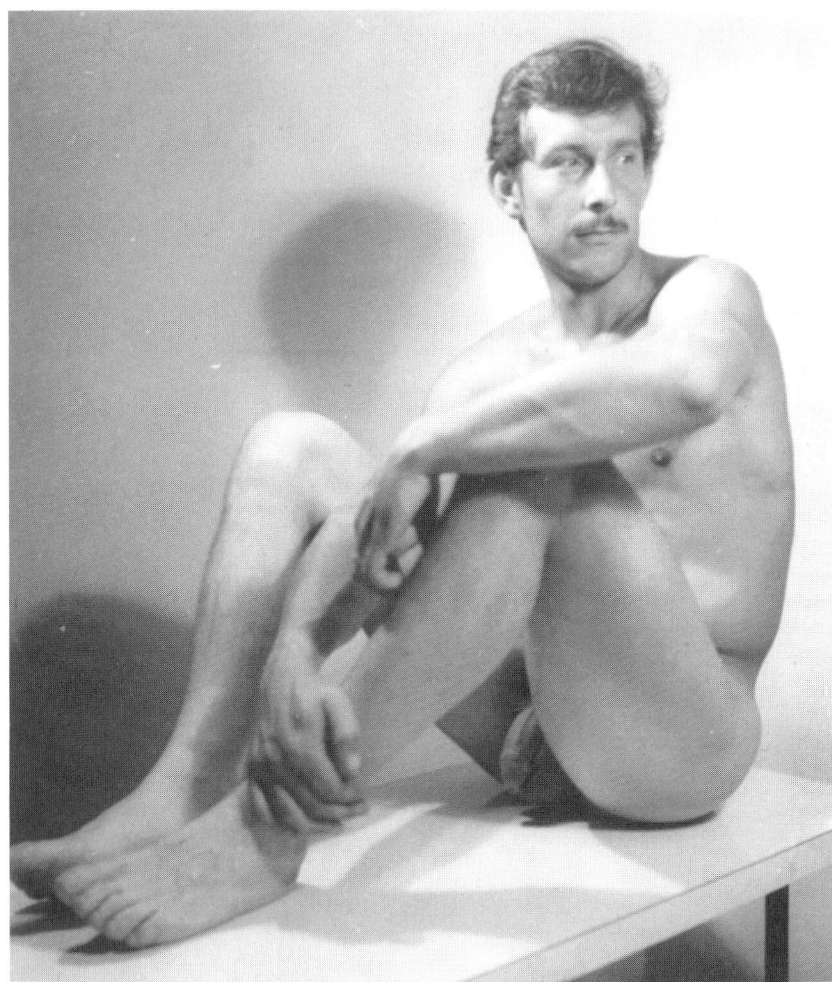

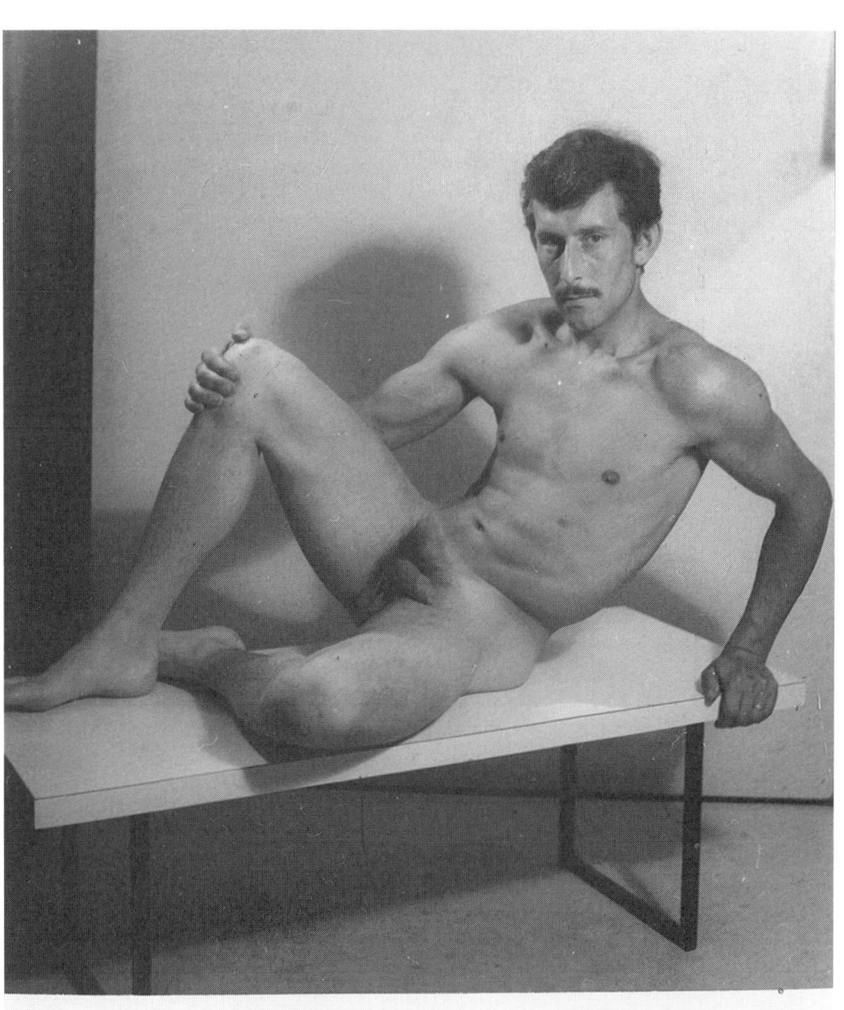

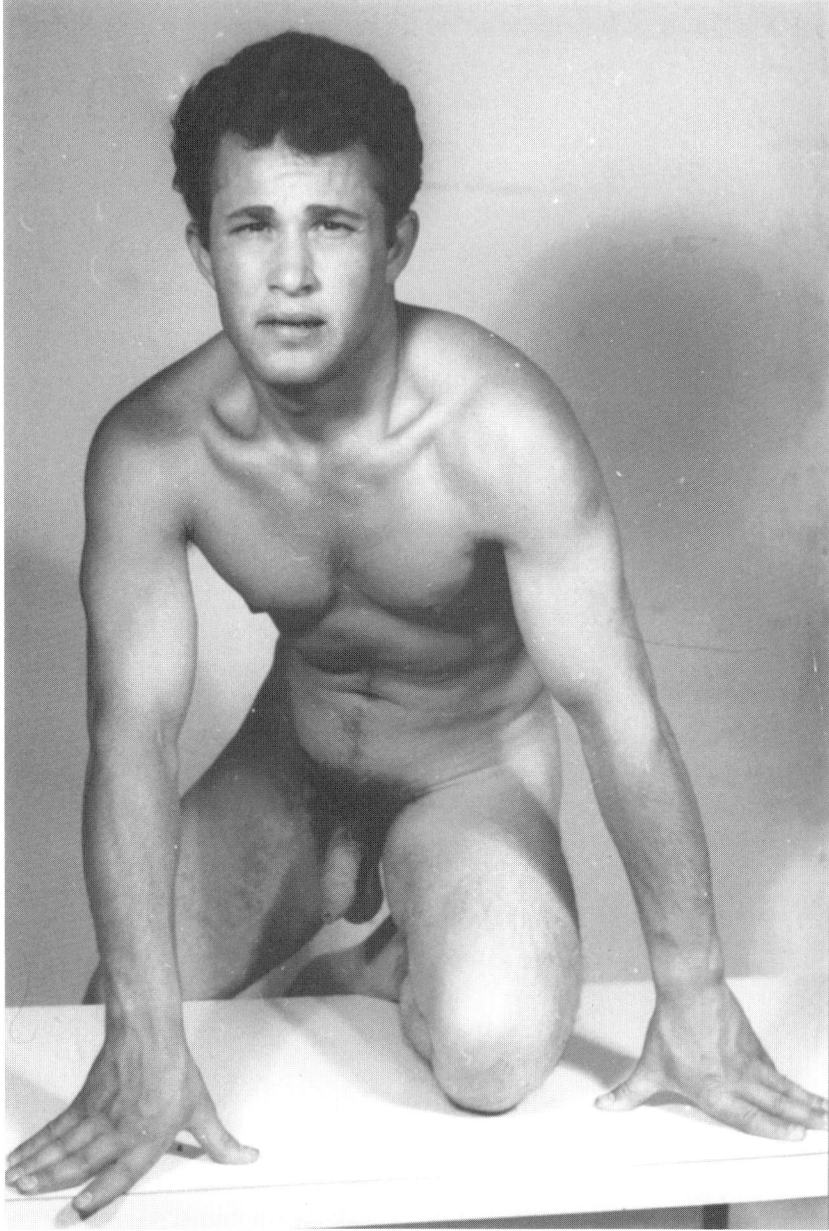

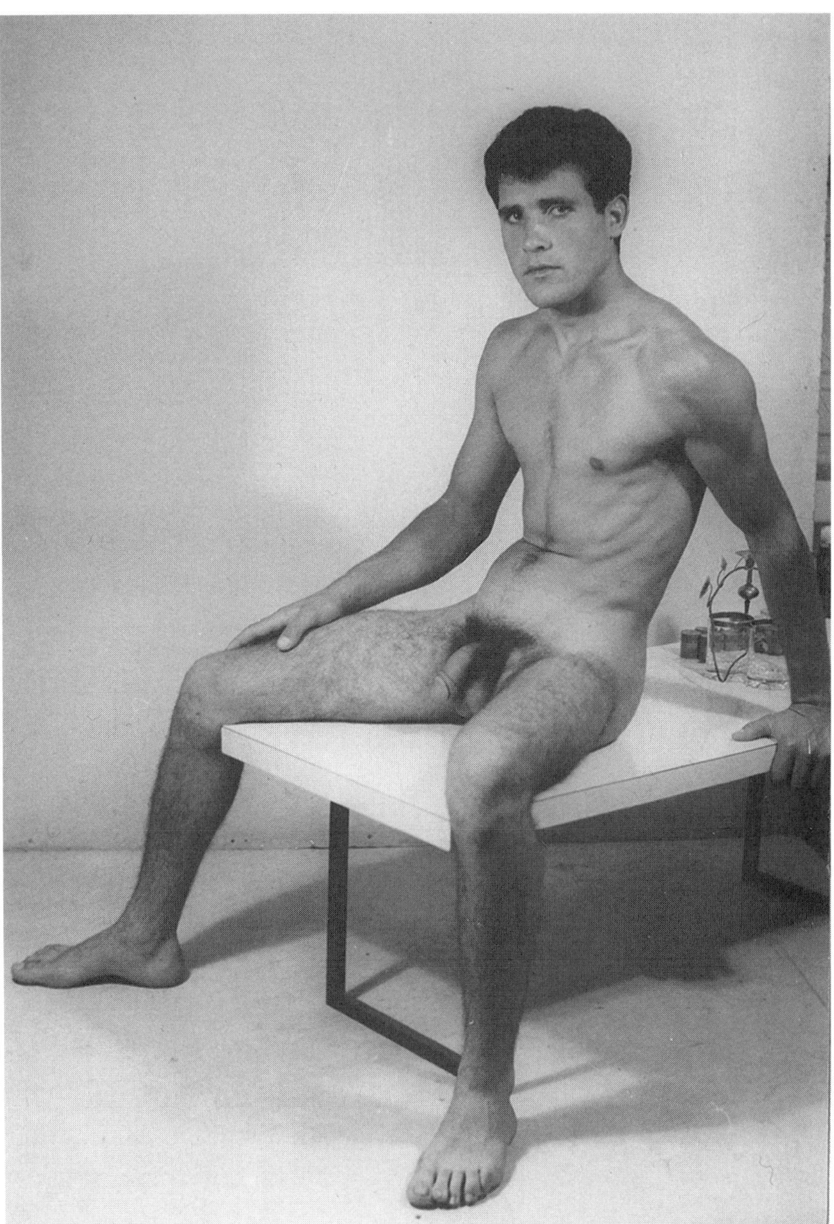

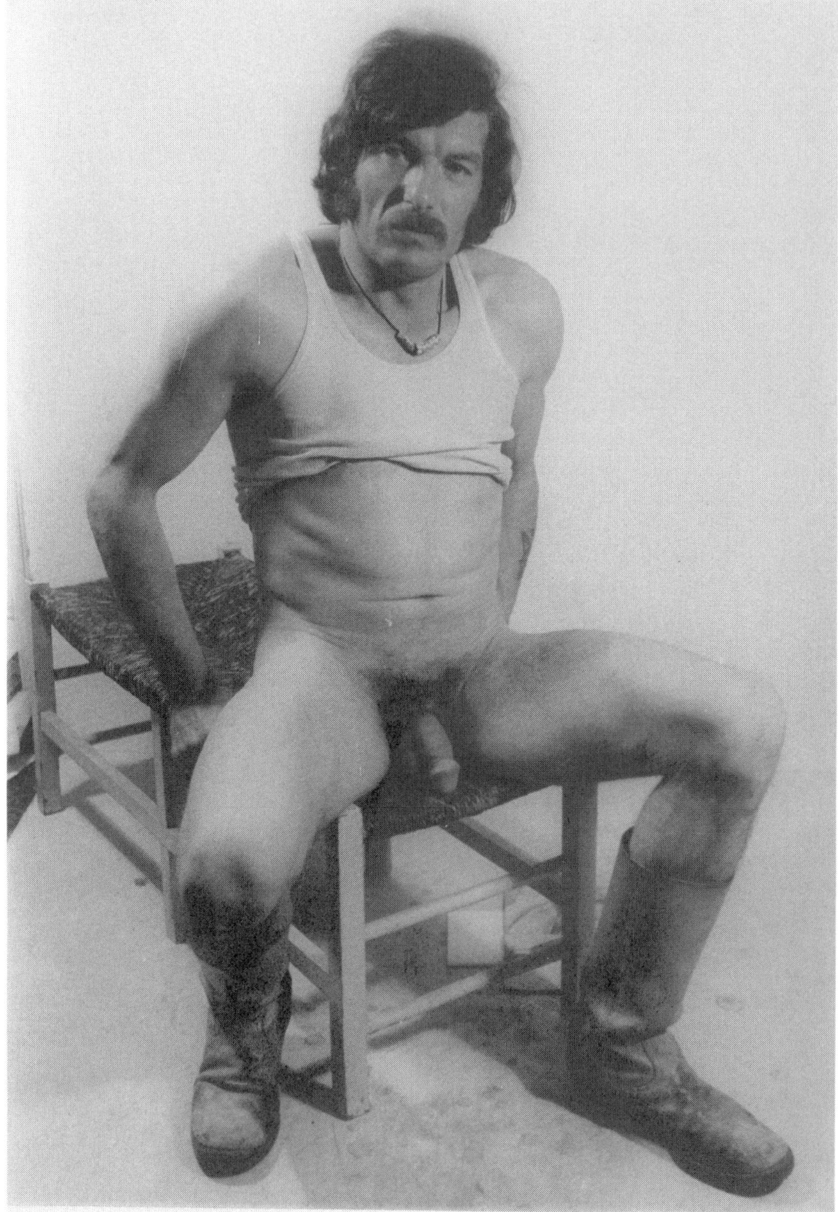

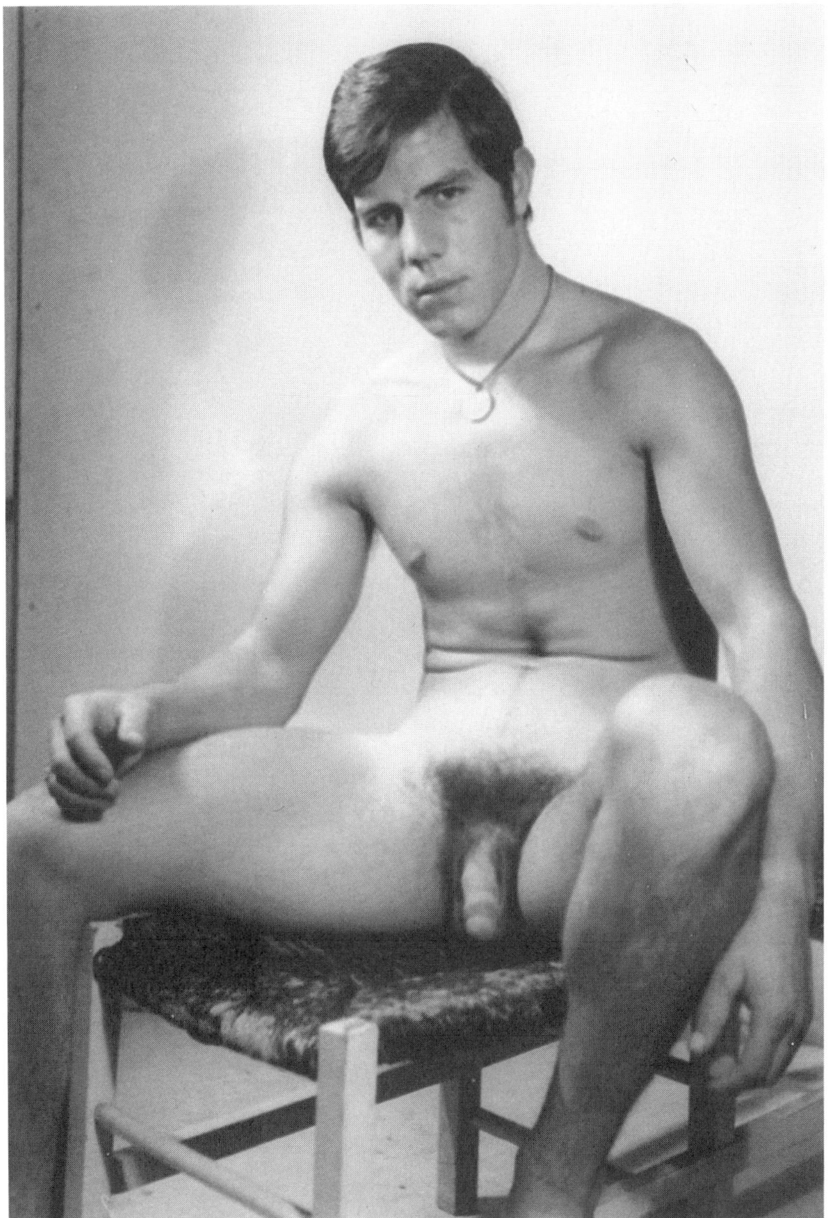

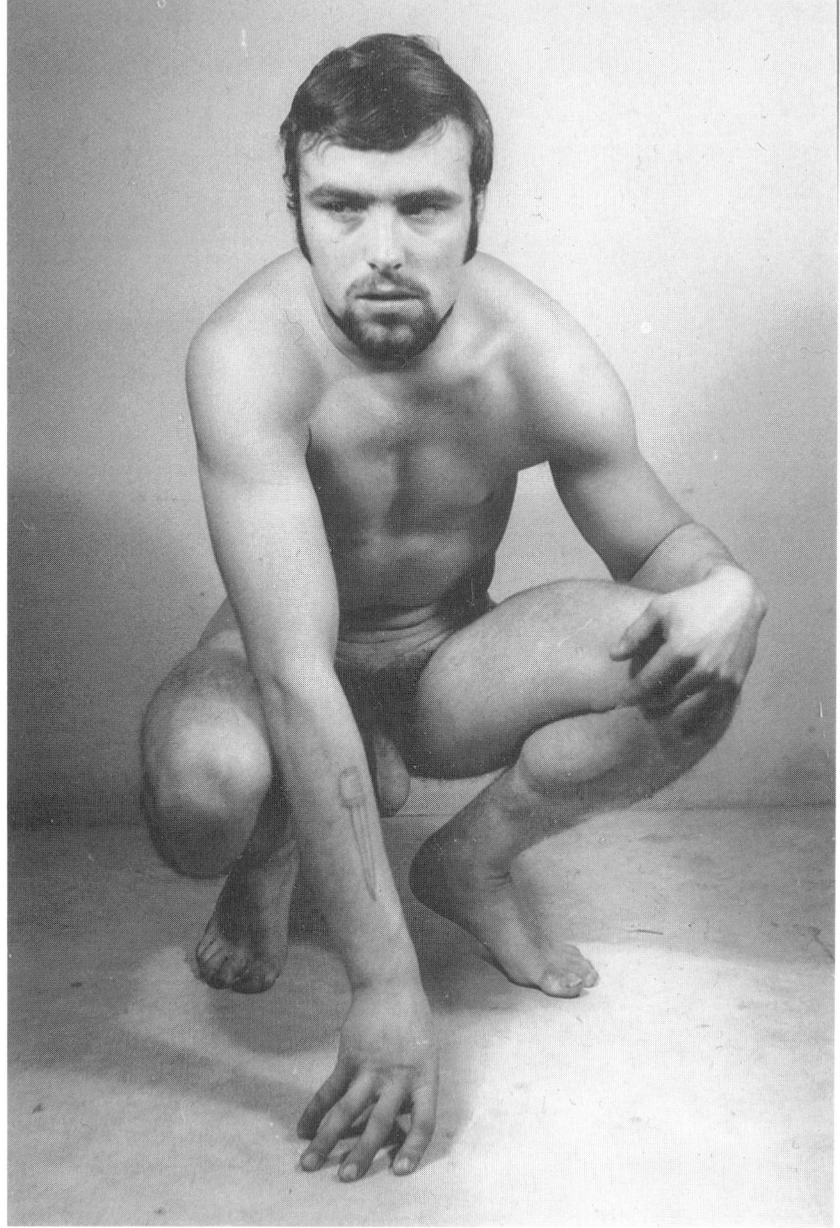

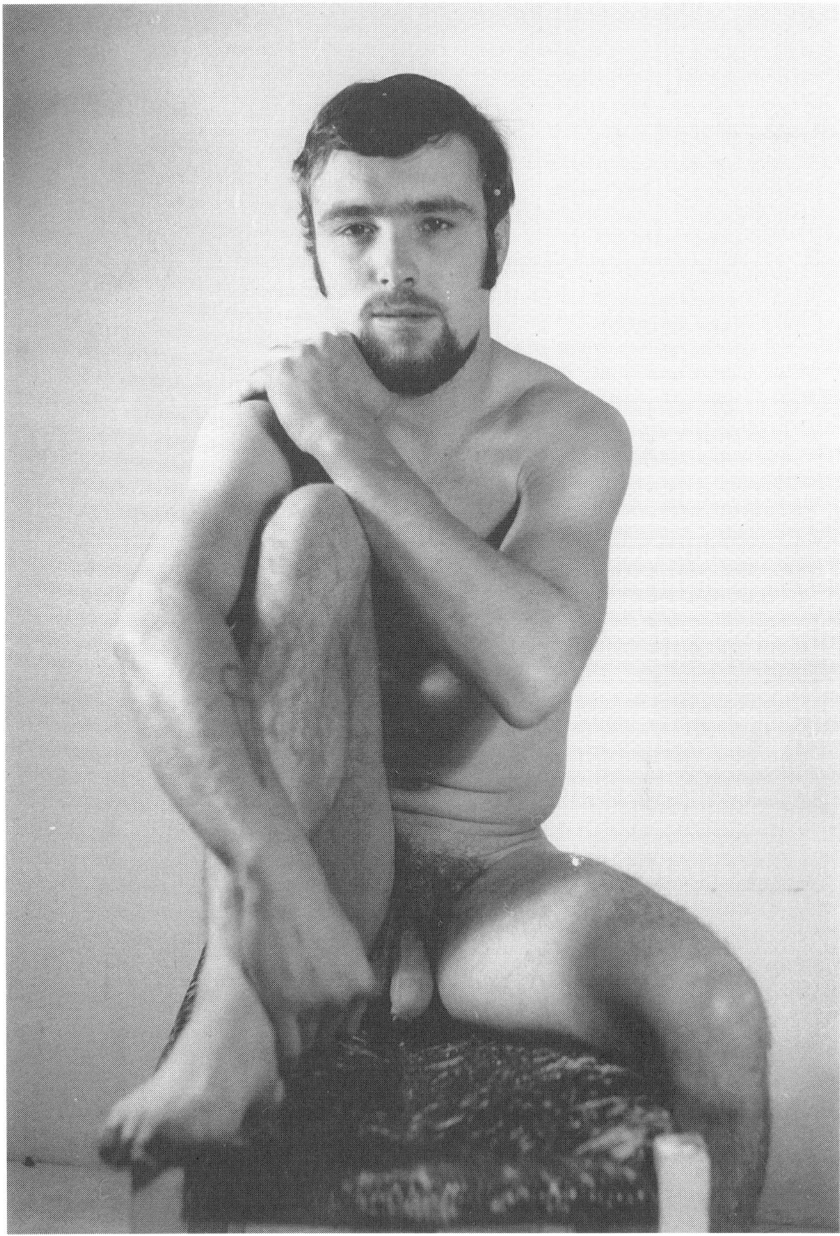

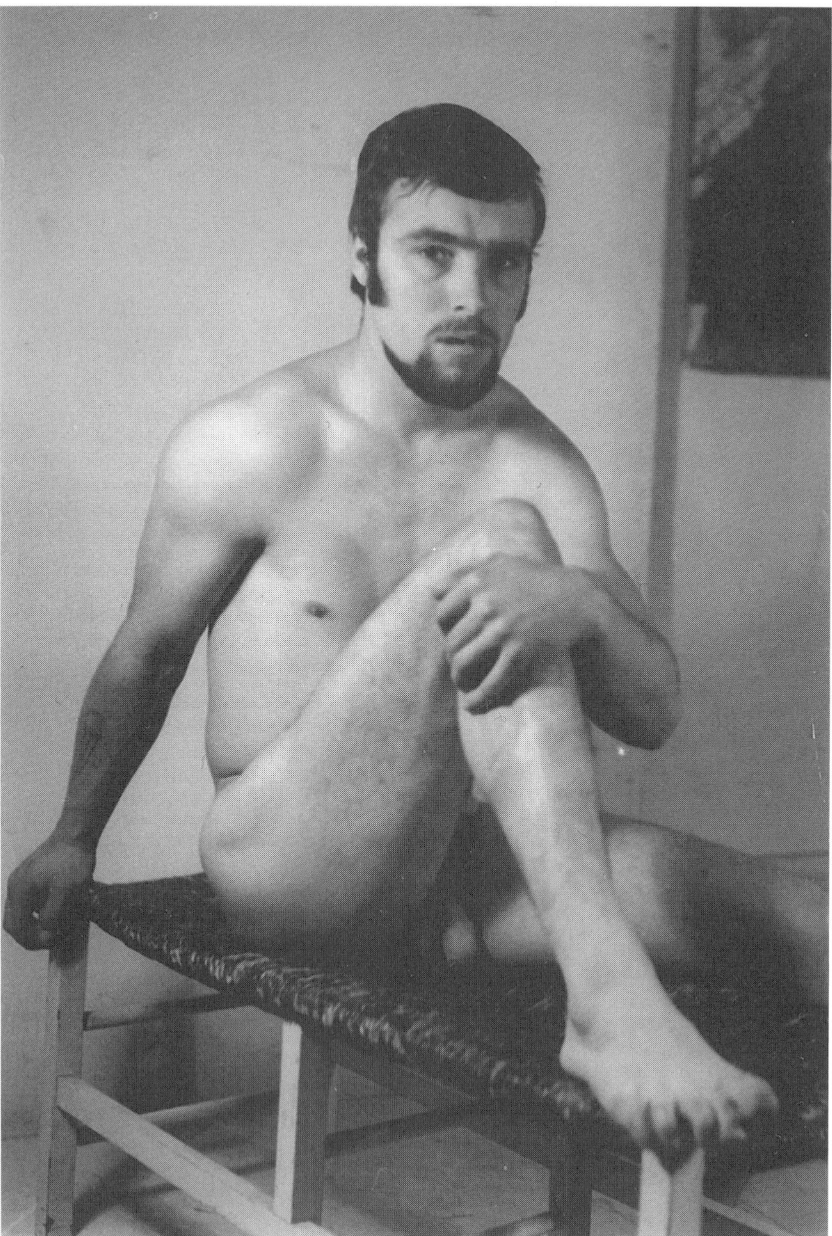

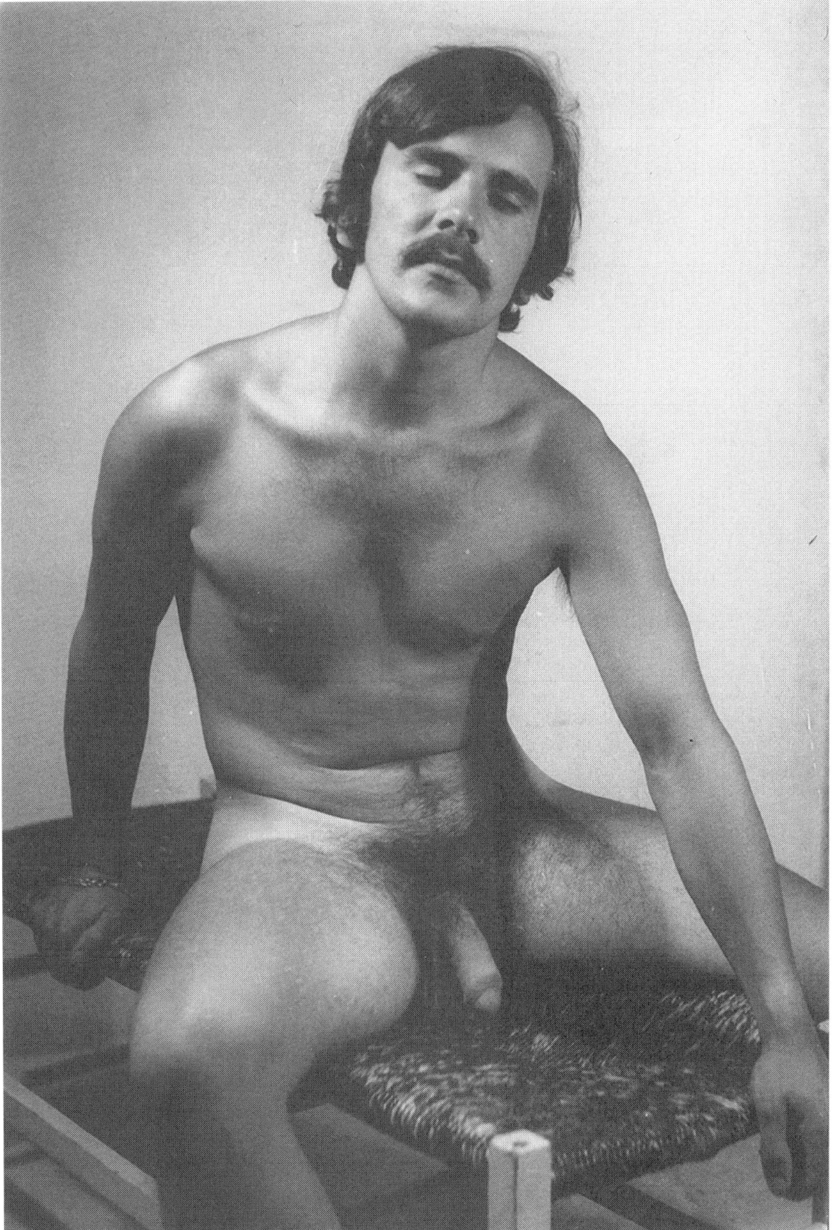

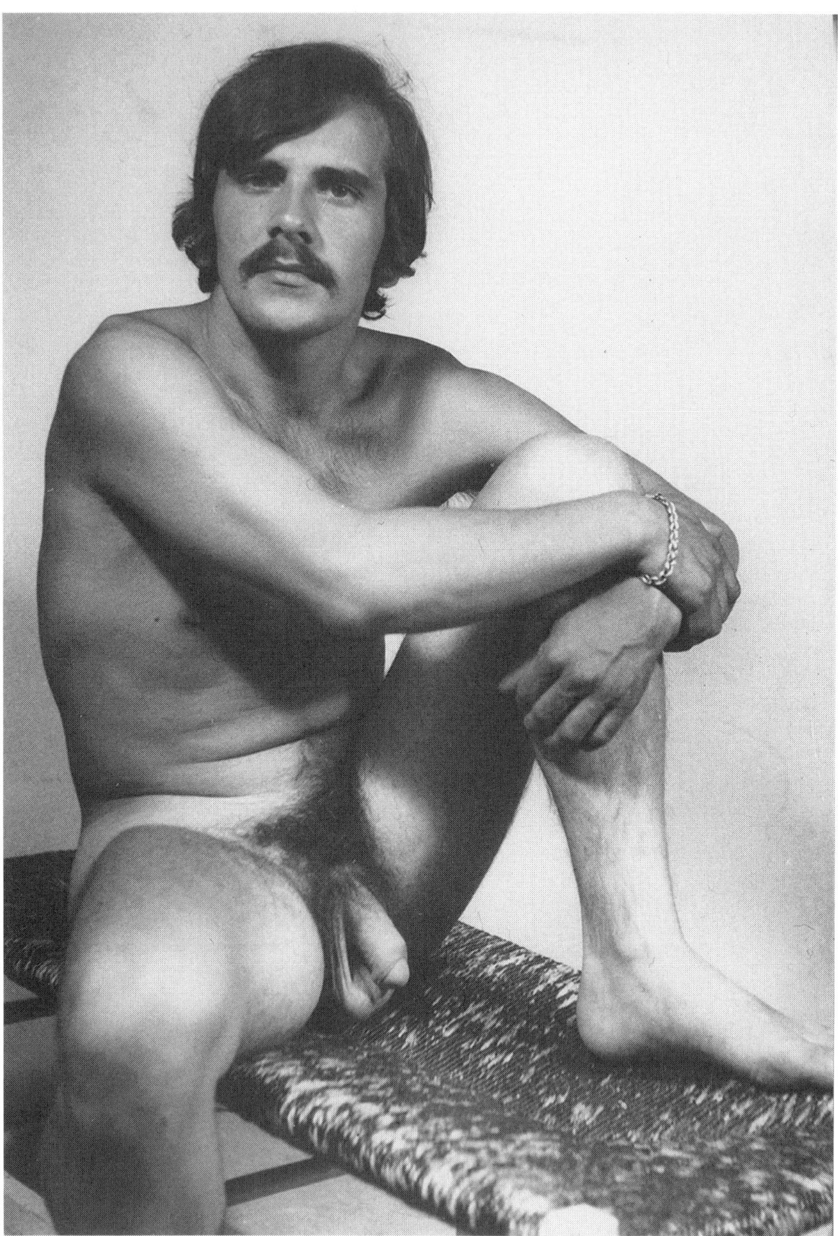

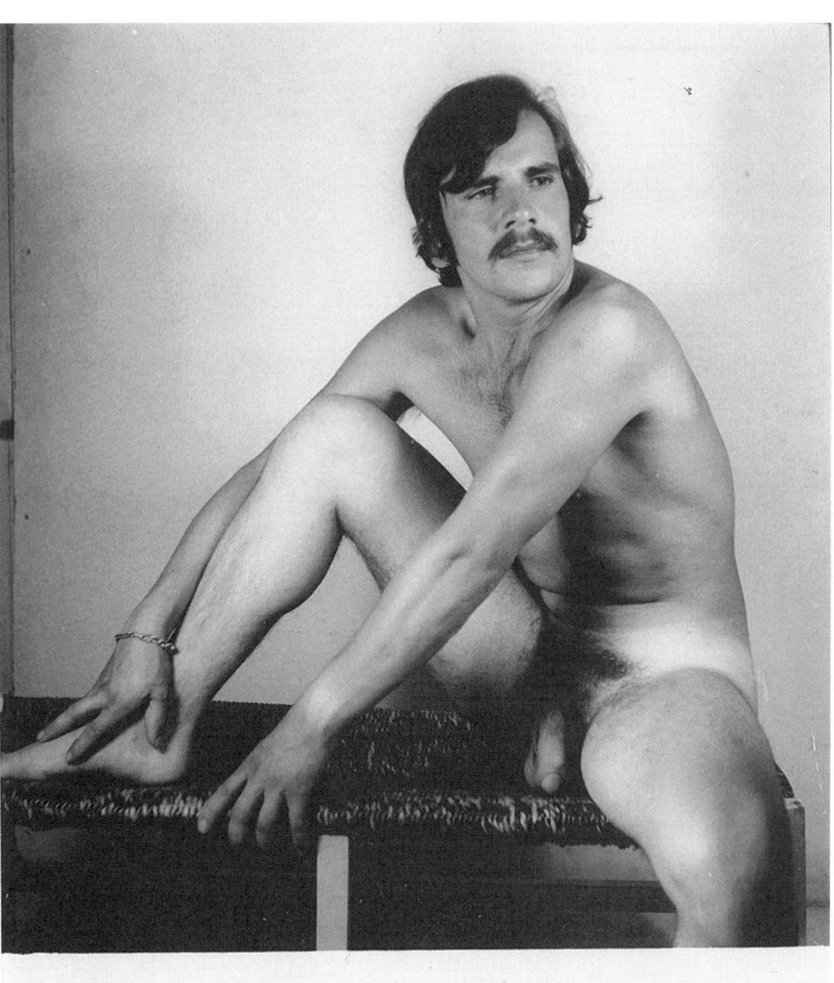

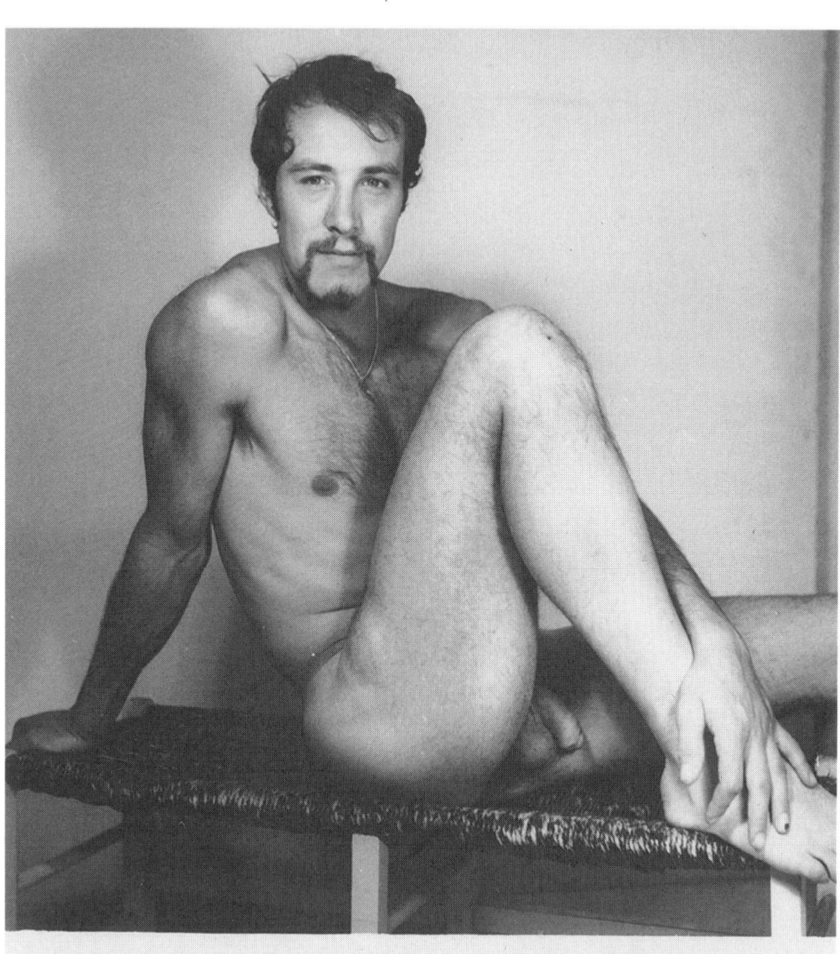

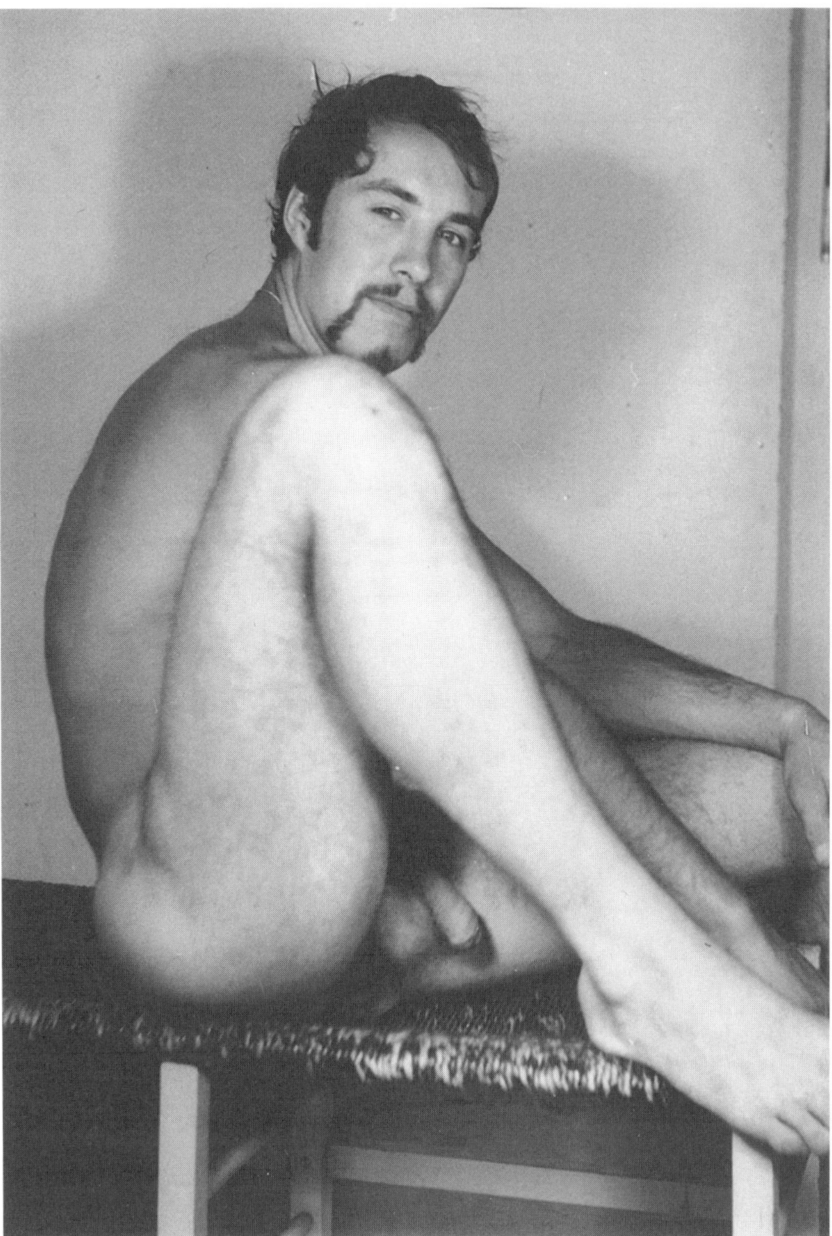

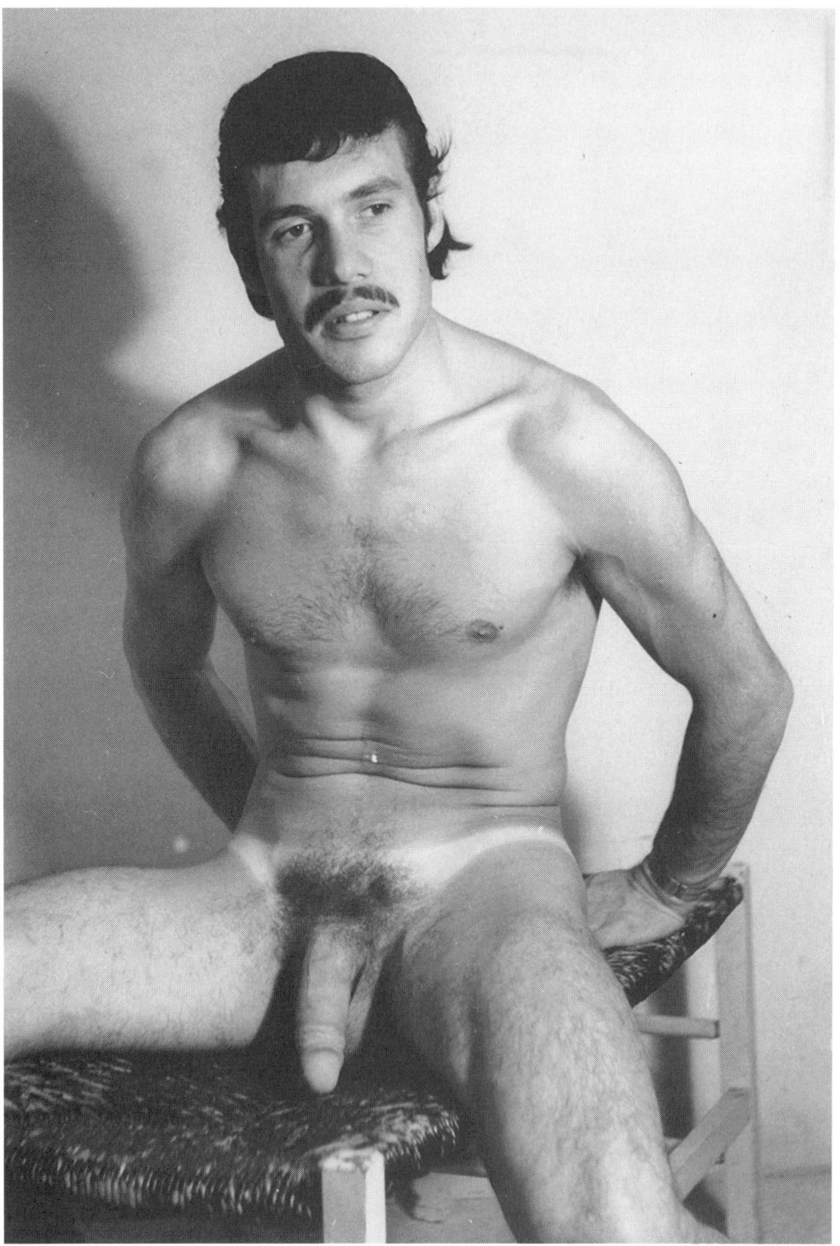

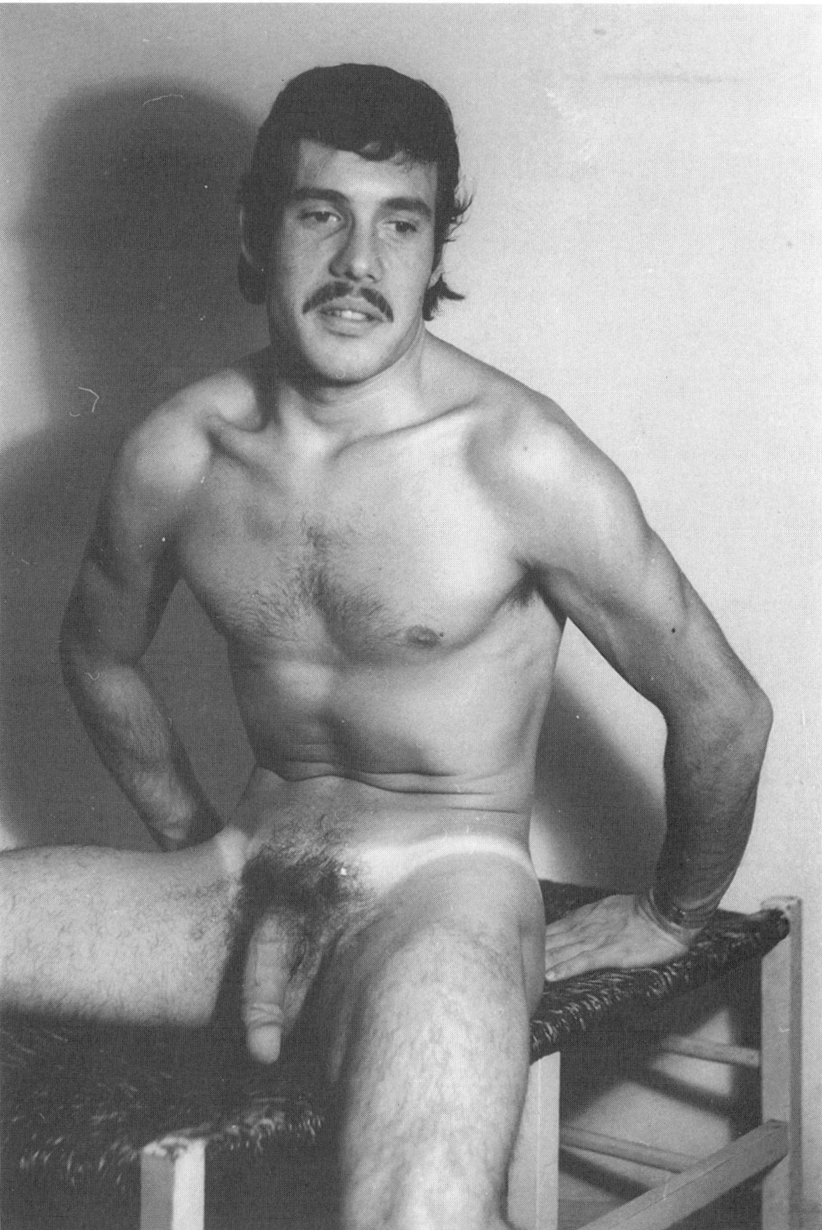

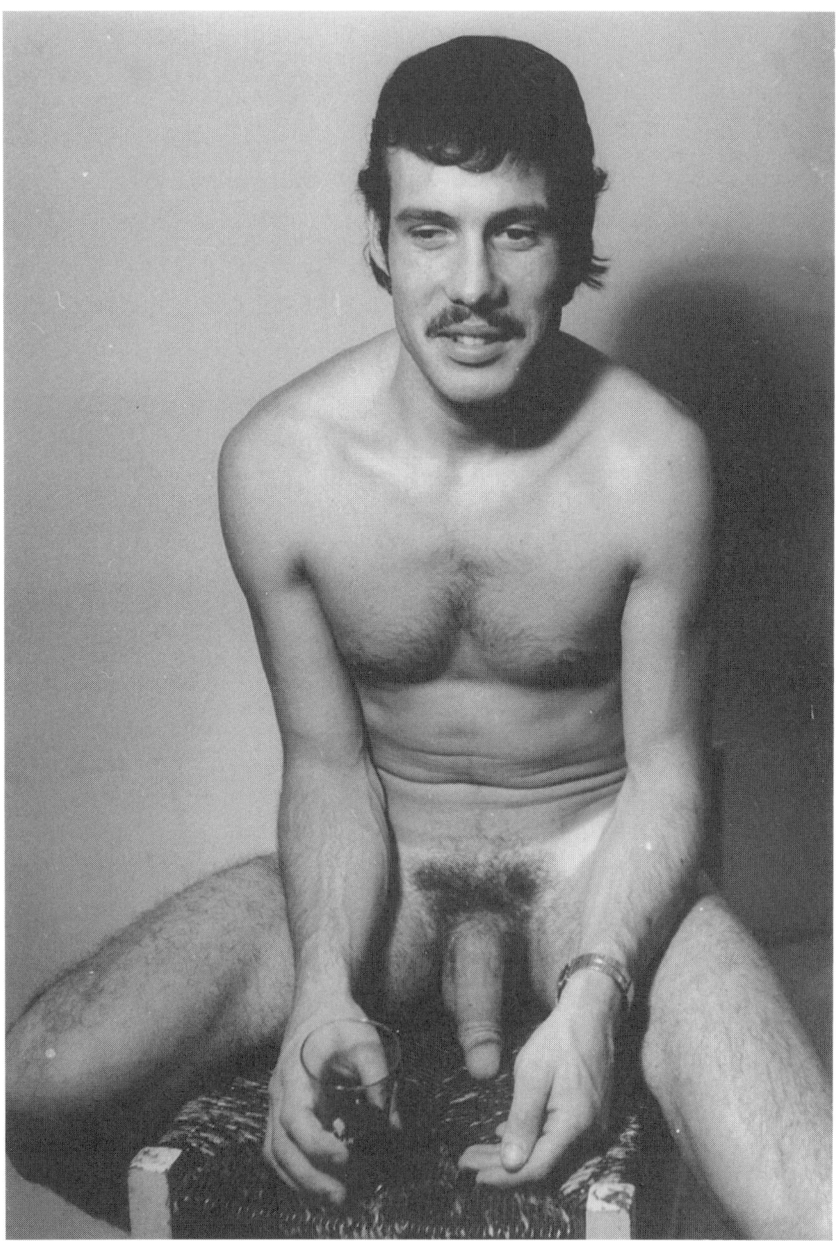

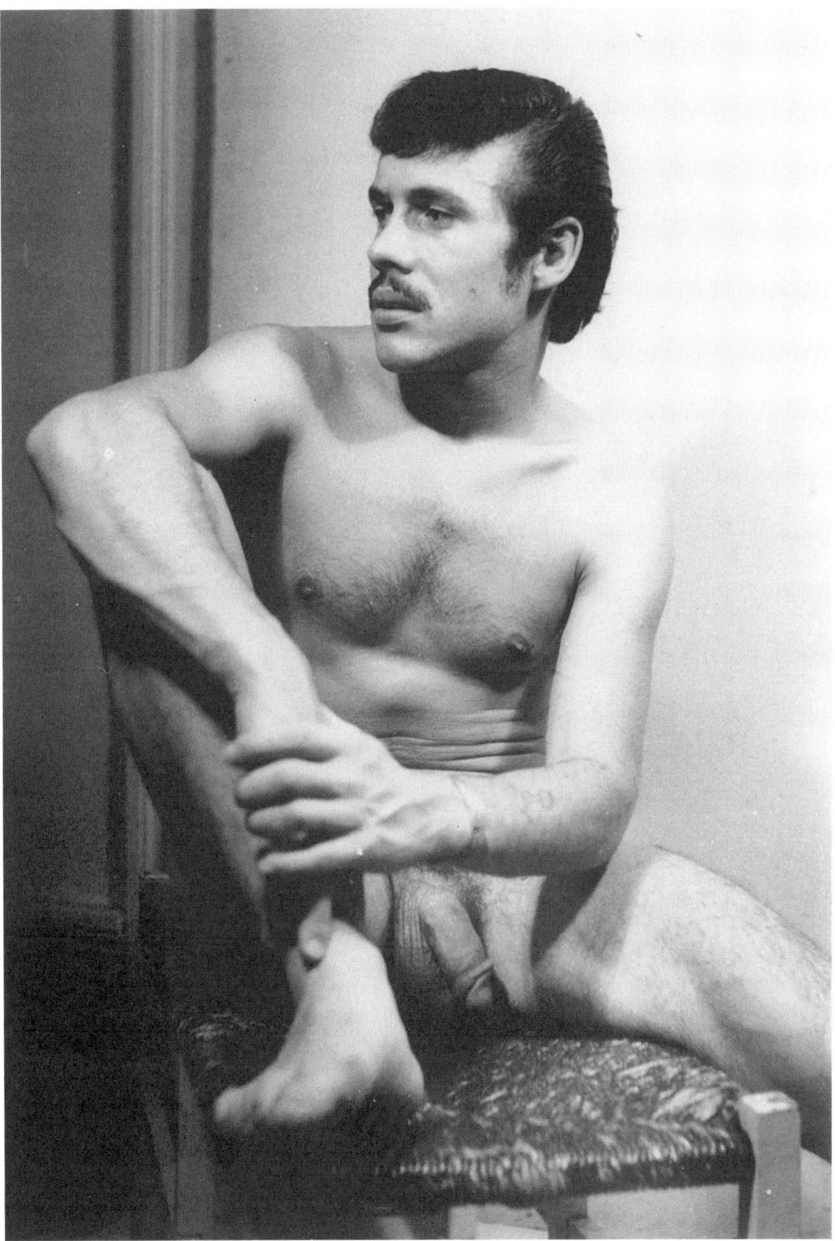

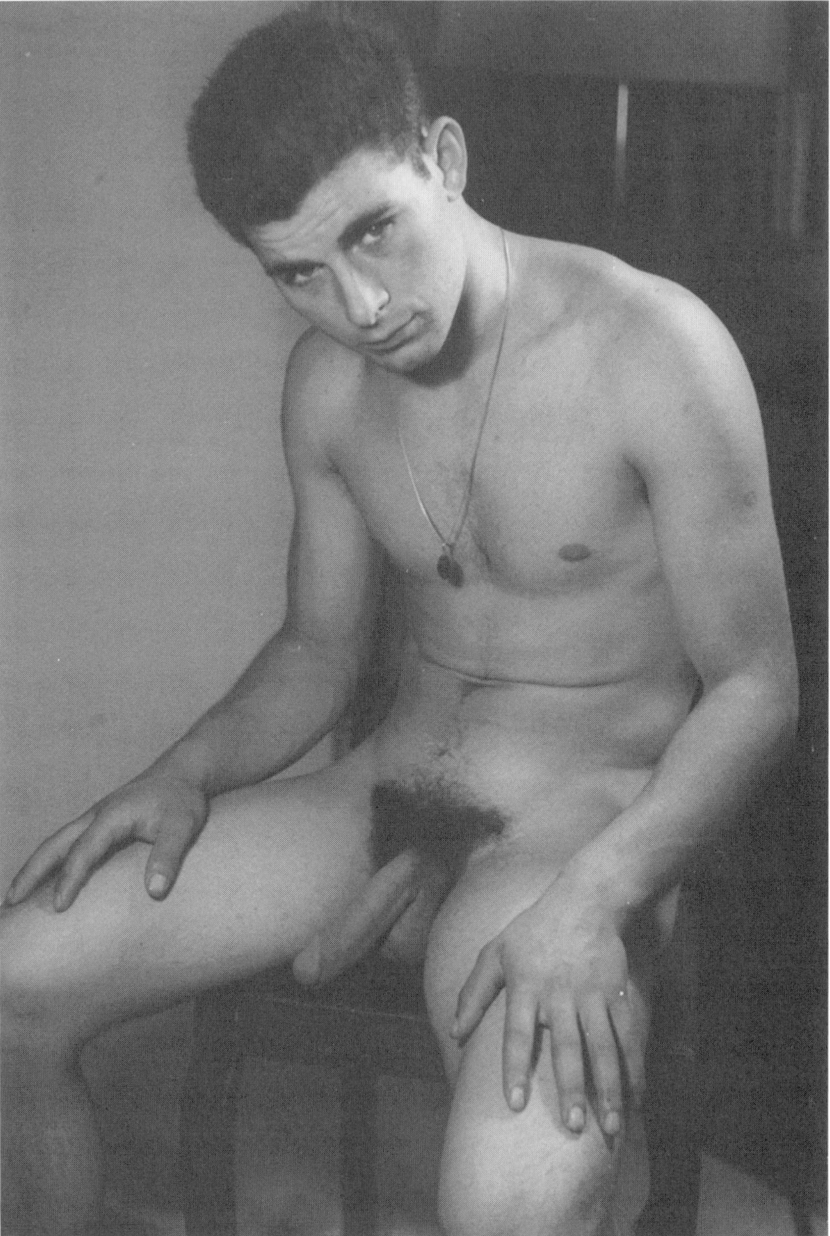

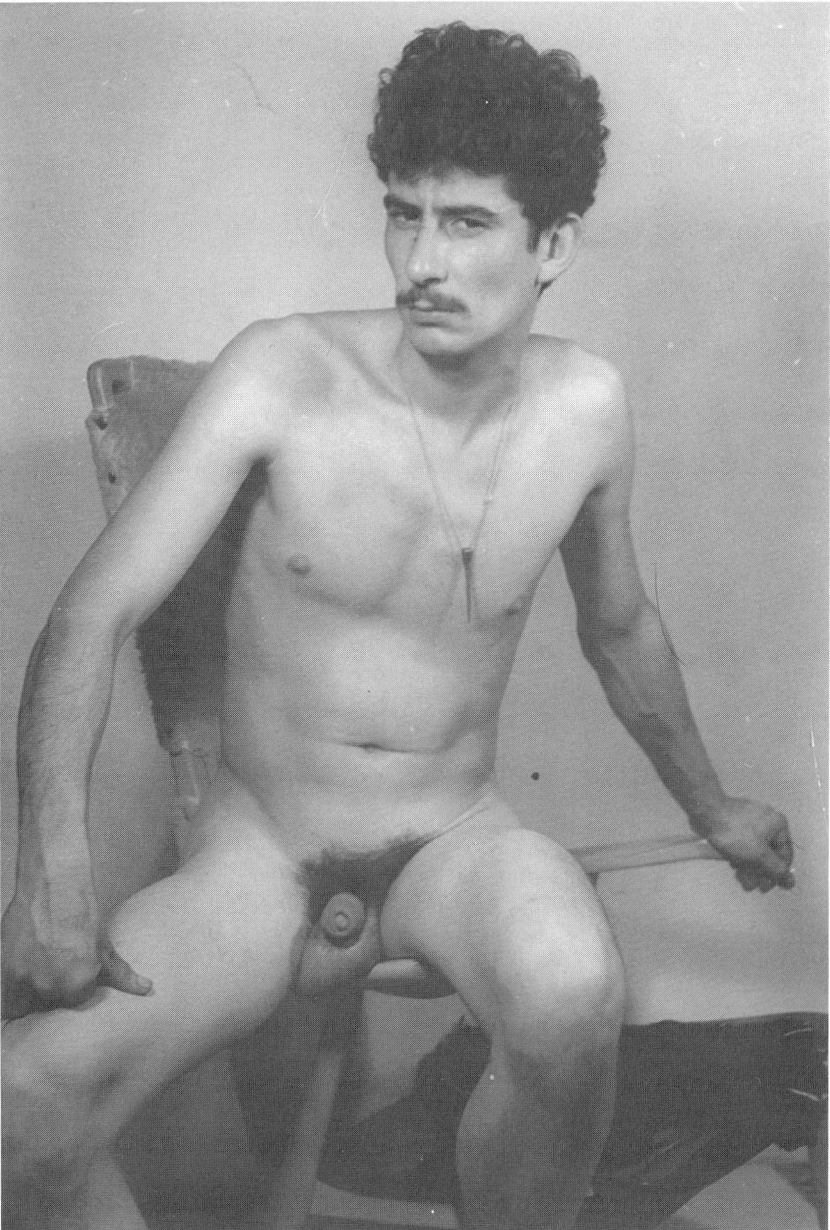

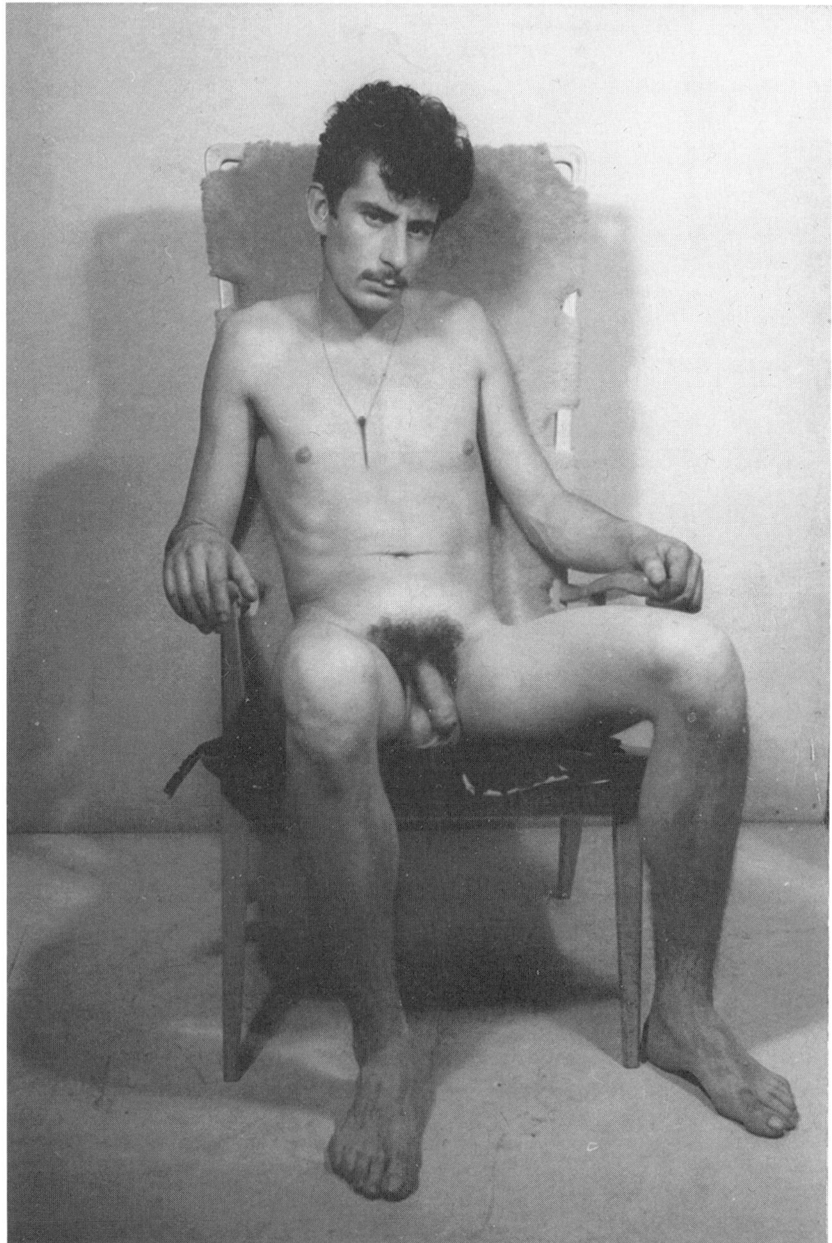

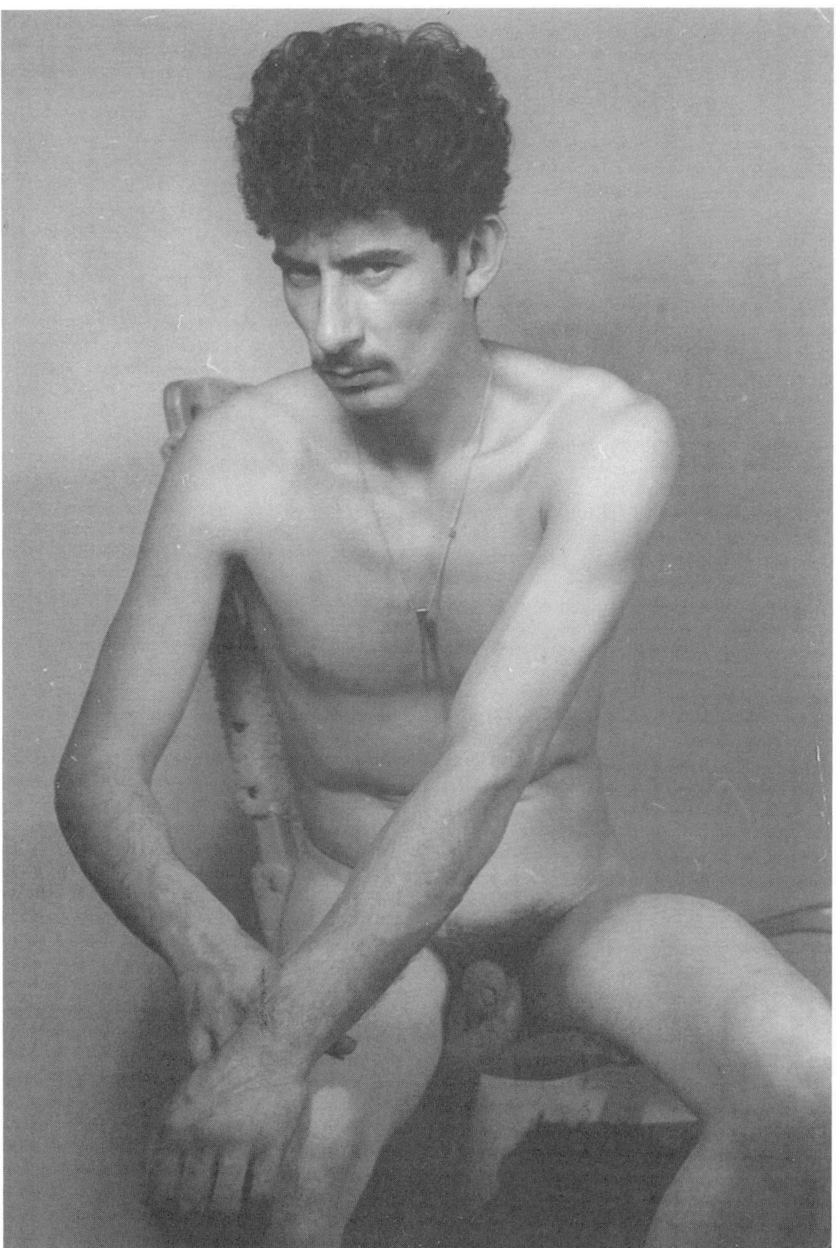

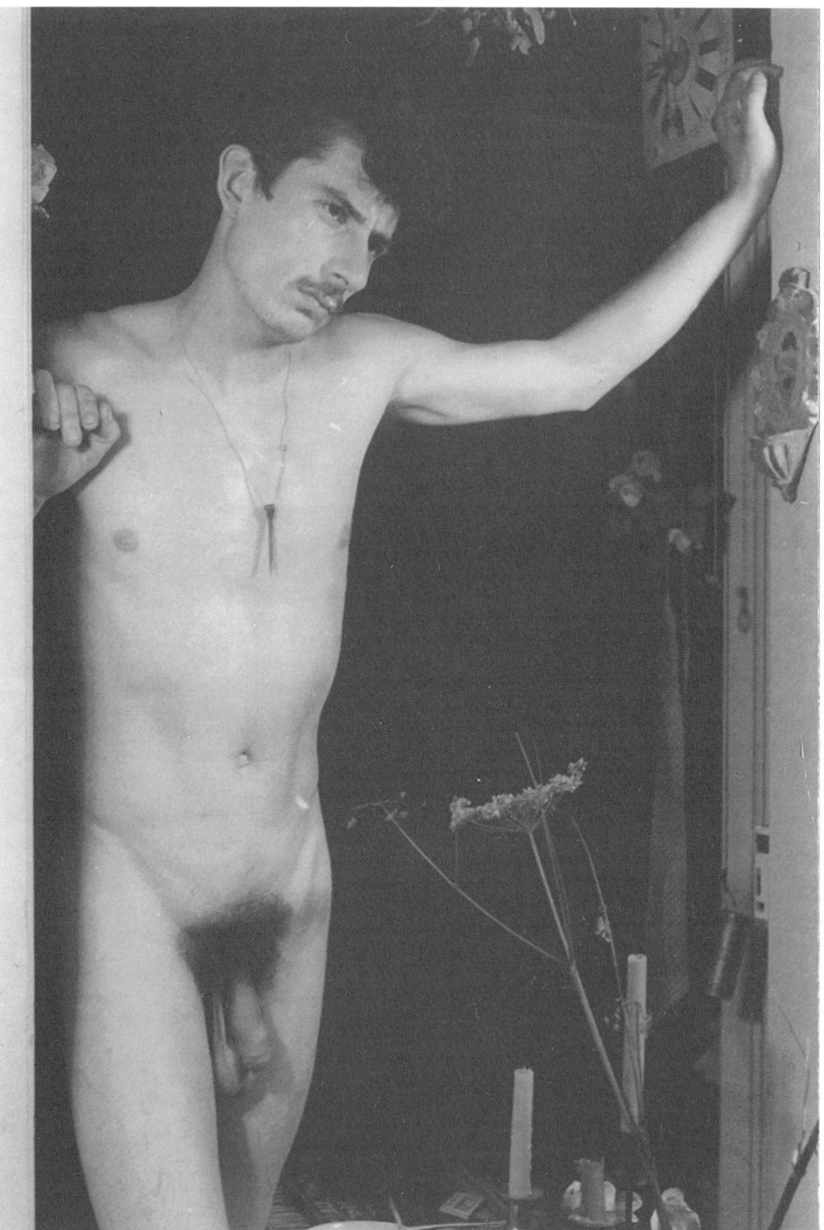

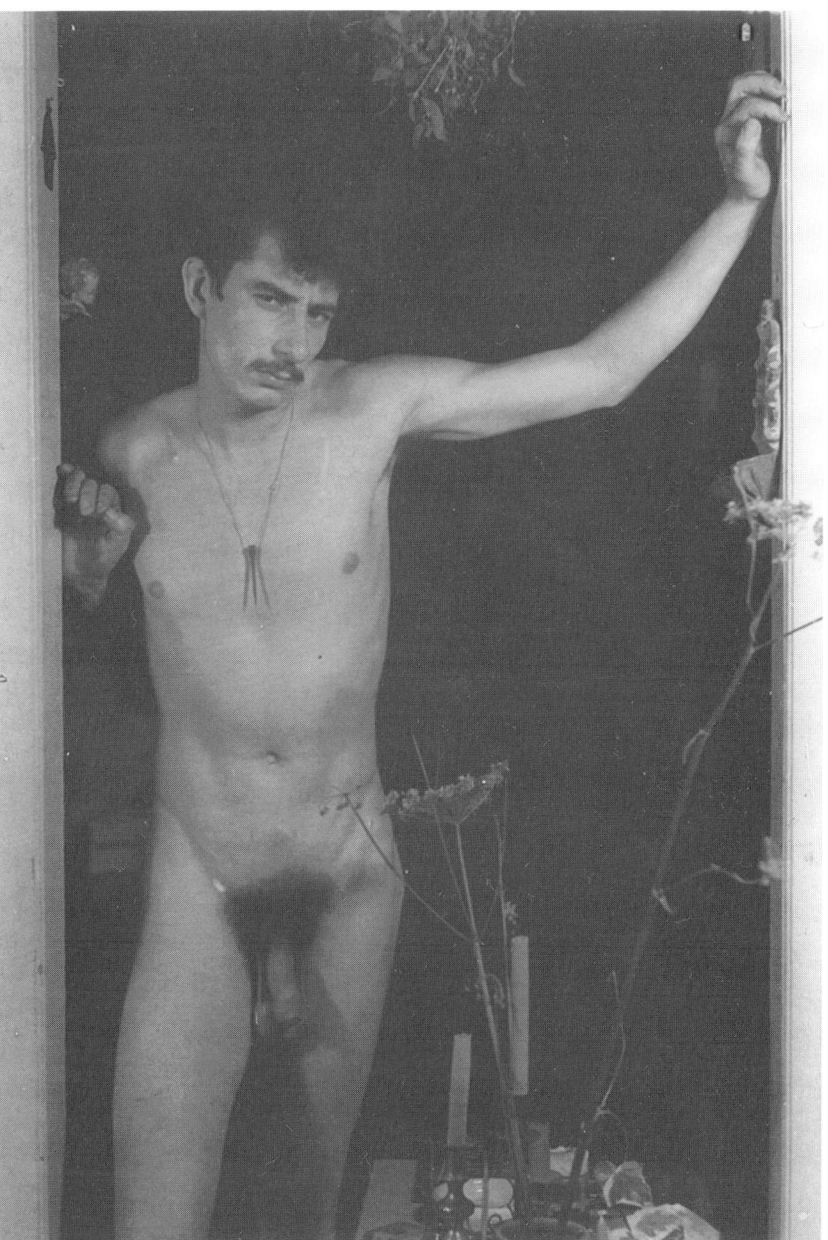

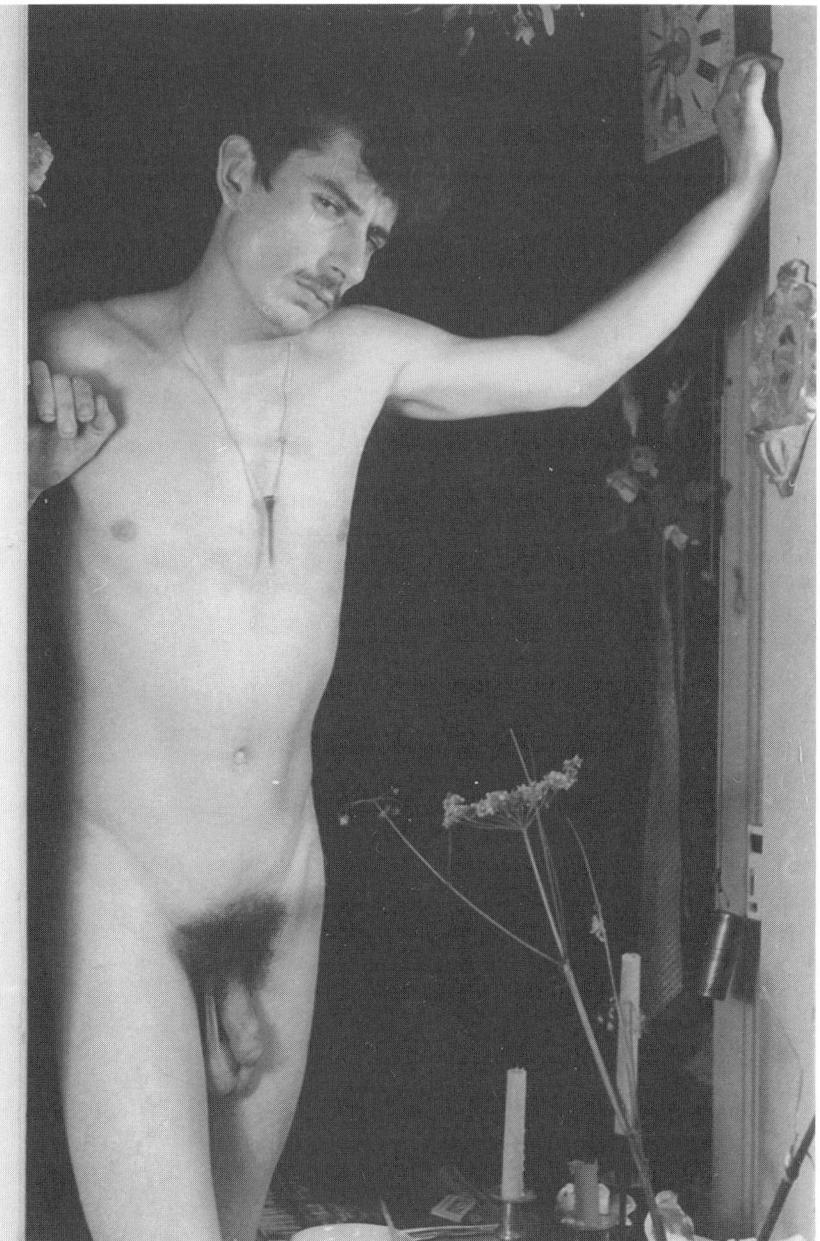

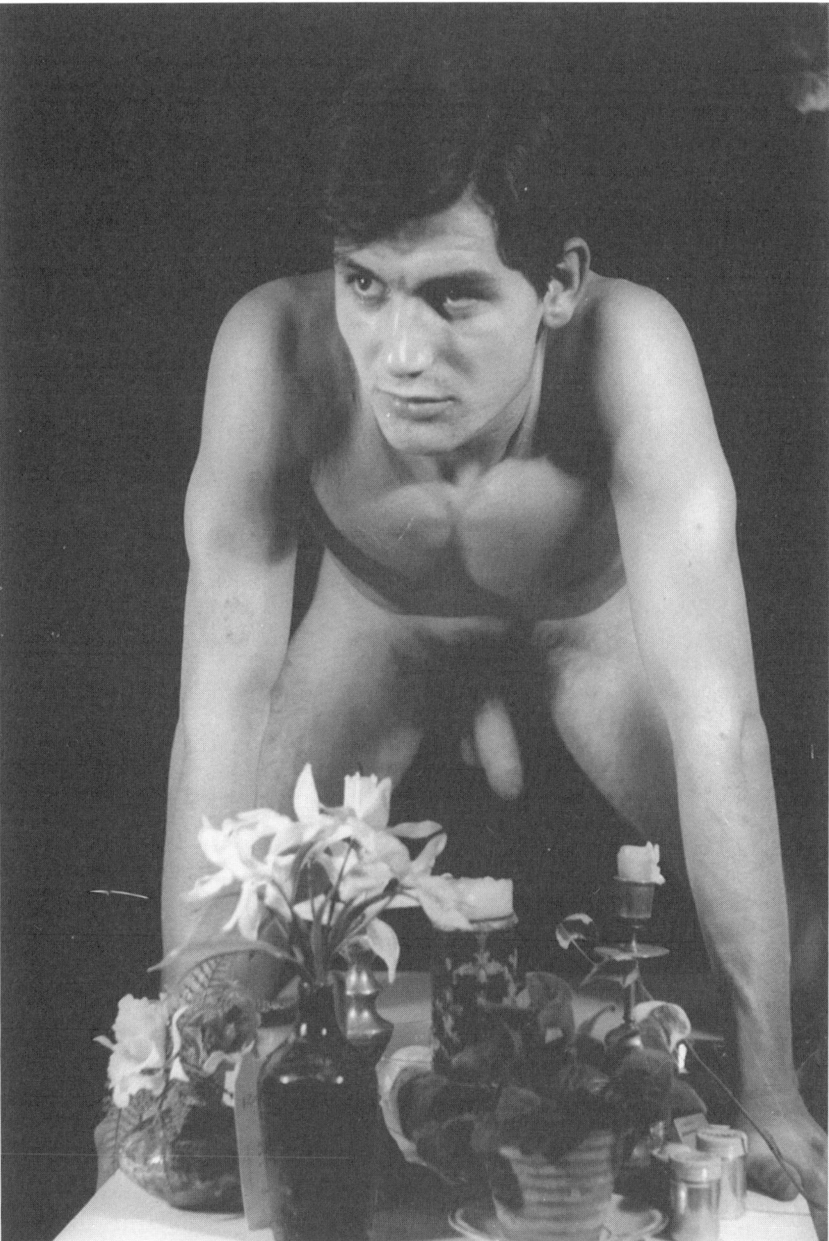

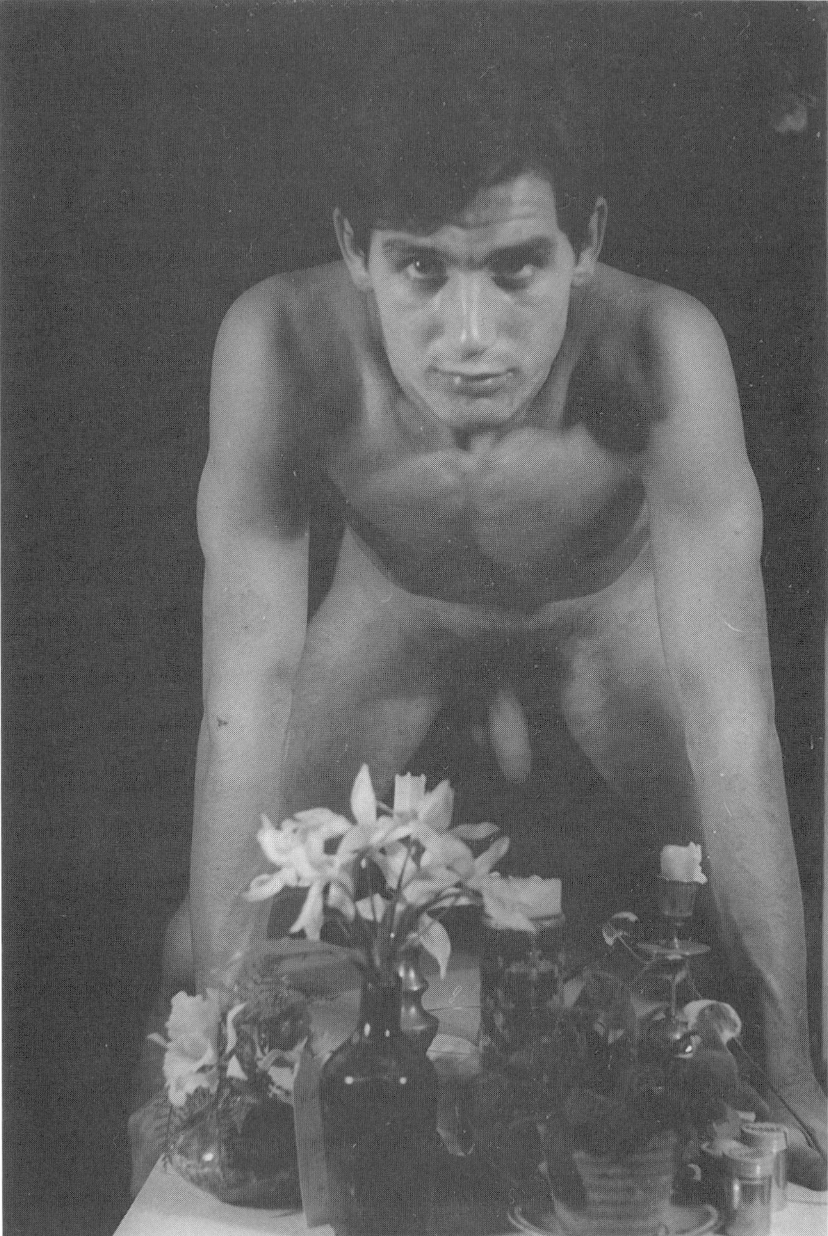

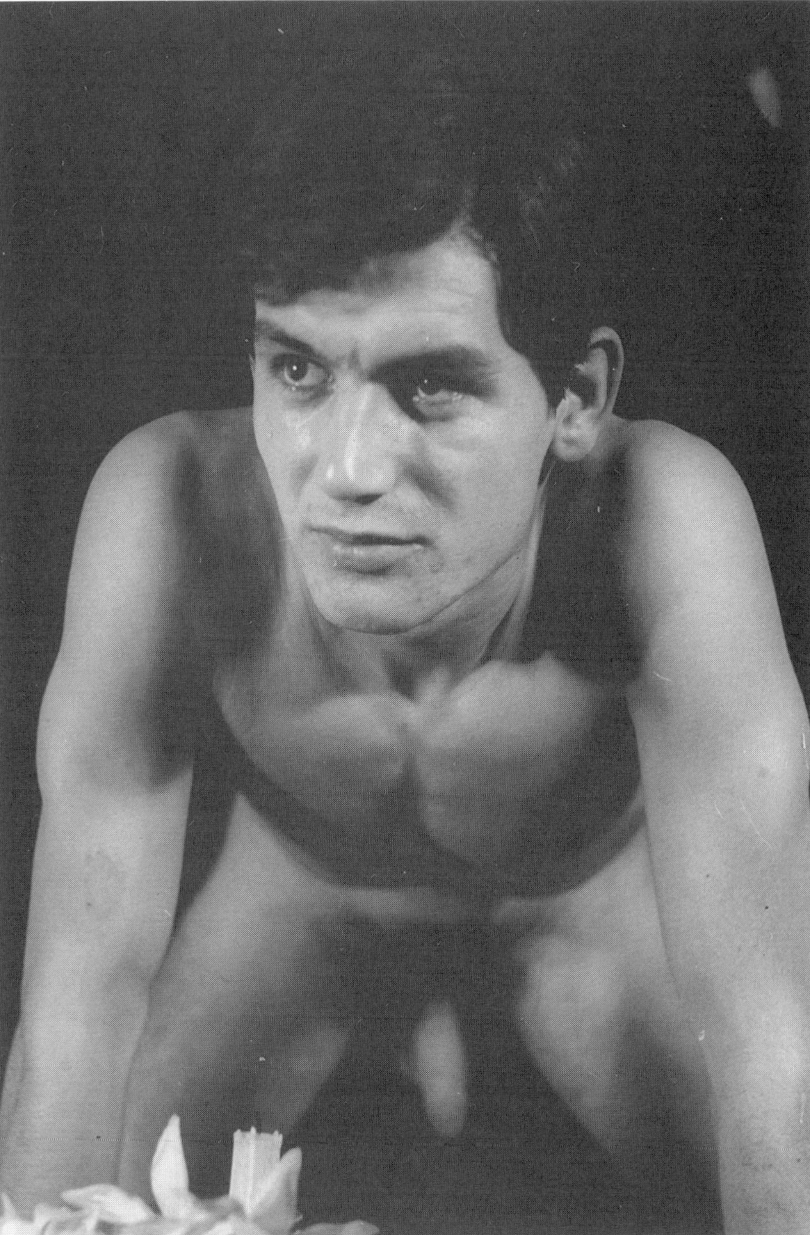

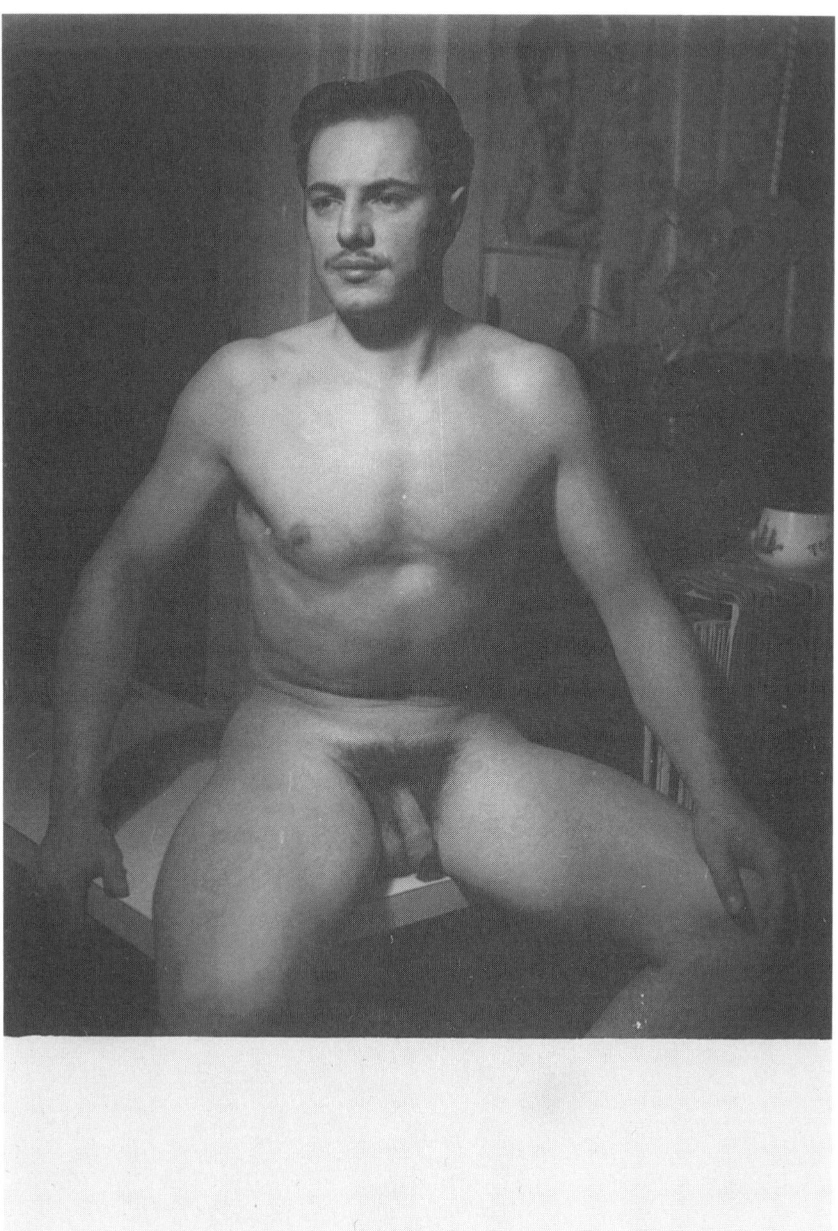

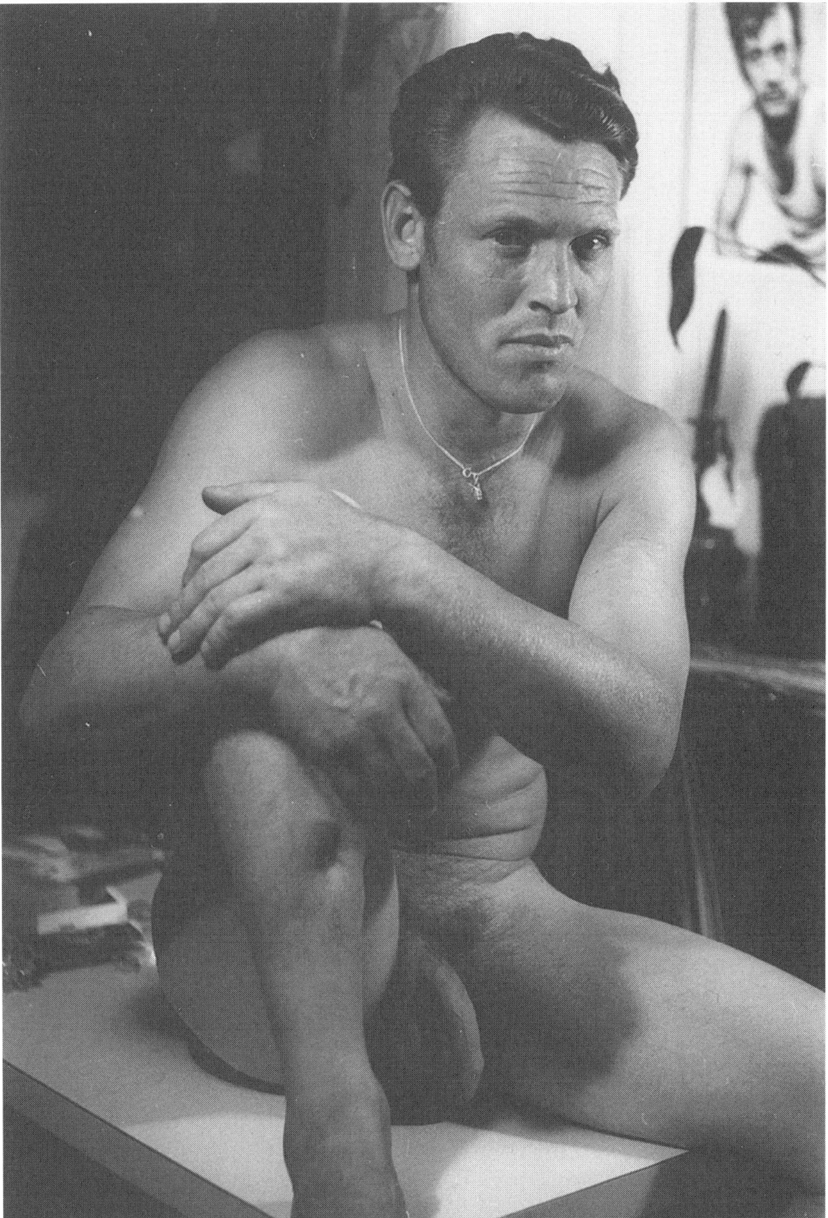

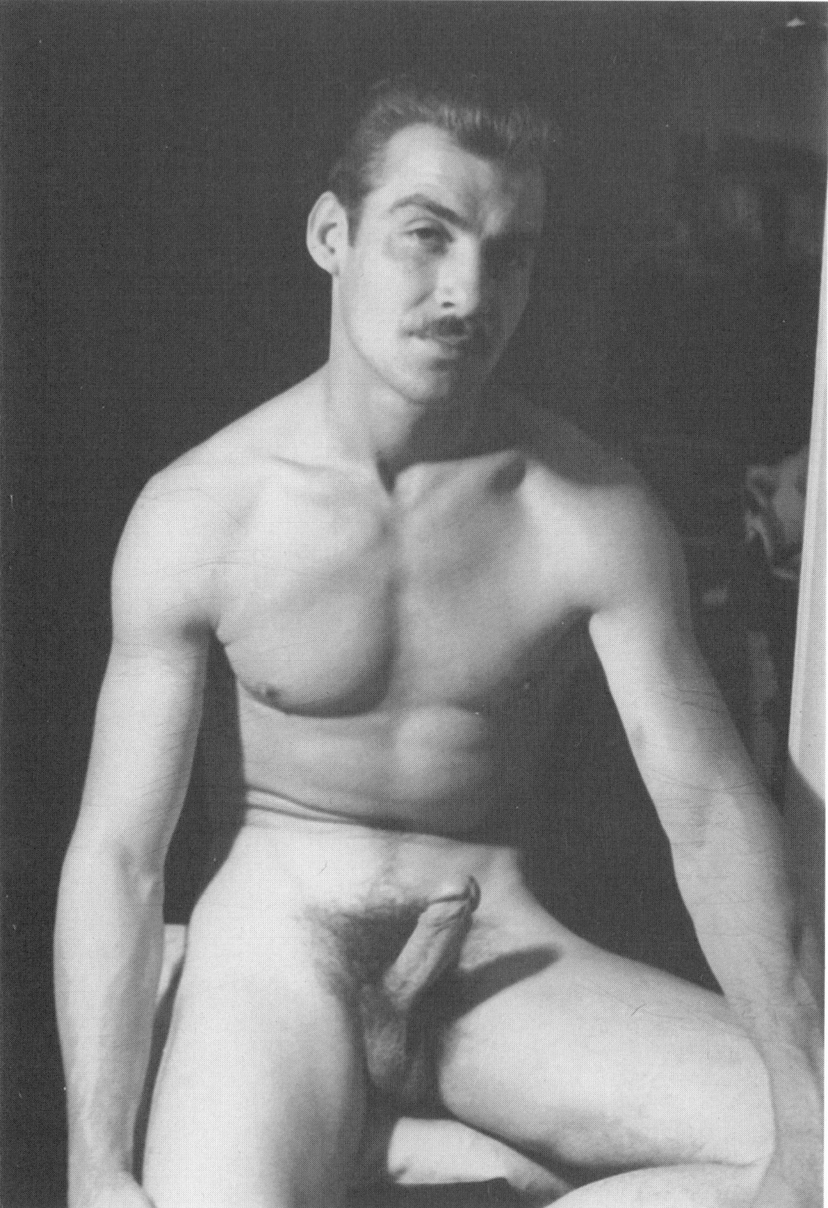

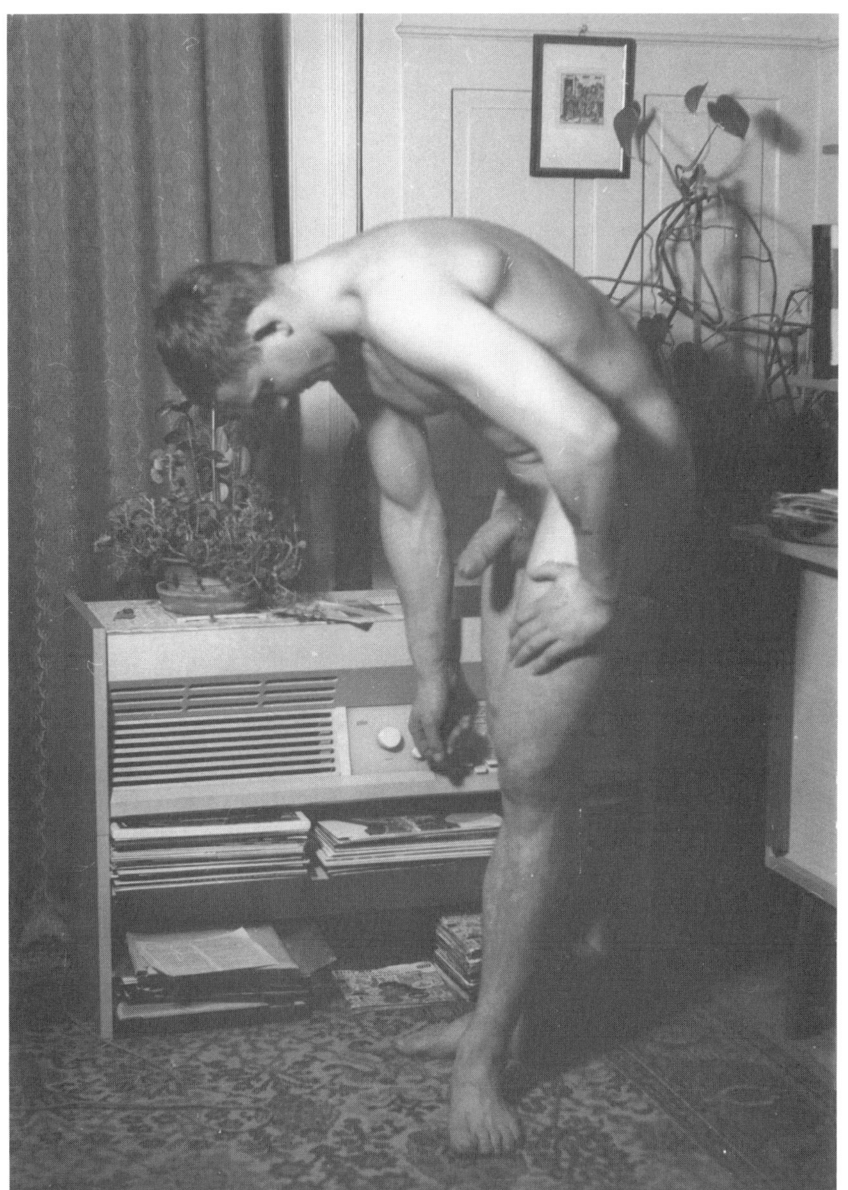

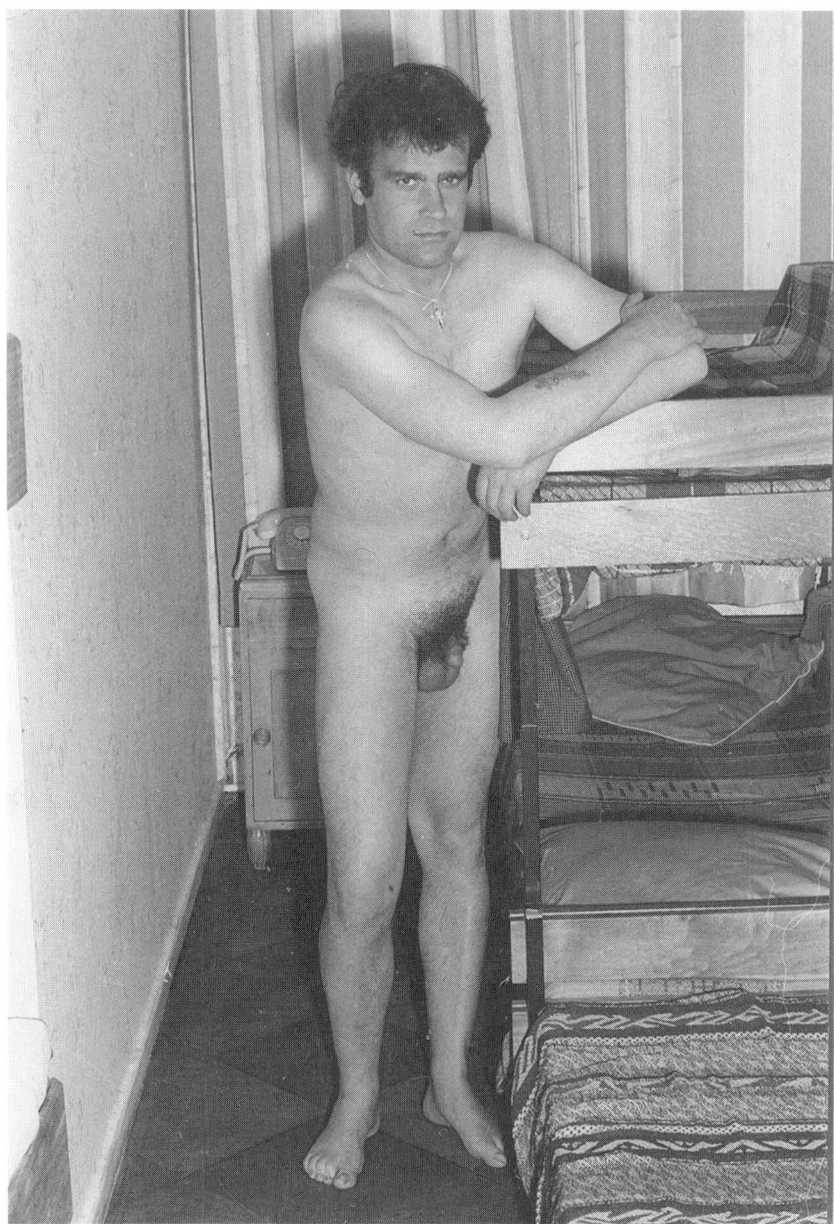

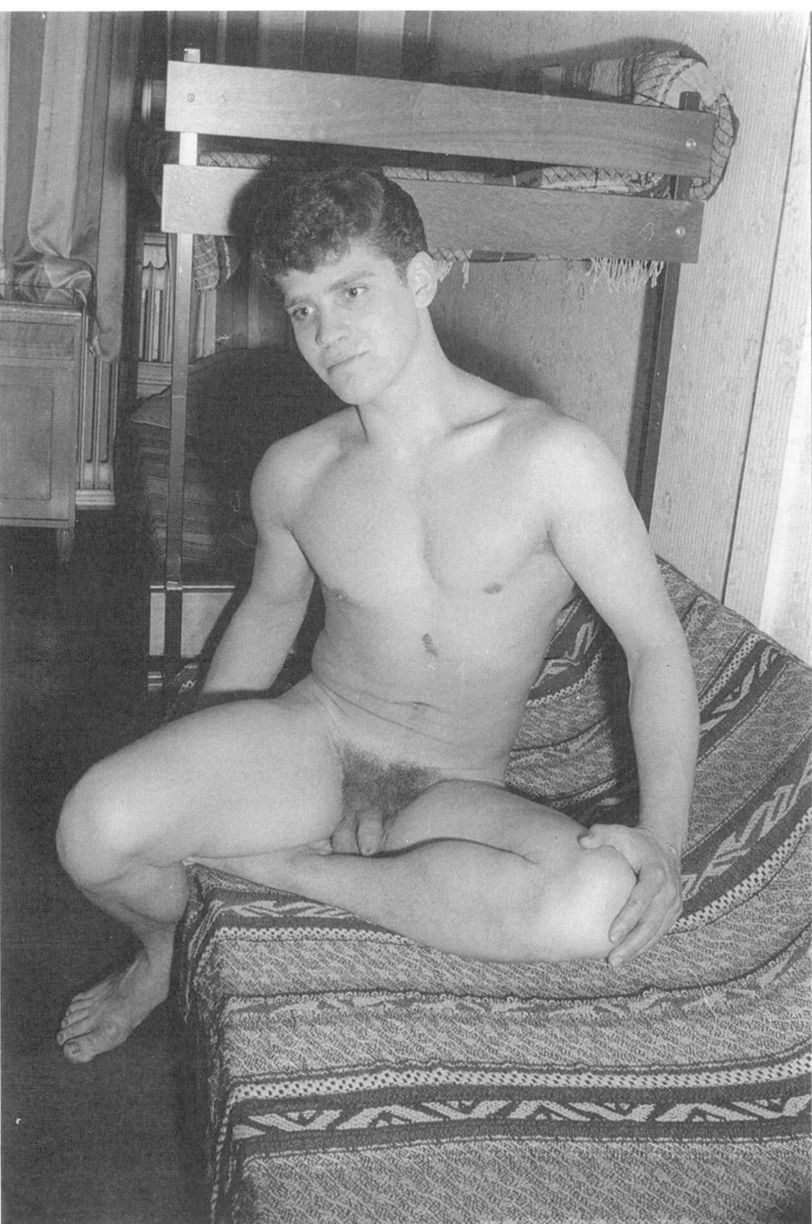

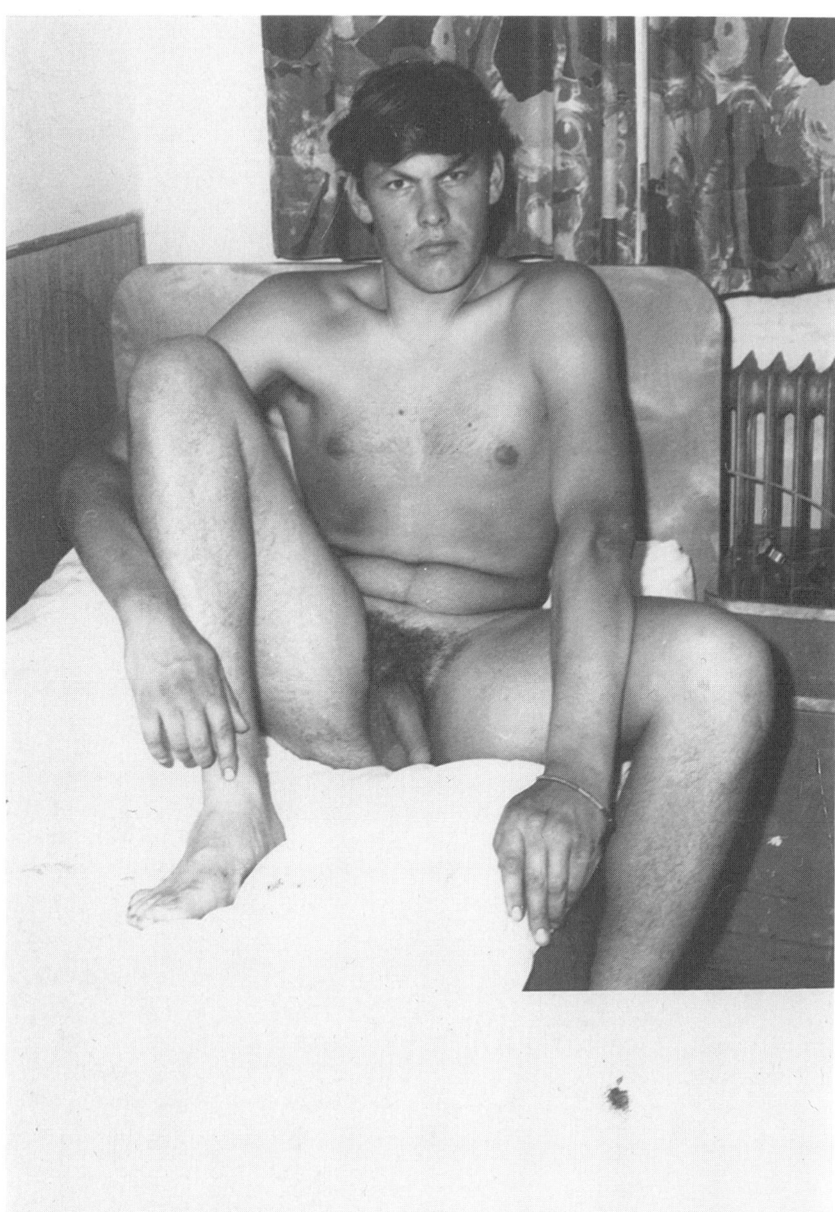

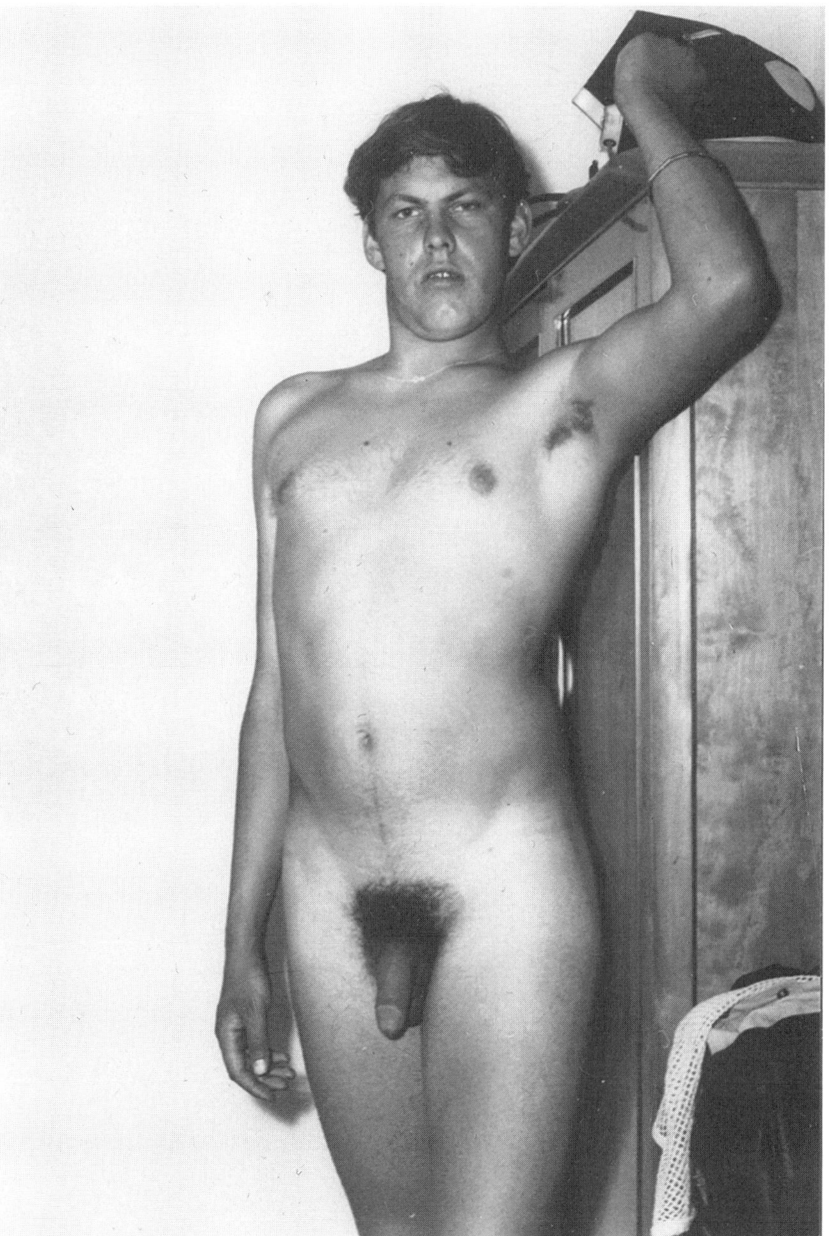

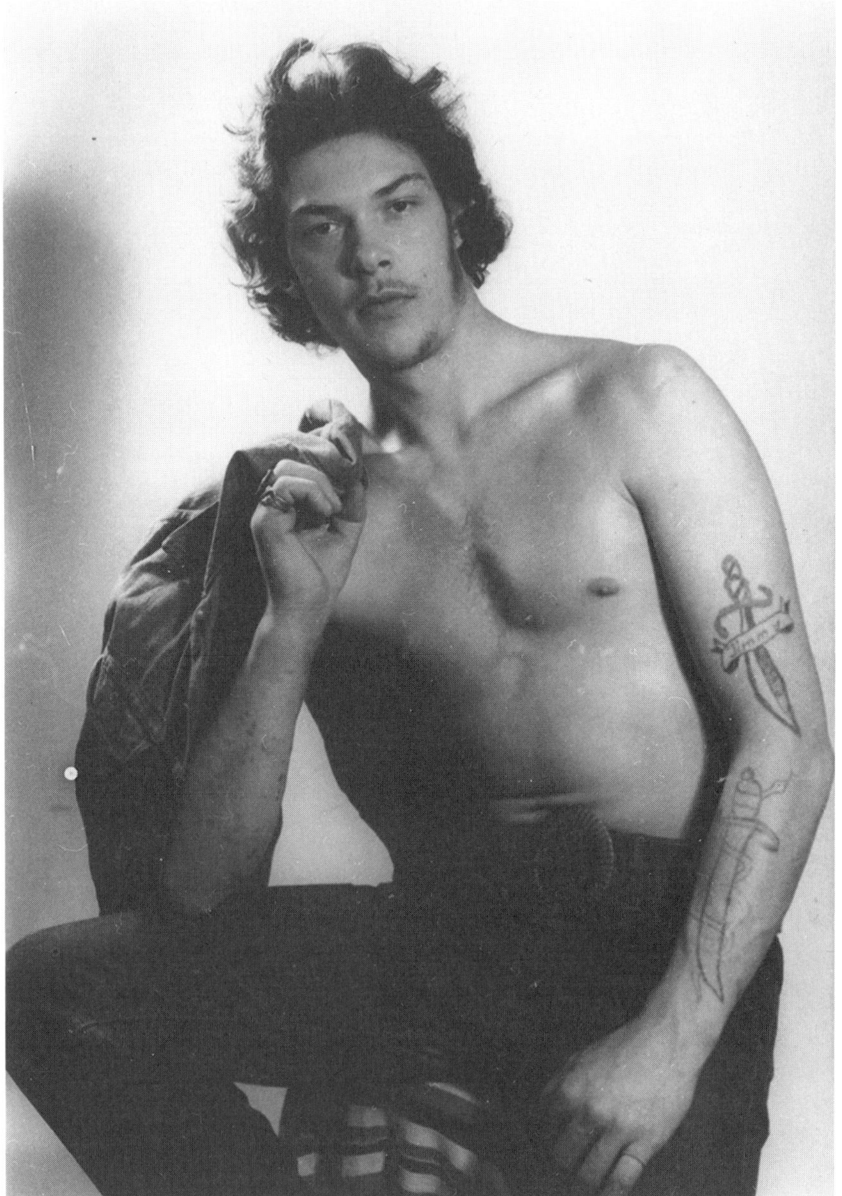

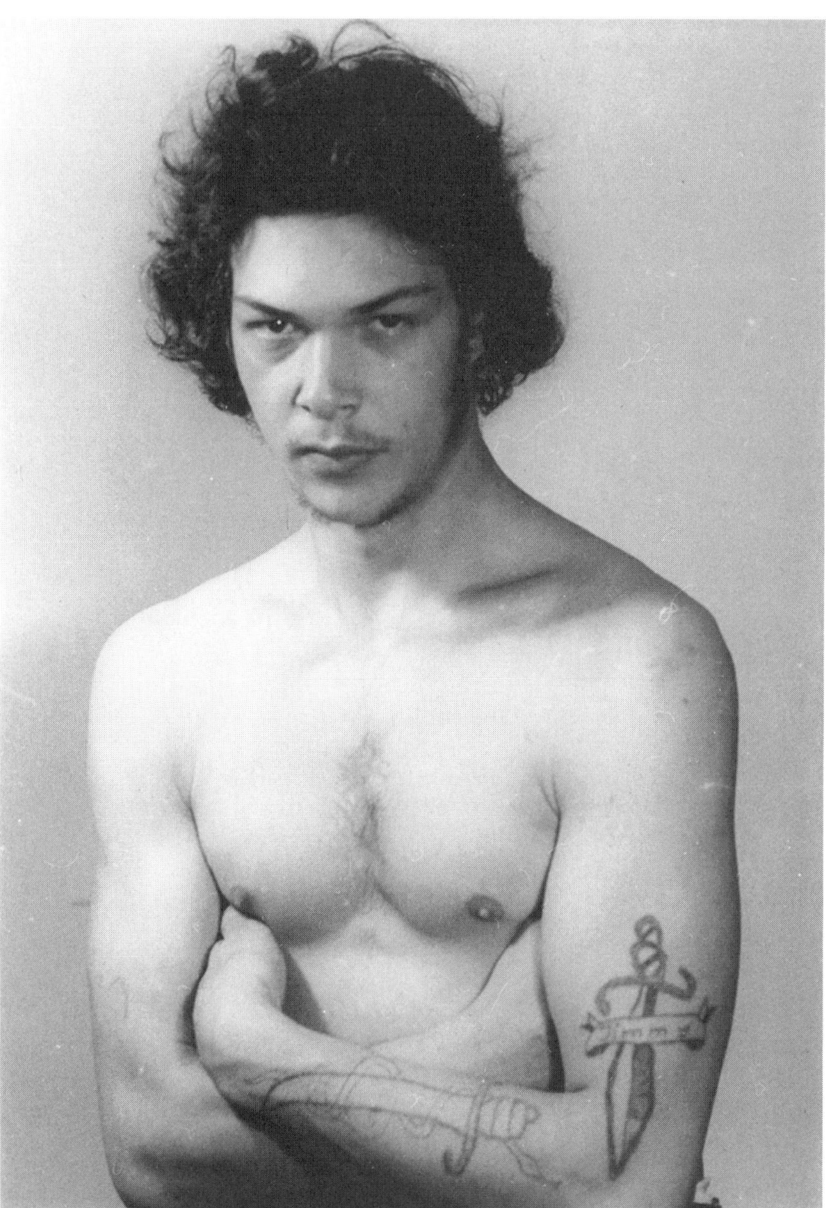

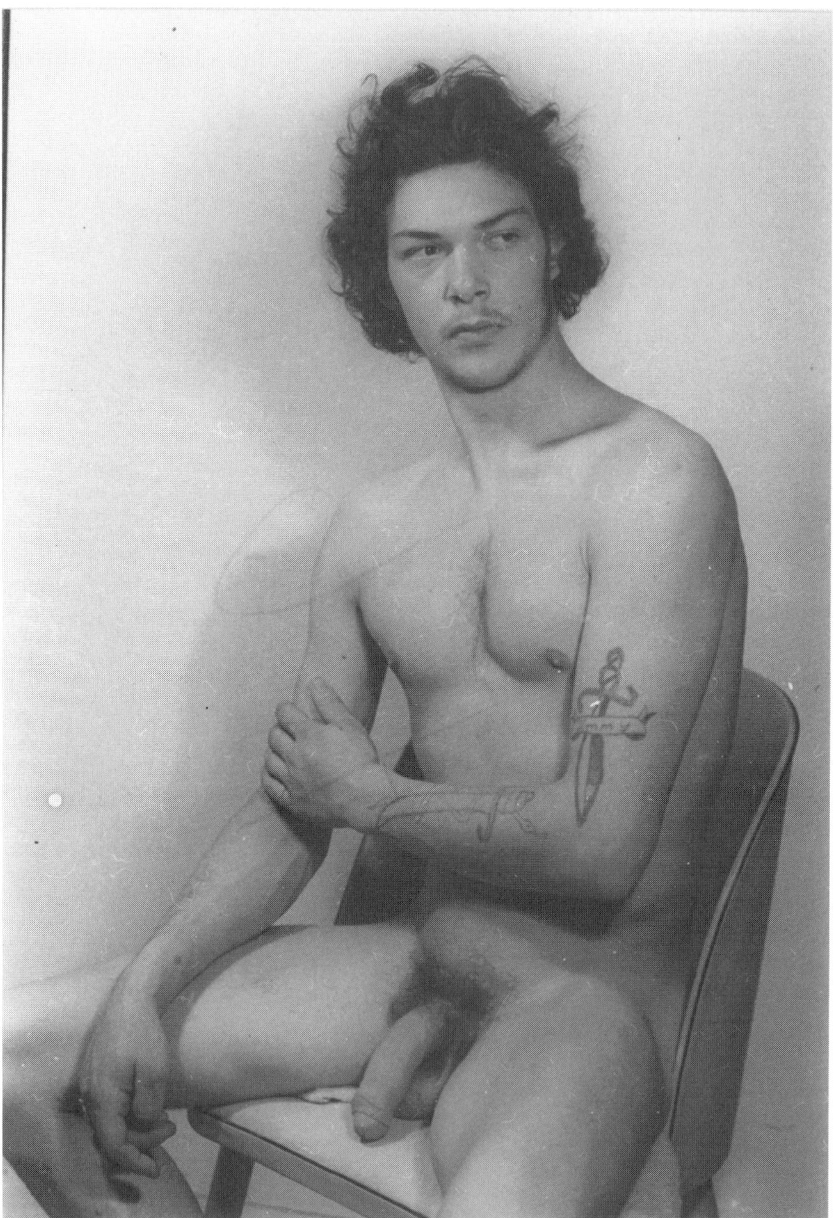

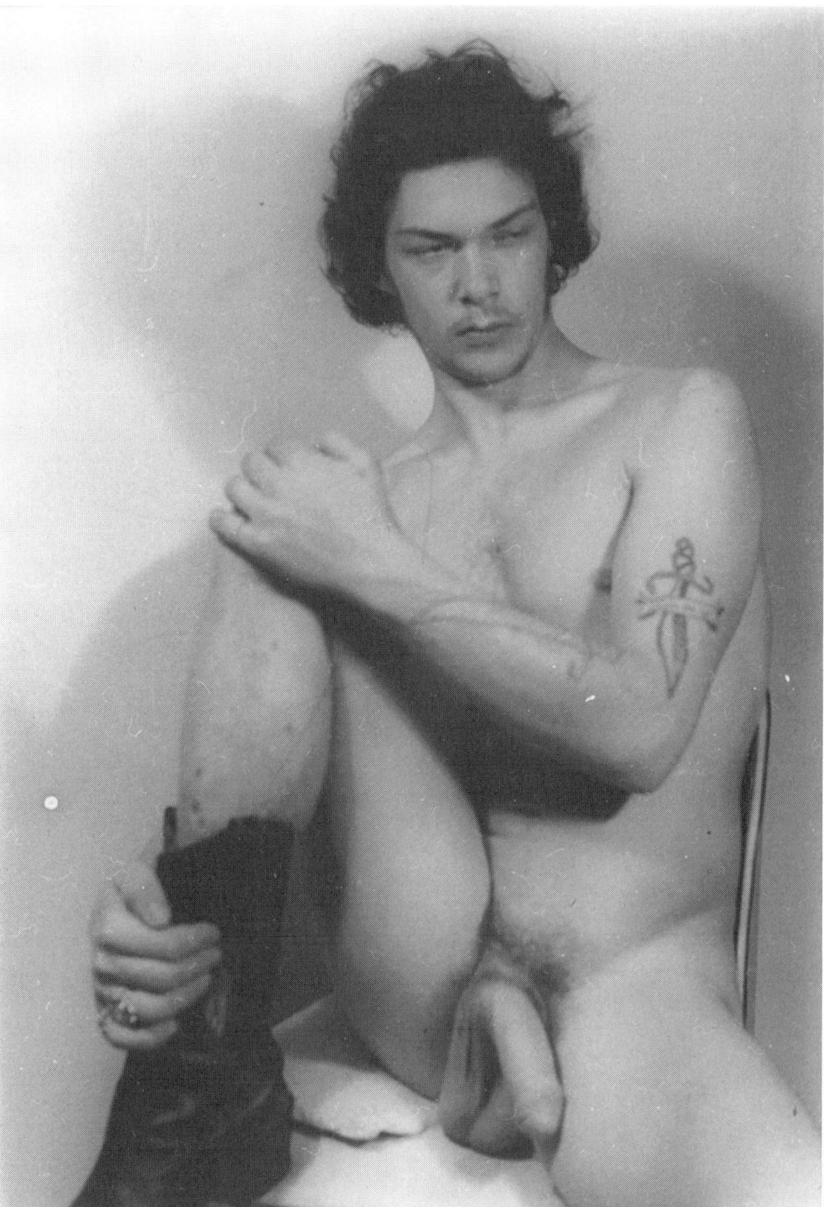

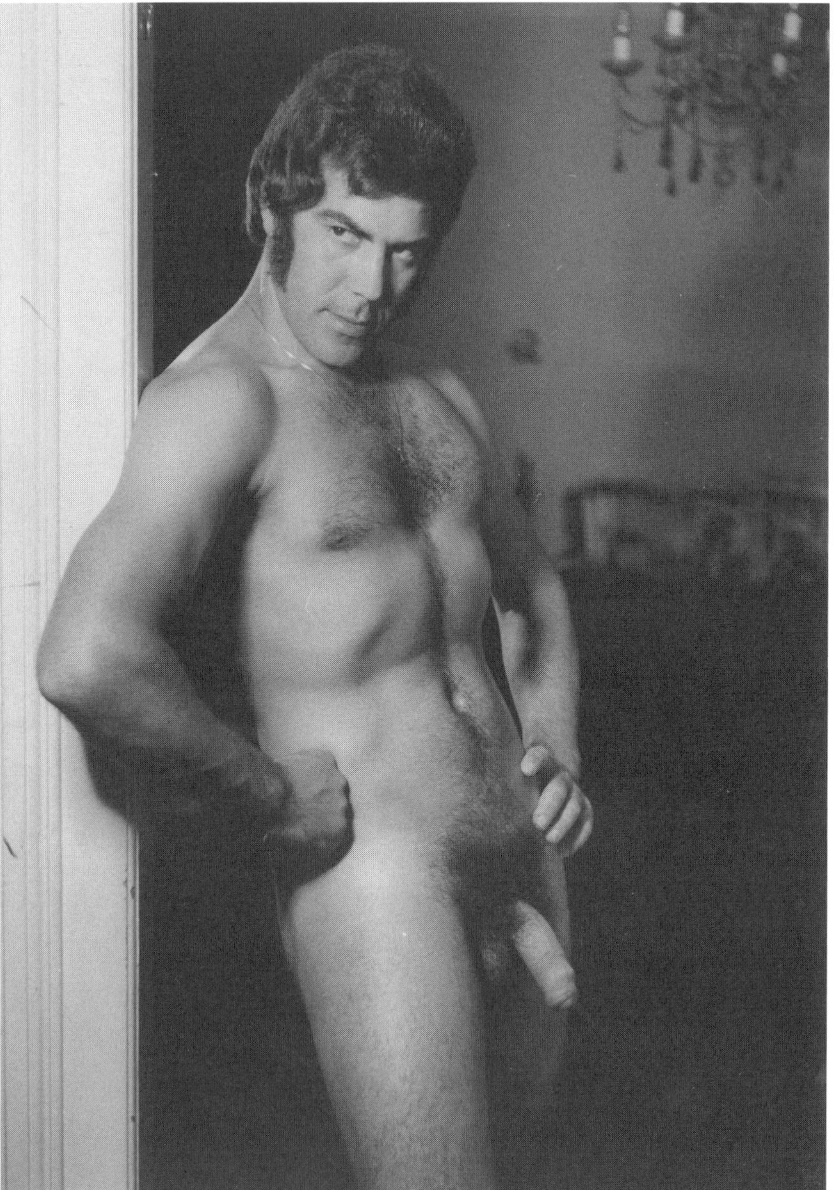

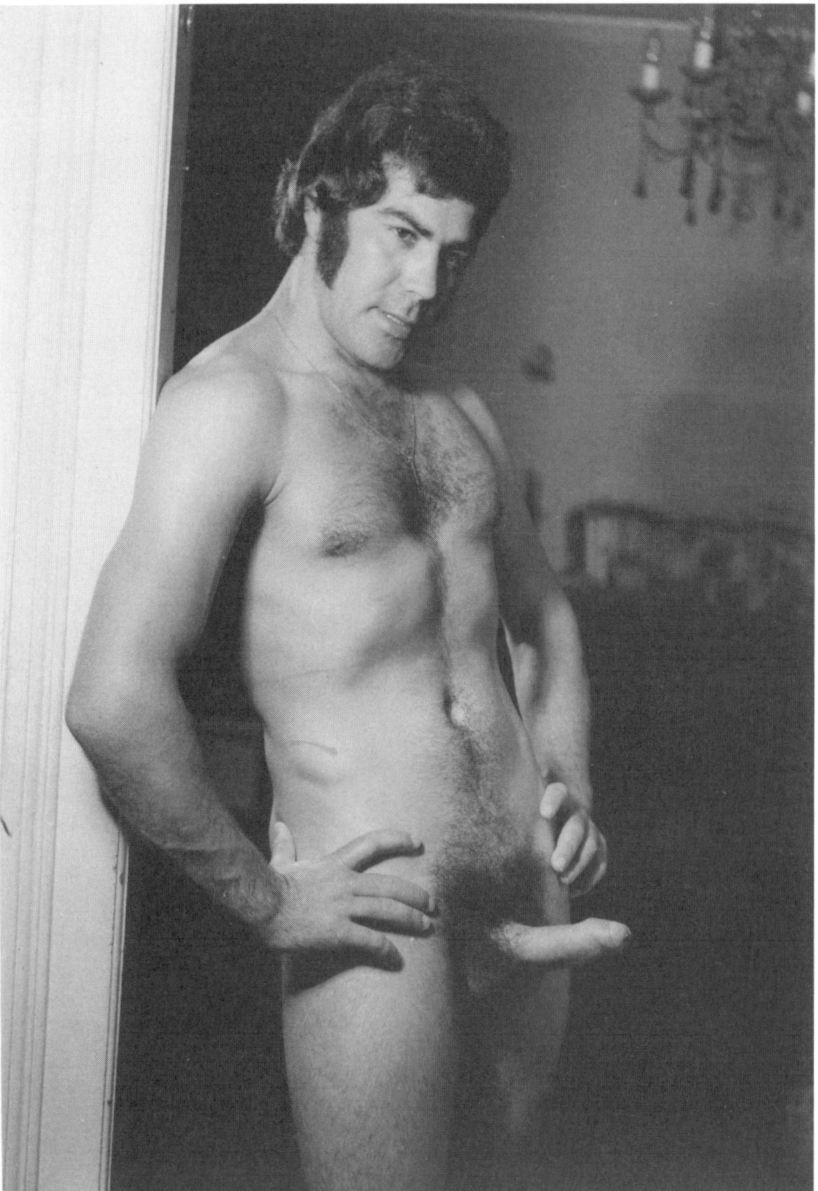

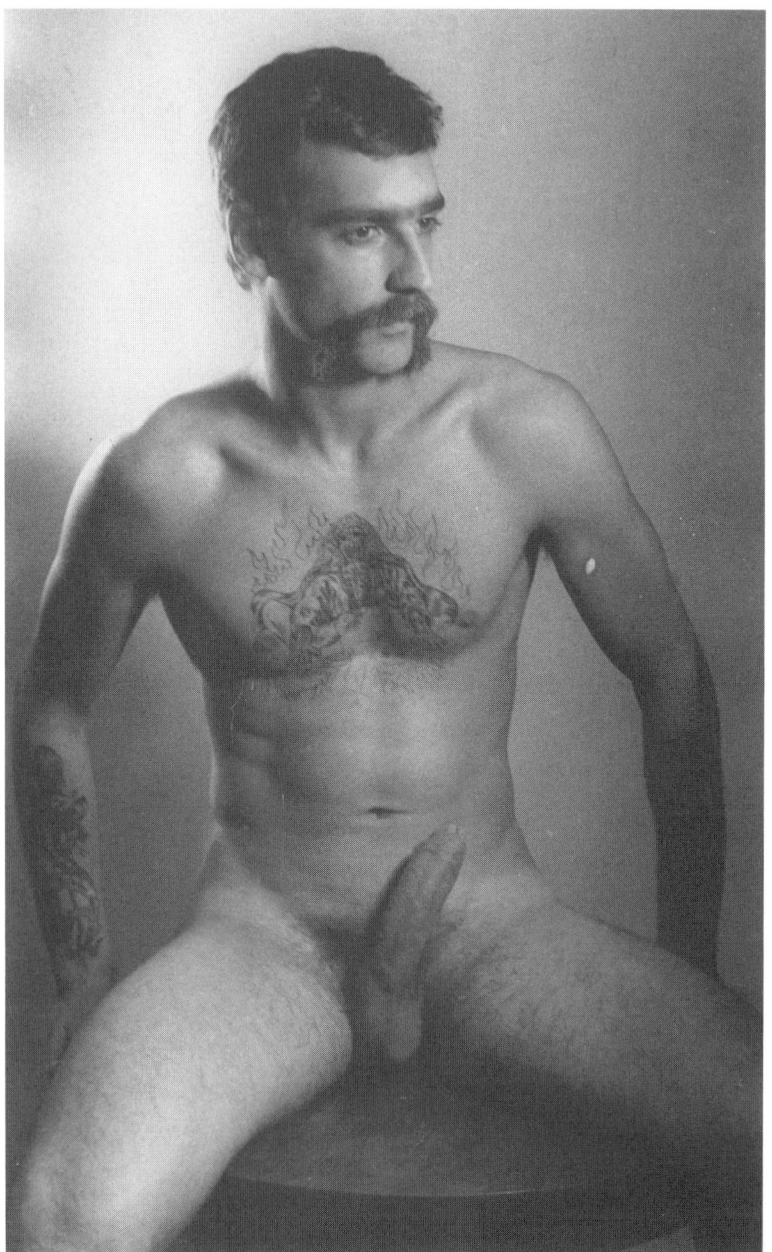

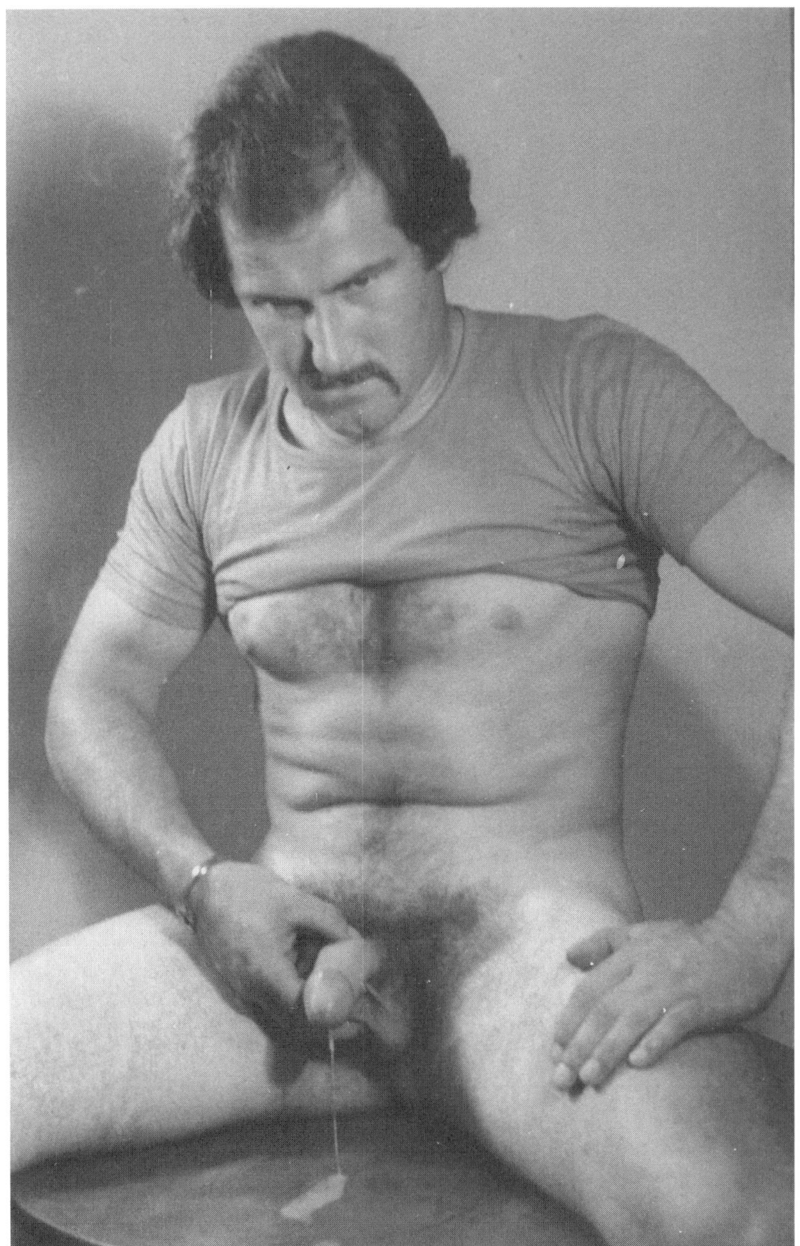

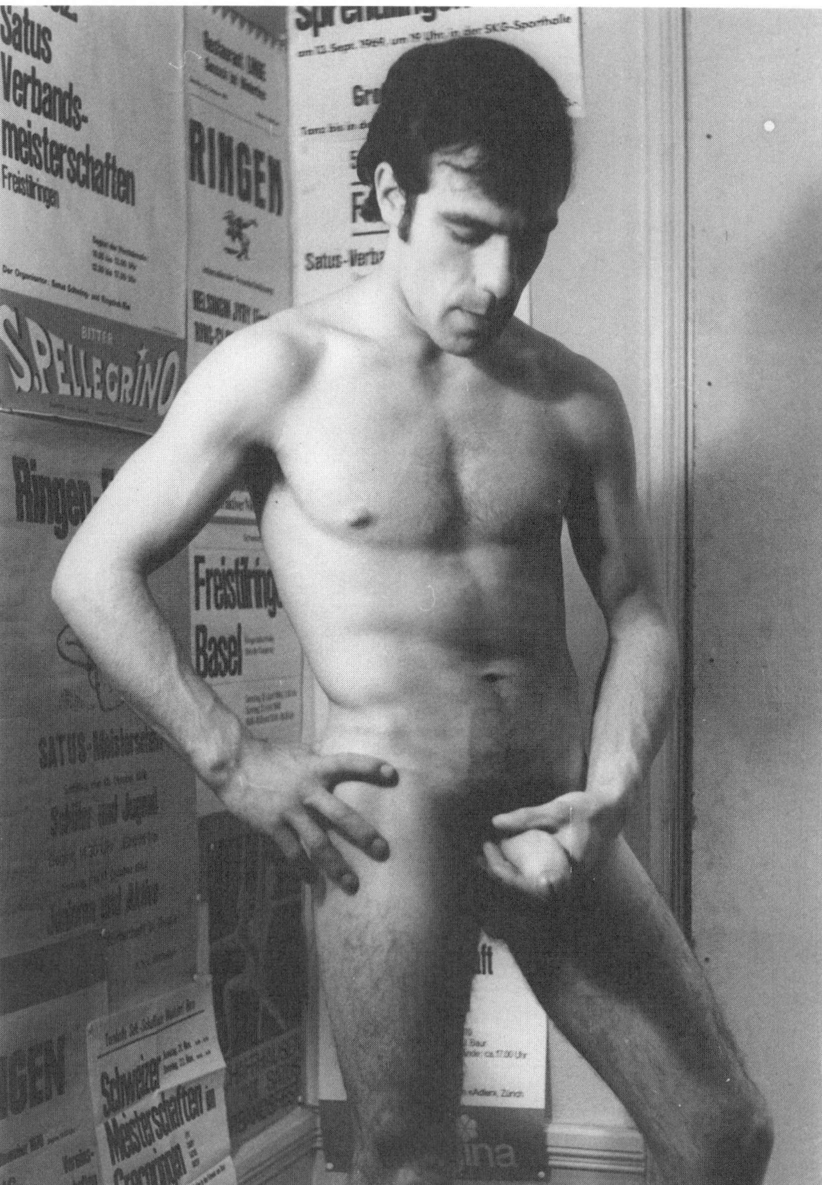
Satus
Verbands-
meisterschaften
Freistilringen
RINGEN
BITTER
S.PELLEGRINO
Basel
Schweizer
Meisterschaften

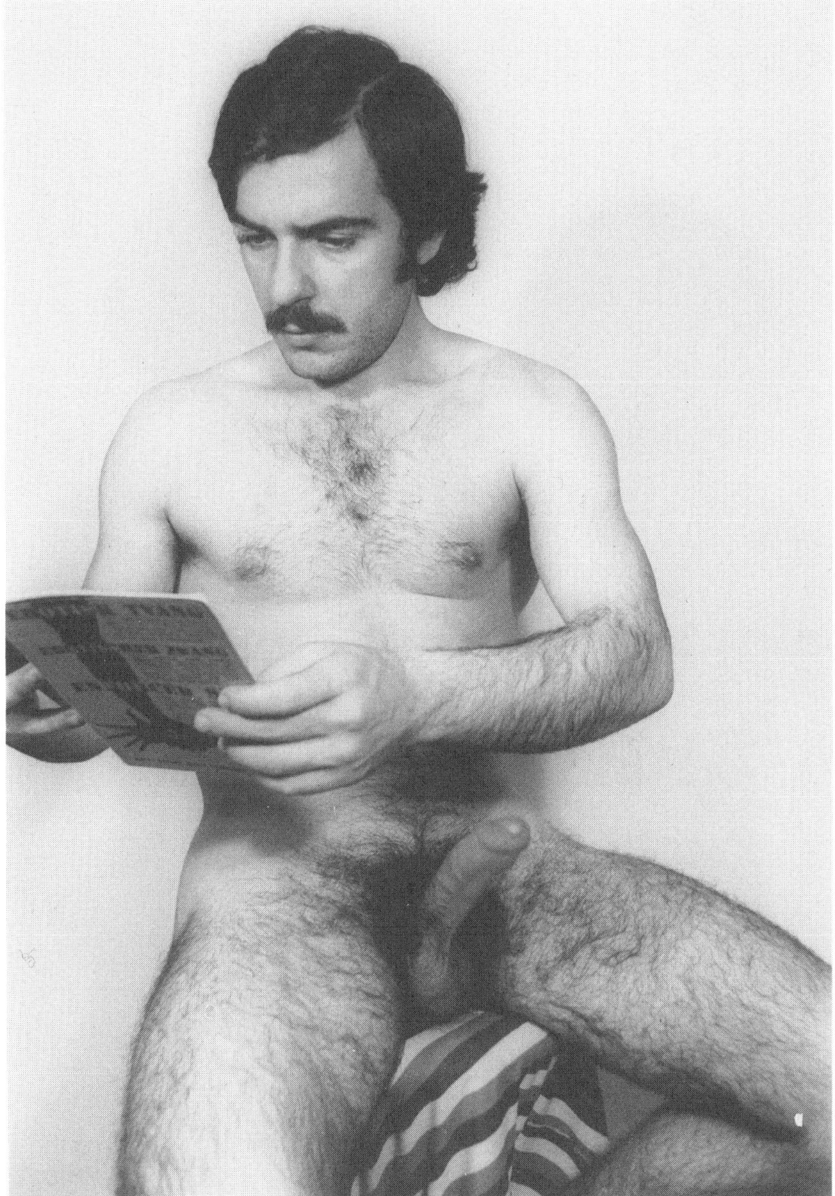

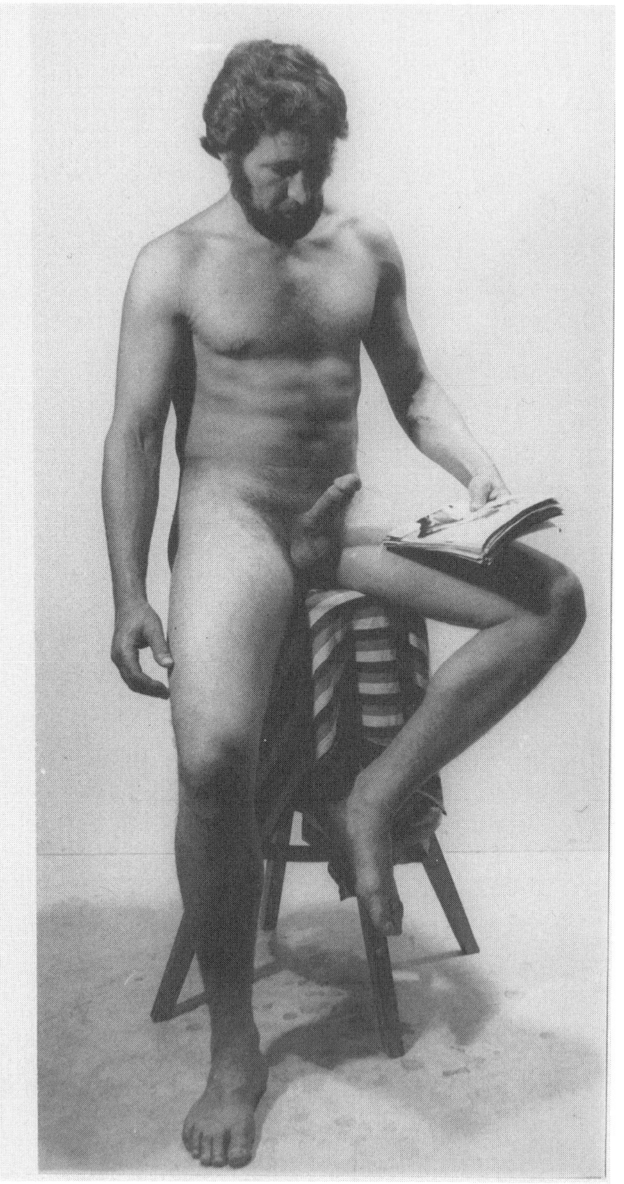

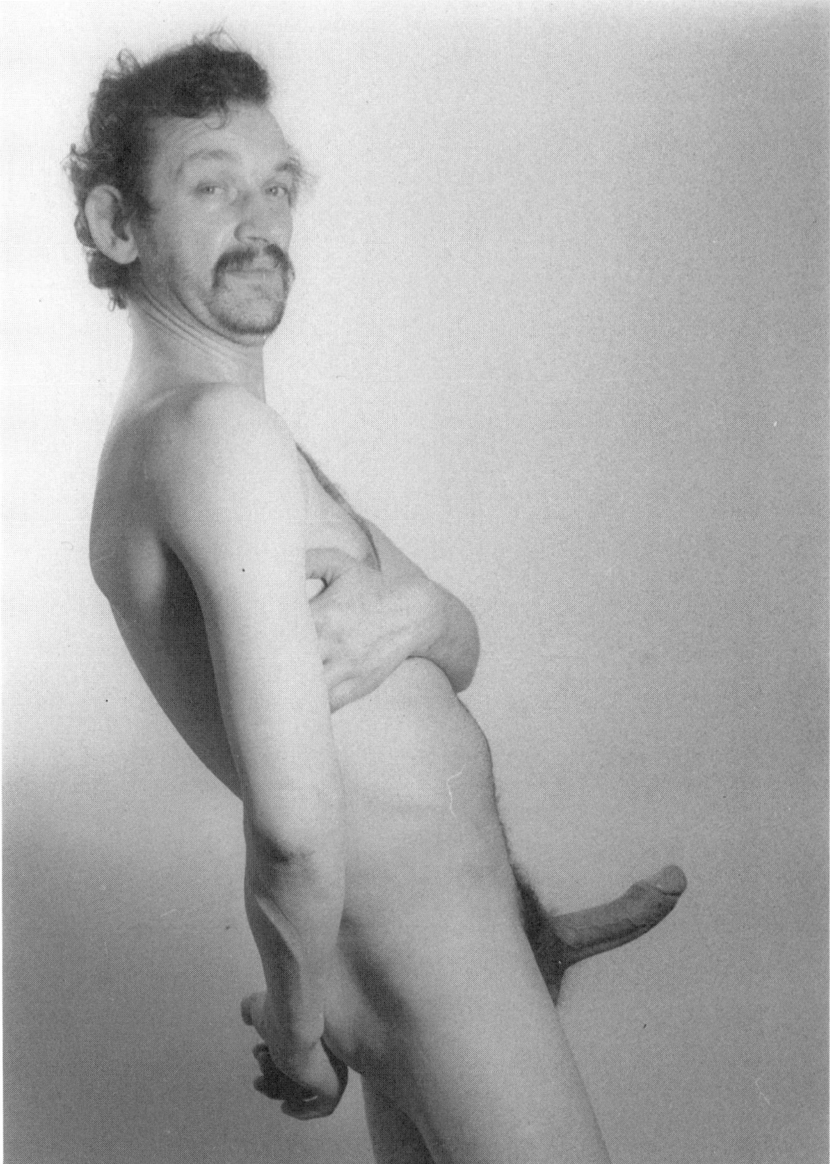

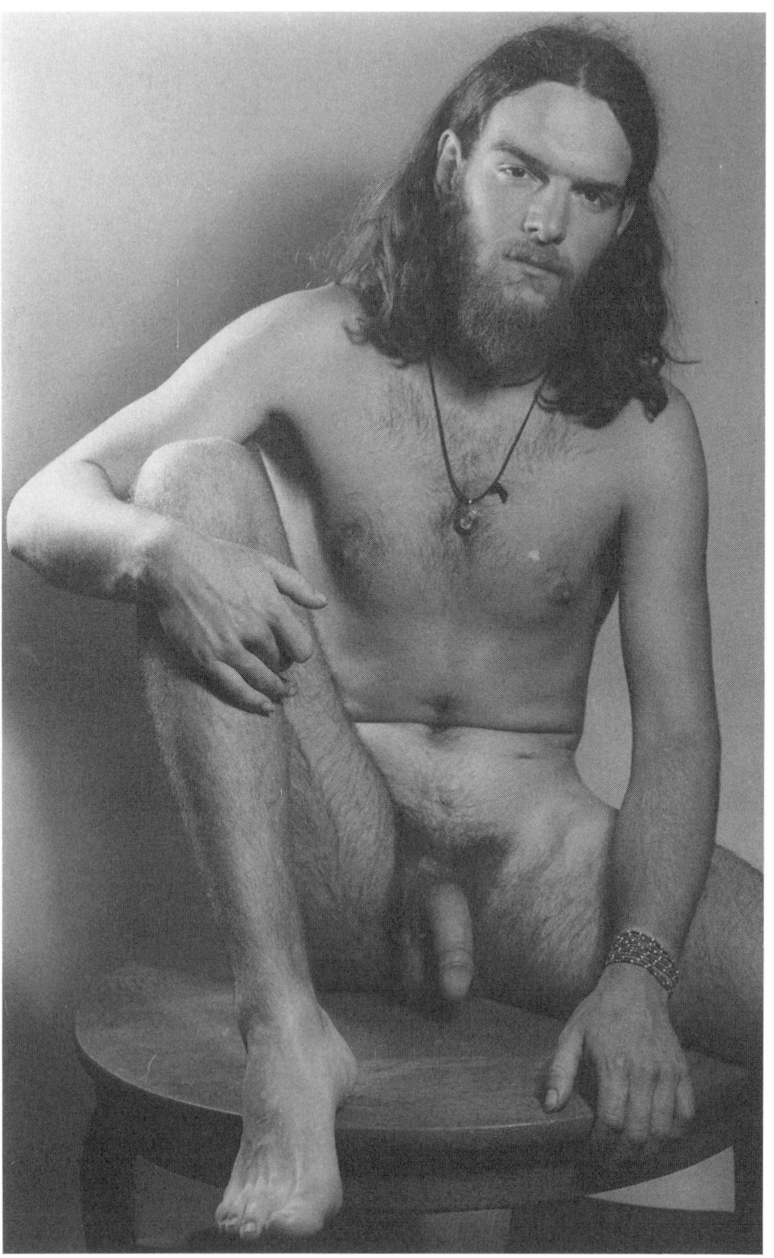

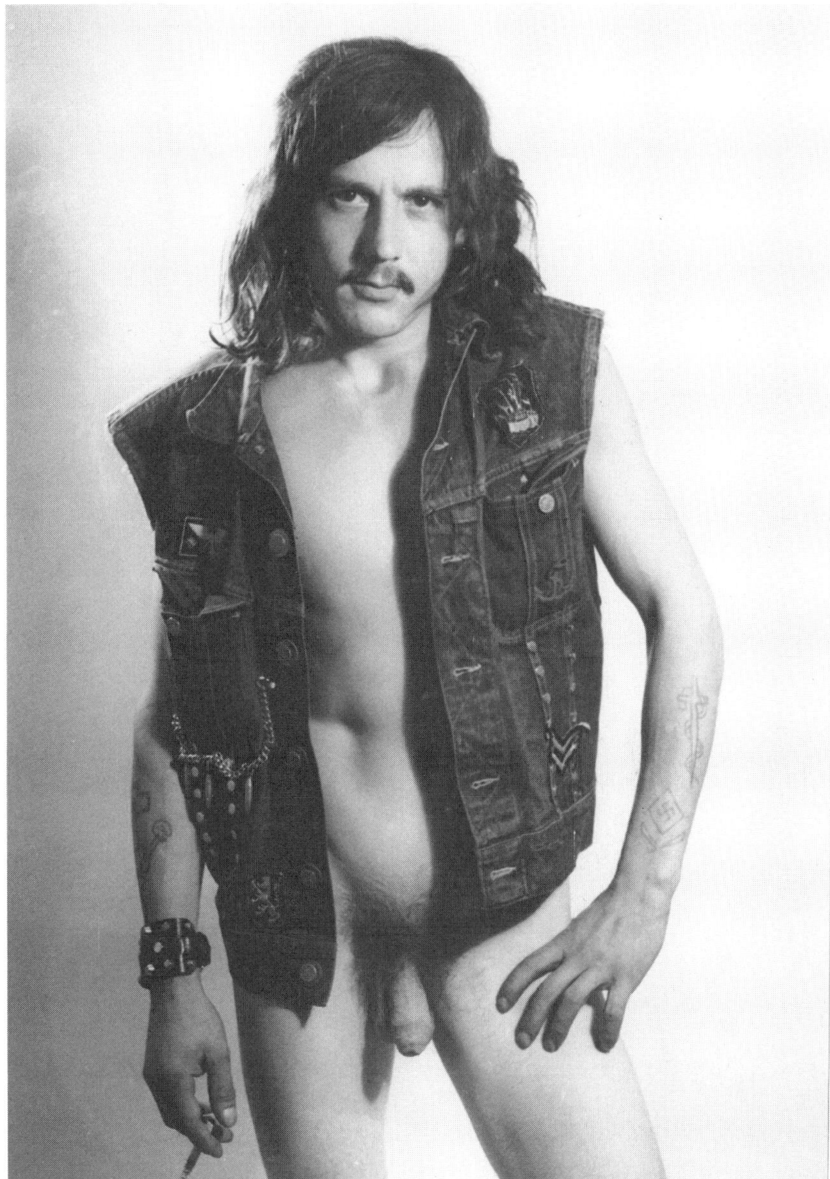

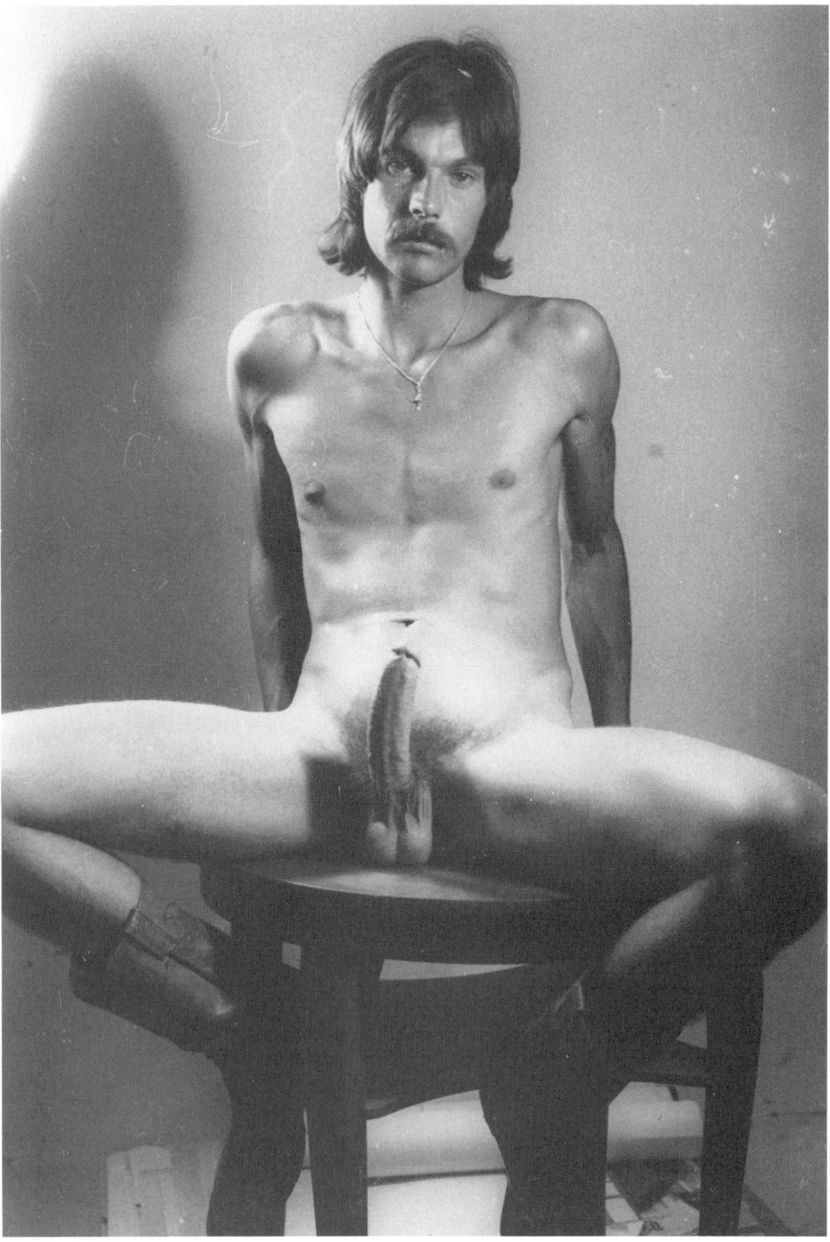

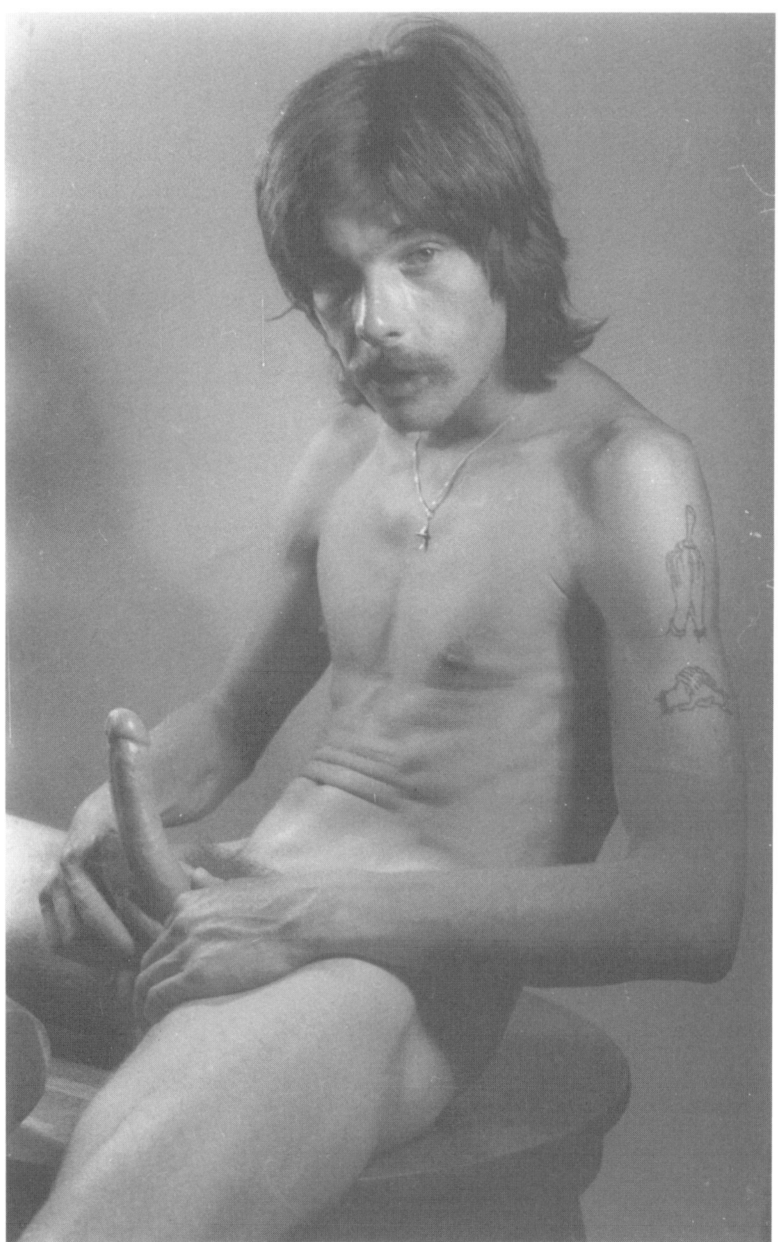

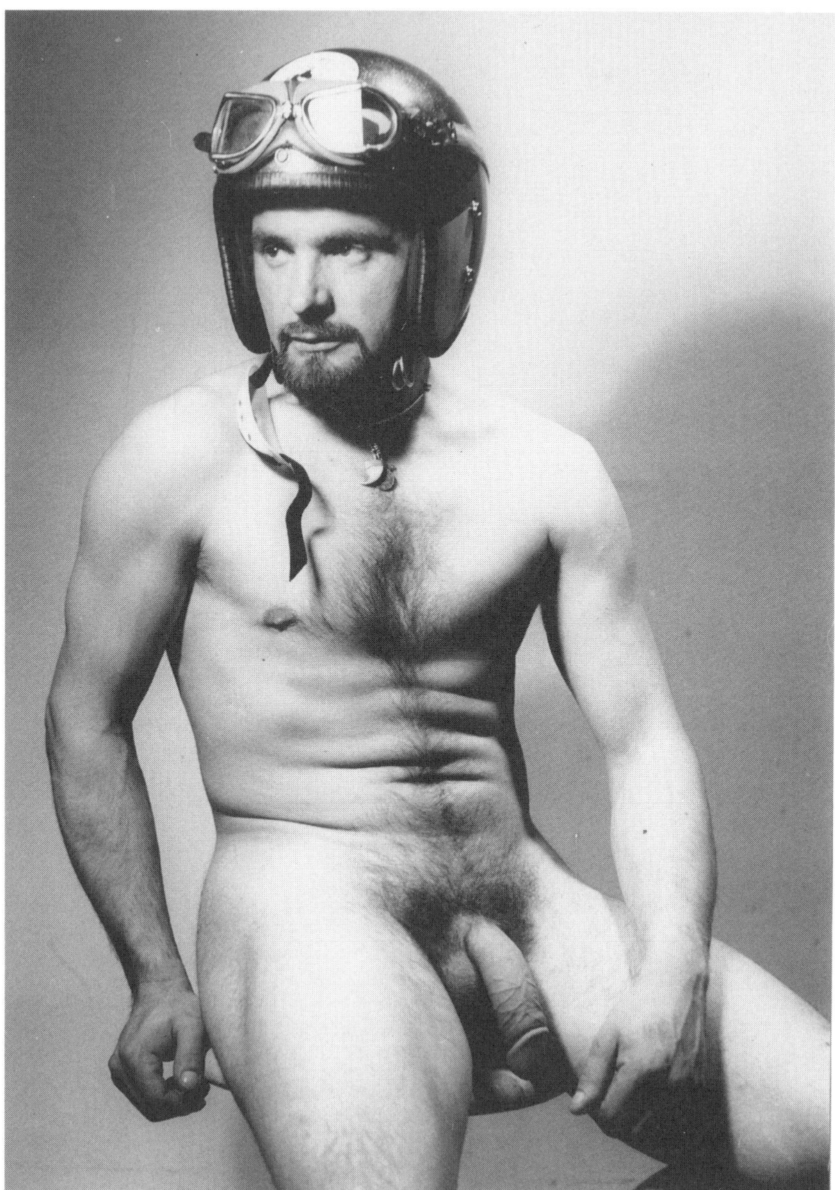

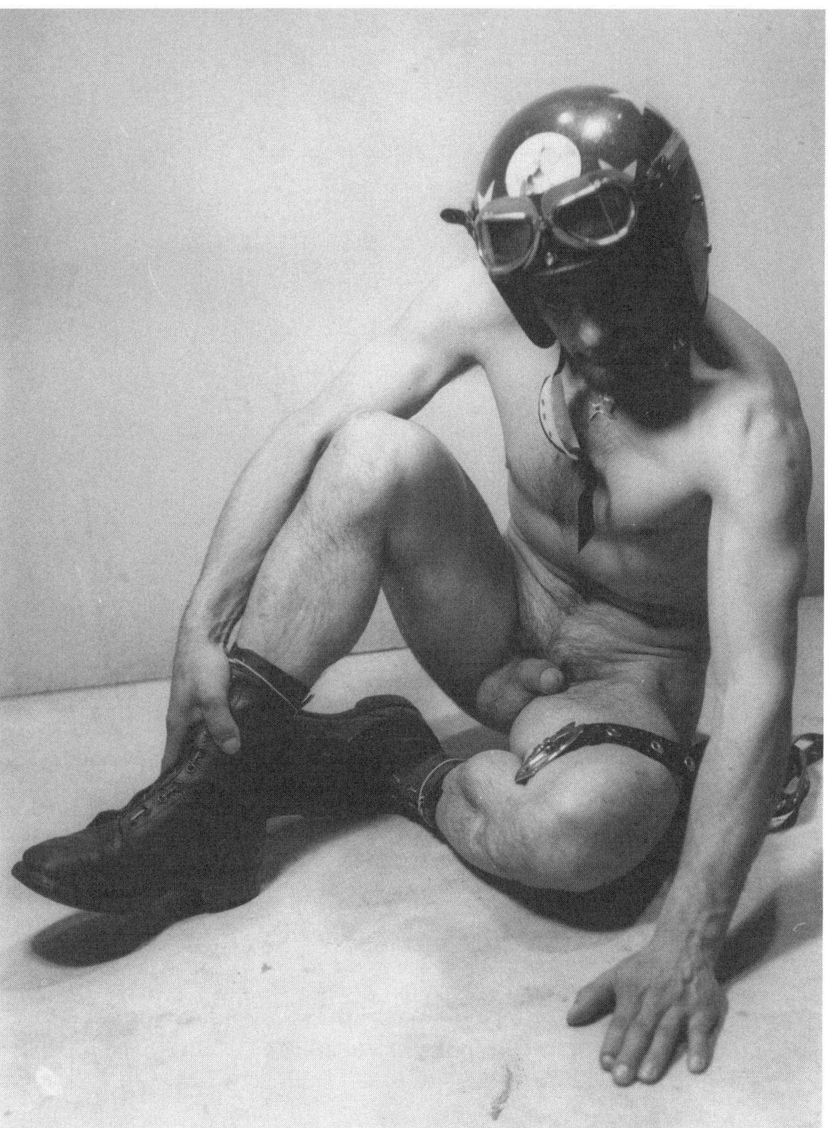

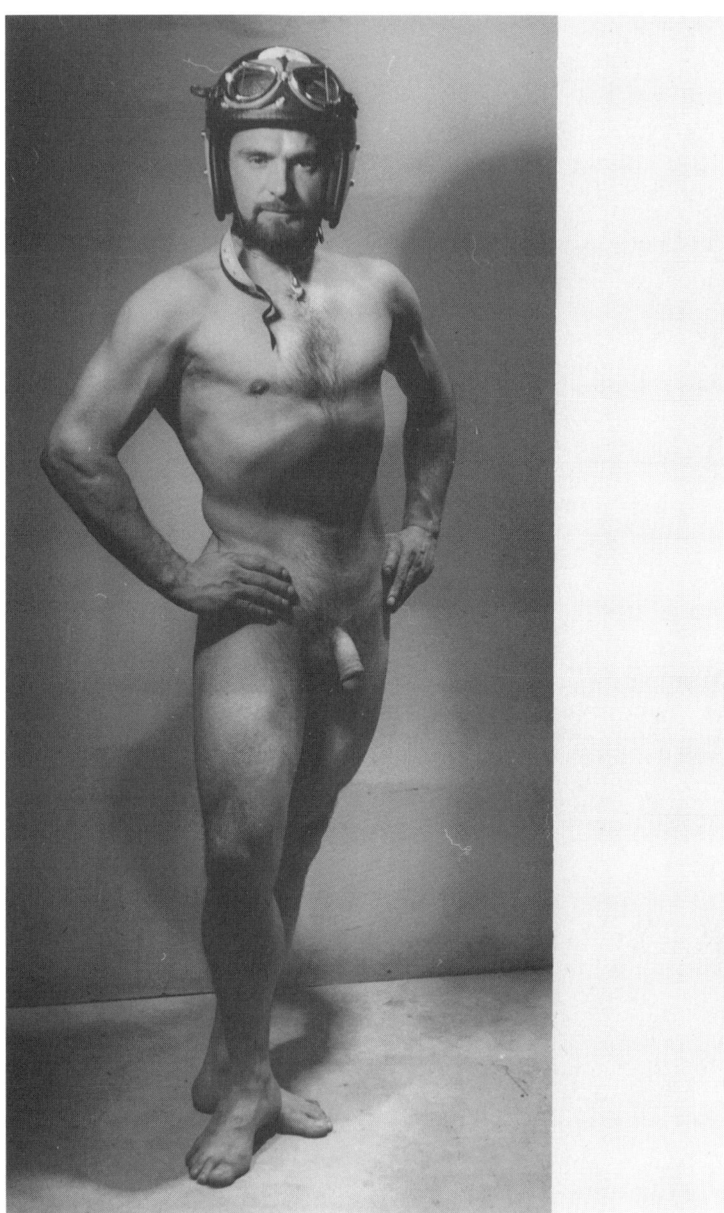

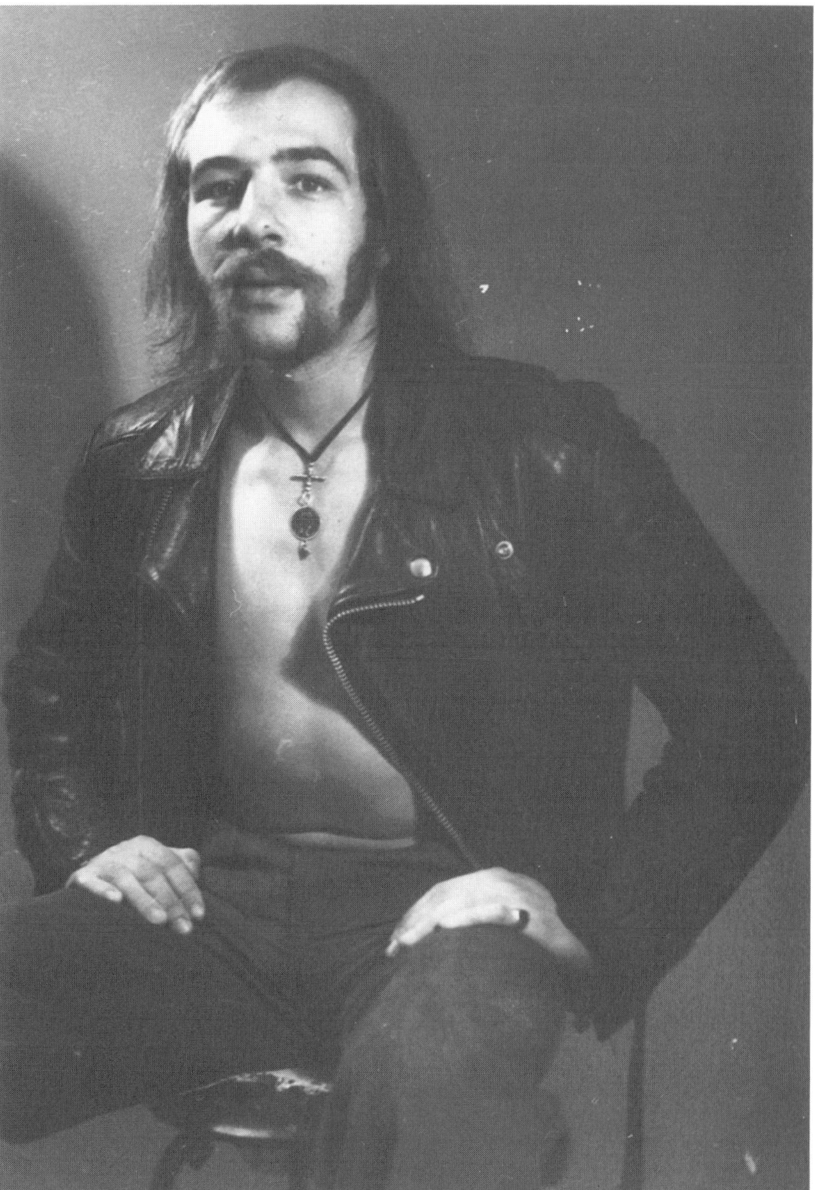

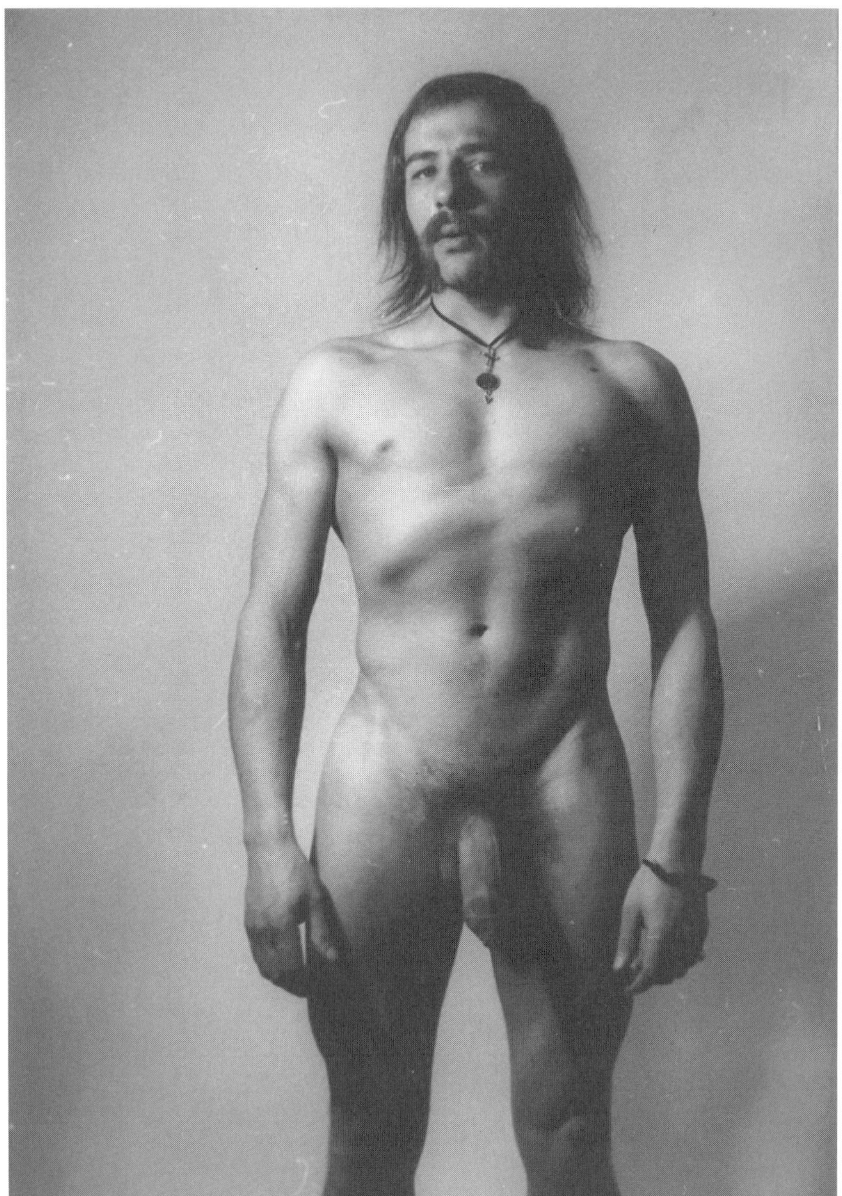

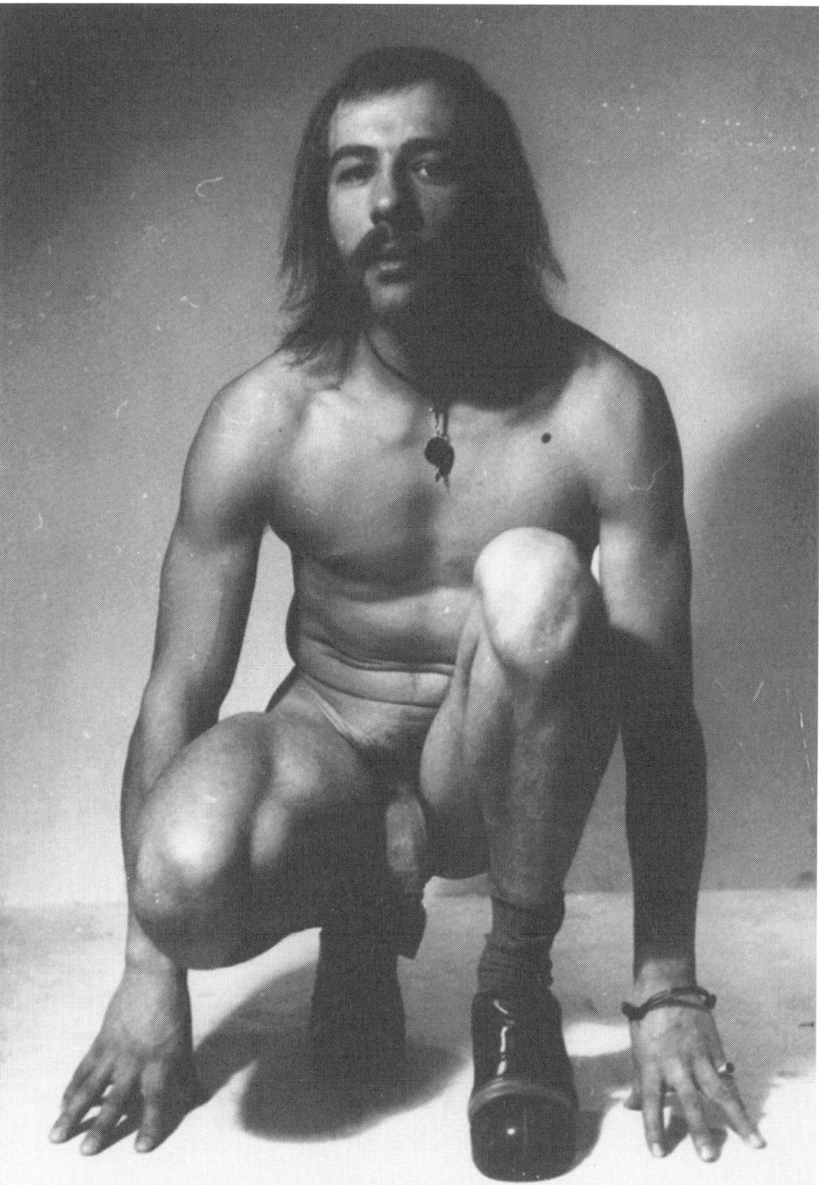

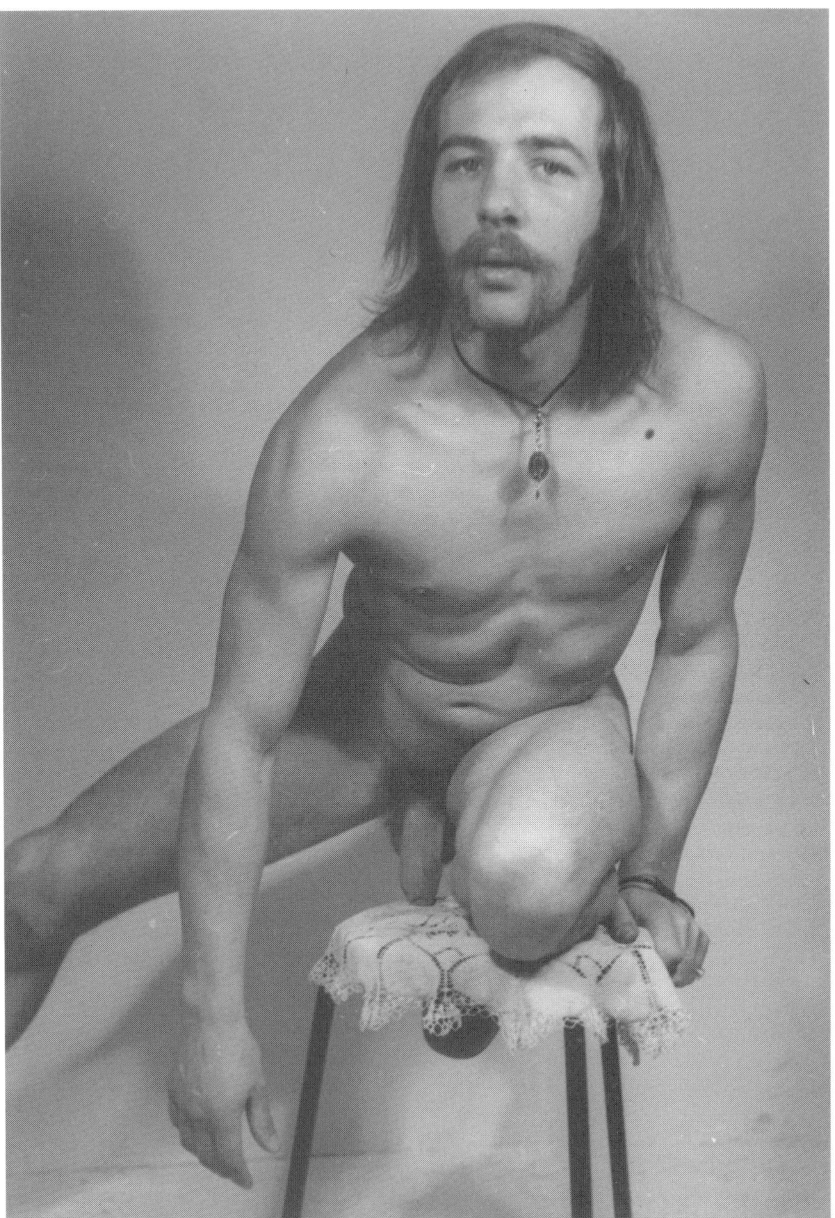

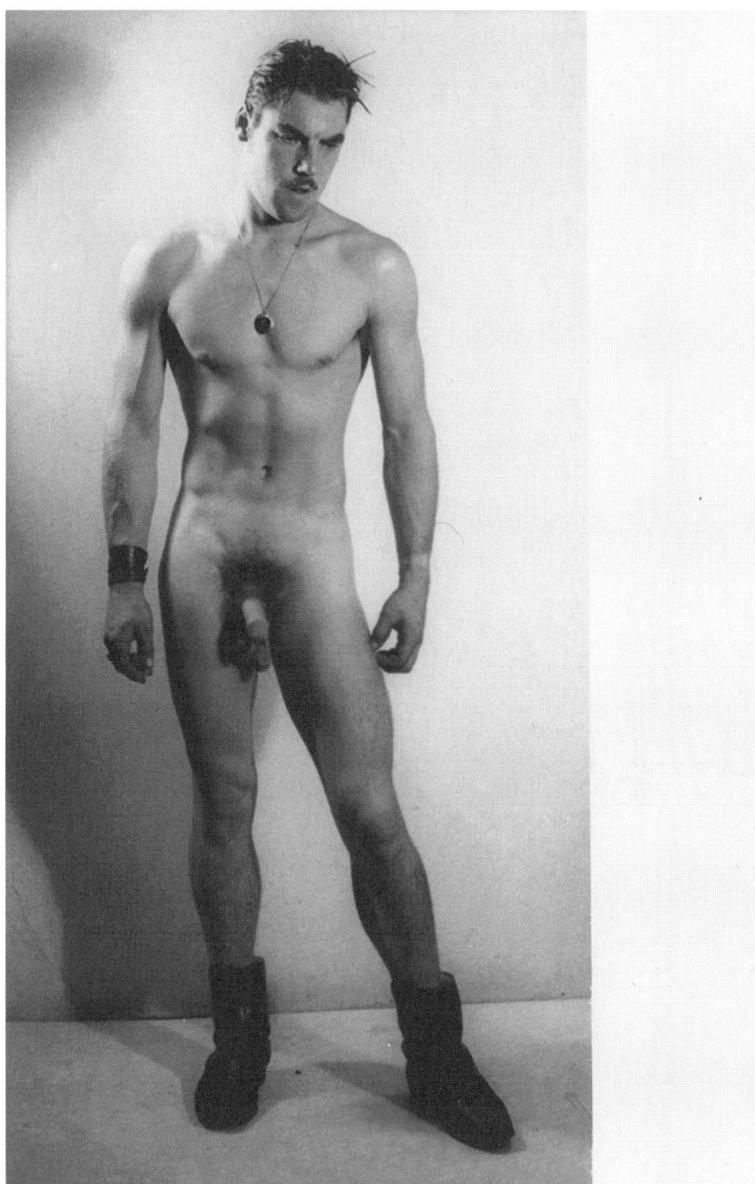

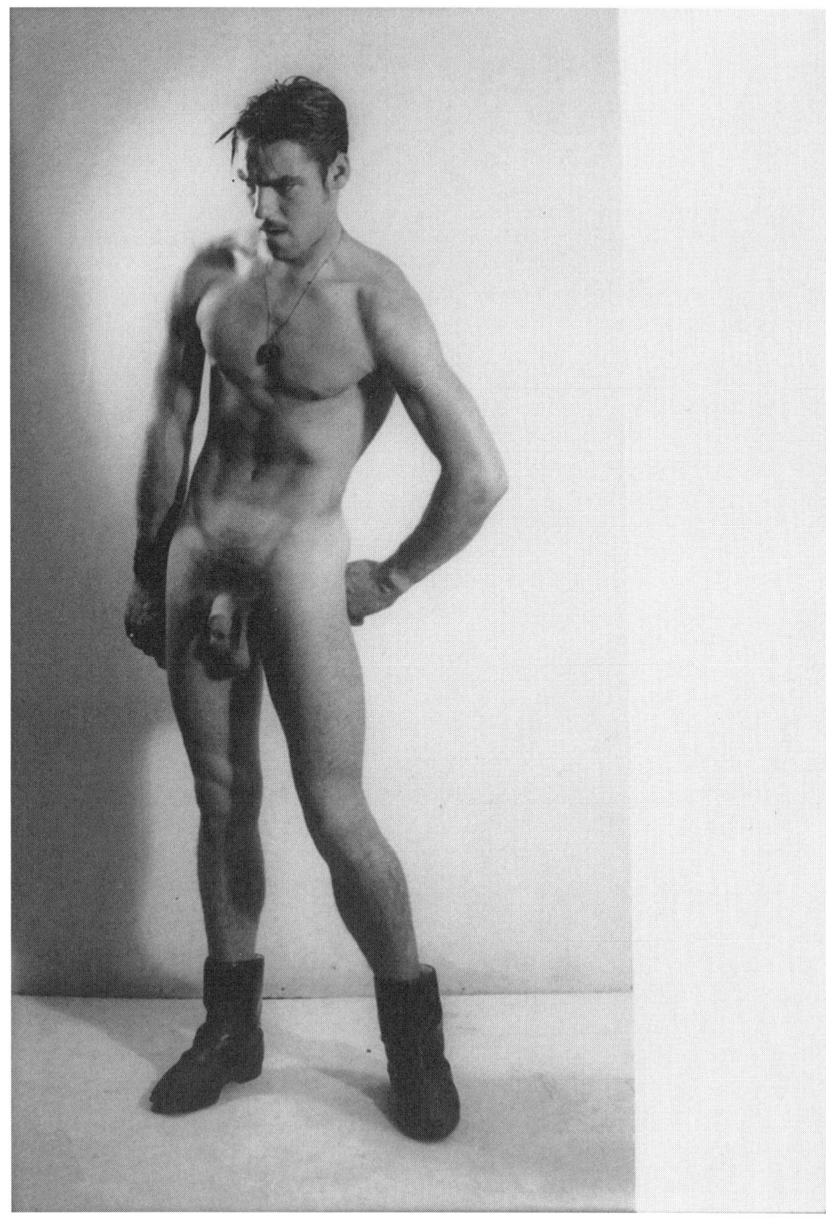

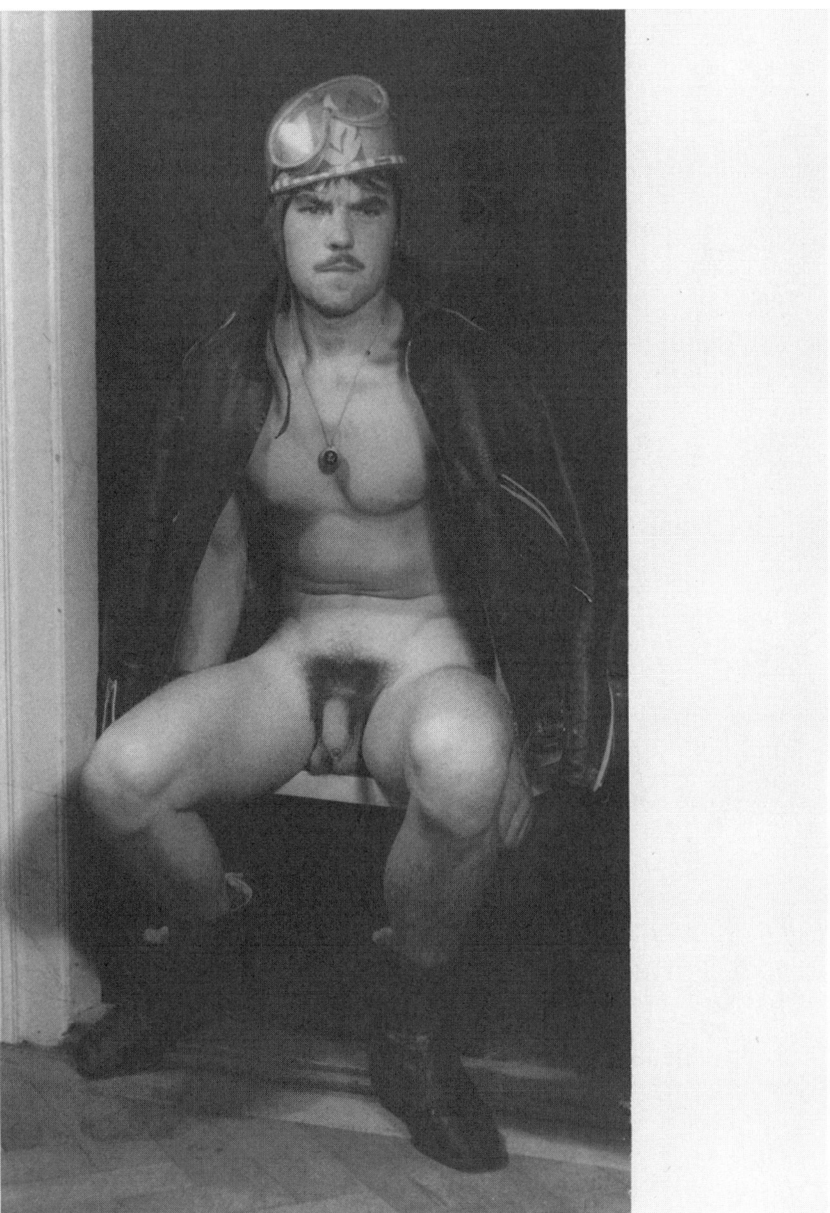

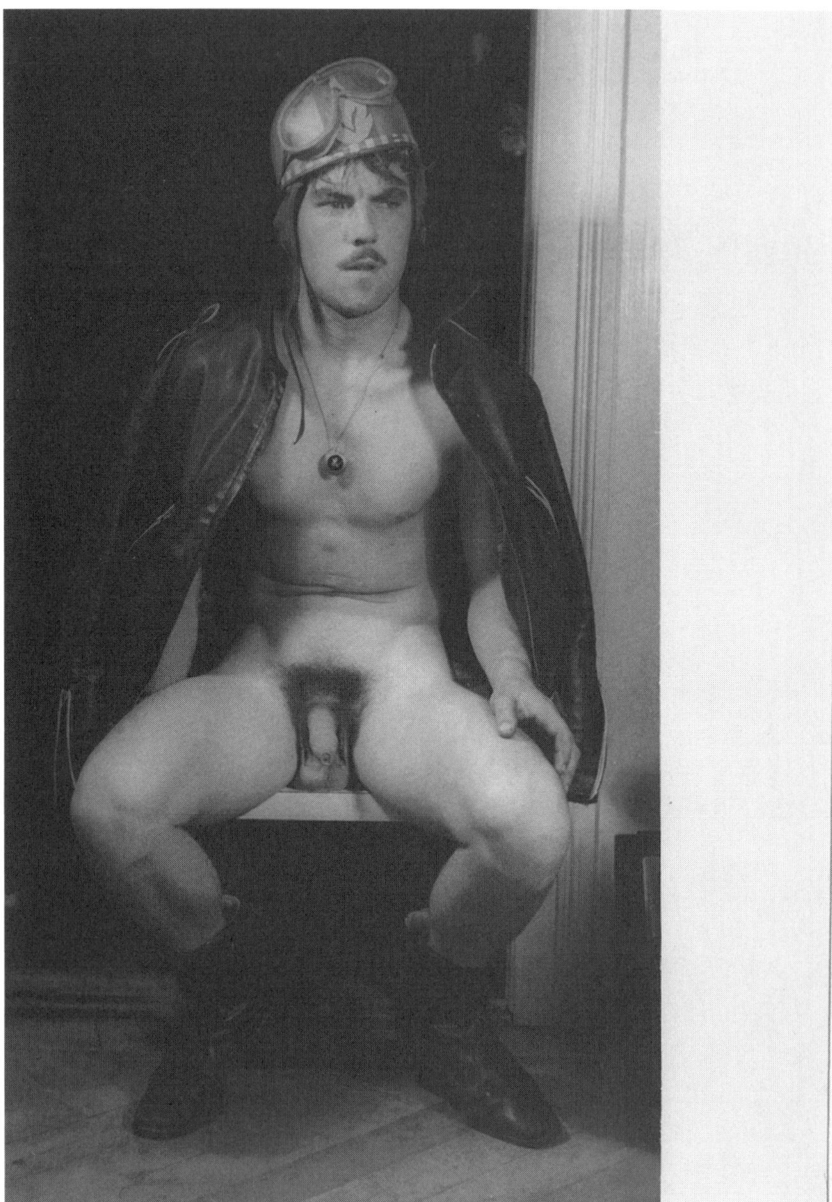

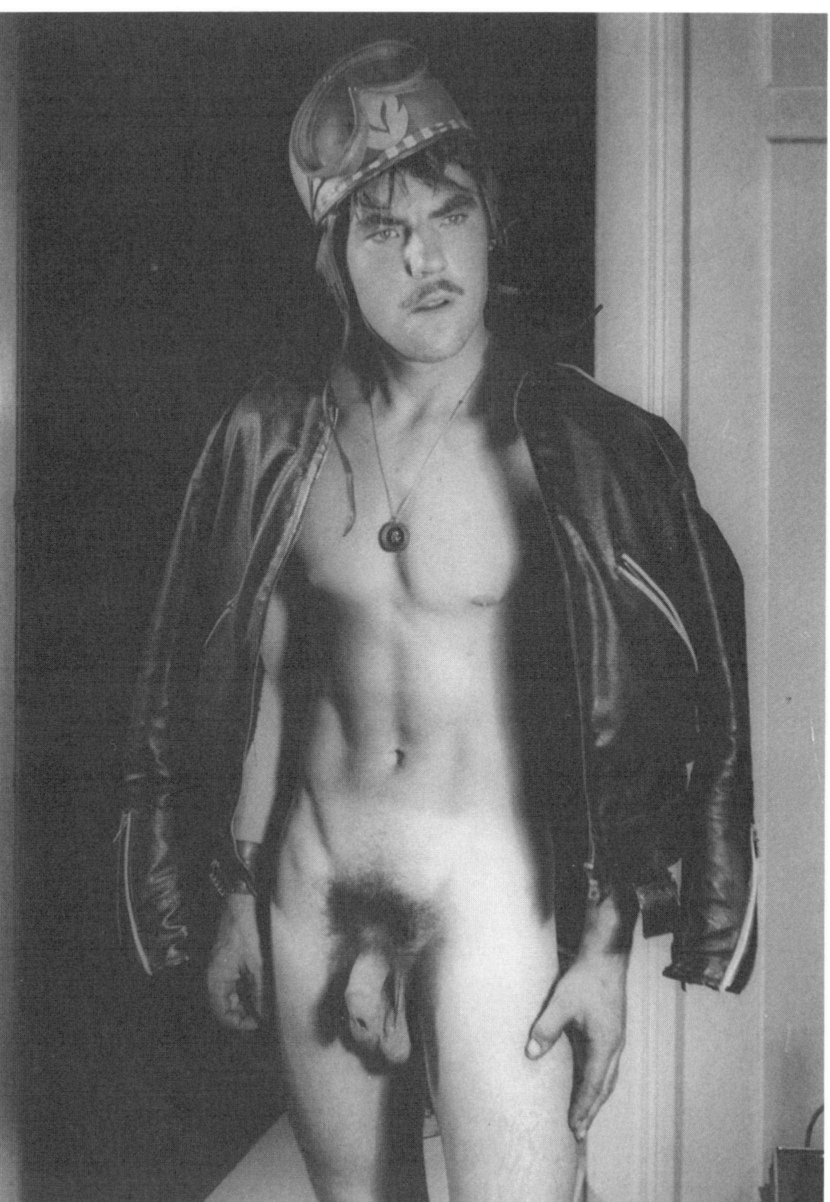

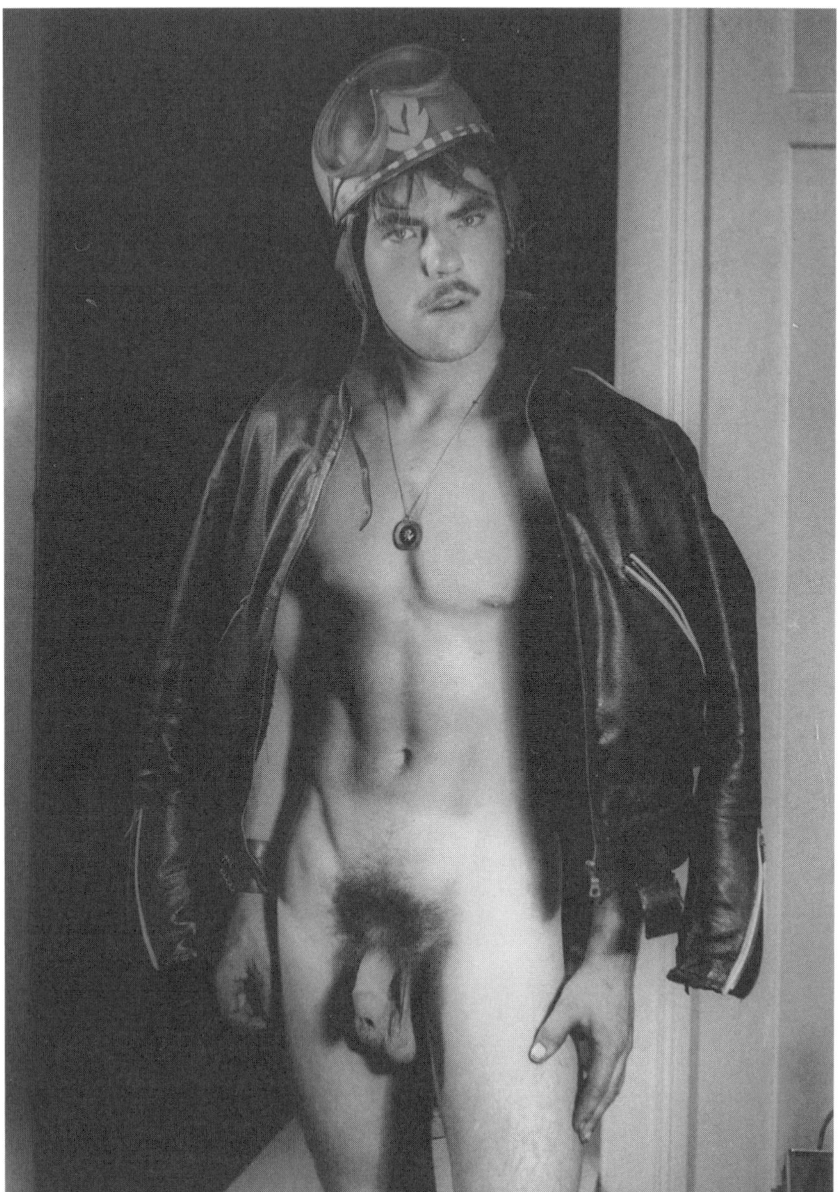

Caption List

The images in this book were reproduced from scans of the vintage photographic prints.

PAGE	TITLE	DATE	SIZE H (inches)	SIZE W (inches)
2	"Elvis", Hardau, Zurich	ca. 1960	4.13	2.55
3	Hardau, Zurich	ca. 1960	4.13	2.95
4	Knabenschiessen, Albisguetli	ca. 1961	4.13	2.55
5	Knabenschiessen, Albisguetli	ca. 1961	4.13	2.95
6	Knabenschiessen, Albisguetli	ca. 1961	2.95	2.55
7	Knabenschiessen, Albisguetli	1962	4.13	2.95
8	Knabenschiessen, Albisguetli	1962	2.95	2.55
9	Knabenschiessen, Albisguetli	1962	2.95	2.55
10	Knabenschiessen, Albisguetli	1962	4.13	2 .95
11	Knabenschiessen, Albisguetli	1962	4.13	2.55
12	Knabenschiessen, Albisguetli	1962	4.13	2.95
13	Knabenschiessen, Albisguetli	1962	4.13	2.55
14	Knabenschiessen, Albisguetli	1962	4.13	2.95
15	Knabenschiessen, Albisguetli	1962	4.13	2.95
16	St. Petersinsel	1964	2.16	2.16
17	St. Petersinsel	1964	2.16	2.16
18	St. Petersinsel	1964	2.16	2.16
19	St. Petersinsel	1964	2.16	2.16
20	St. Petersinsel	1964	2.16	2.16
21	St. Petersinsel	1964	2.16	2.16
22	"Vampir", St. Petersinsel	1964	2.16	2.16
24	St. Petersinsel	1964	2.95	2.95
25	St. Petersinsel	1964	2.95	2.95
26	St. Petersinsel	1964	2.95	2.95
27	St. Petersinsel	1964	2.95	2.95
28	St. Petersinsel	1964	2.95	2.95
29	St. Petersinsel	1964	2.95	2.95
30	St. Petersinsel	1964	2.95	2.95
31	St. Petersinsel	1964	2.95	2.95

PAGE	TITLE	DATE	SIZE H (inches)	SIZE W (inches)
32	St. Petersinsel	1964	2.95	2.95
33	St. Petersinsel	1964	2.95	2.95
34	St. Petersinsel	1964	2.95	2.95
35	St. Petersinsel	1964	2.95	2.95
36	St. Petersinsel	1964	2.95	2.95
37	St. Petersinsel	1964	2.95	2.95
38	St. Petersinsel	1964	2.95	2.95
39	St. Petersinsel	1964	2.95	2.95
40	St. Petersinsel	1964	2.95	2.95
41	St. Petersinsel	1964	2.95	2.95
42	St. Petersinsel	1964	2.95	2.95
43	St. Petersinsel	1964	2.95	2.95
44	St. Petersinsel	1964	2.95	2.95
45	St. Petersinsel	1964	2.95	2.95
46	St. Petersinsel	1964	2.95	2.95
47	St. Petersinsel	1964	2.95	2.95
48	St. Petersinsel	1964	2.95	2.95
49	St. Petersinsel	1964	2.95	2.95
50	St. Petersinsel	1964	2.95	2.95
51	St. Petersinsel	1964	2.95	2.95
52	St. Petersinsel	1964	2.95	2.95
53	St. Petersinsel	1964	2.95	2.95
56	Portrait, Zurich	c. mid 1950's	4.13	2.95
57	Portrait, Zurich	c. mid 1950's	4.13	2.95
58	Portrait, Zurich	c. mid 1950's	4.13	2.95
59	Portrait, Zurich	c. mid 1950's	4.13	2.95
60	Portrait, Zurich	c. mid 1950's	4.13	2.95
61	Portrait, Zurich	c. mid 1950's	4.13	2.95
62	Portrait, Zurich	c. mid 1950's	4.13	2.95
63	Portrait, Zurich	c. mid 1950's	4.13	2.95
64	Portrait, Zurich	c. mid 1950's	4.13	2.95
65	Portrait, Zurich	c. mid 1950's	4.13	2.95
66	Portrait, Zurich	c. mid 1950's	4.13	2.95
67	Portrait, Zurich	c. mid 1950's	4.13	2.95
68	Portrait, Zurich	c. mid 1950's	4.13	2.95
69	Portrait, Zurich	c. mid 1950's	4.13	2.95
70	Portrait, Zurich	c. mid 1950's	4.13	2.95
71	Portrait, Zurich	c. mid 1950's	4.13	2.95

PAGE	TITLE	DATE	SIZE H (inches)	SIZE W (inches)
72	Portrait, Zurich	c. mid 1950's	4.13	2.95
73	Portrait, Zurich	c. mid 1950's	4.13	2.95
74	Portrait, Zurich	c. late 1950's	4.13	2.95
75	Portrait, Zurich	c. late 1950's	4.13	2.95
76	Portrait, Zurich	c. late 1950's	4.13	2.95
77	Portrait, Zurich	c. late 1950's	4.13	2.95
78	Portrait, Zurich	c. late 1950's	4.13	2.95
79	Portrait, Zurich	c. late 1950's	4.13	2.95
80	Portrait, Zurich	c. late 1950's	4.13	2.95
81	Portrait, Zurich	c. late 1950's	4.13	2.95
82	Portrait, Zurich	c. late 1950's	4.13	2.95
83	Portrait, Zurich	c. late 1950's	4.13	2.95
84	Portrait, Zurich	c. late 1950's	4.13	2.95
85	Portrait, Zurich	c. late 1950's	4.13	2.95
86	Portrait, Zurich	c. late 1950's	4.13	2.95
87	Portrait, Zurich	c. late 1950's	4.13	2.95
88	Portrait, Zurich	c. late 1950's	4.13	2.95
89	Portrait, Zurich	c. late 1950's	4.13	2.95
90	Portrait, Zurich	c. late 1950's	4.13	2.95
91	Portrait, Zurich	c. late 1950's	4.13	2.95
92	Portrait, Zurich	c. late 1950's	4.13	2.95
93	Portrait, Zurich	c. late 1950's	4.13	2.95
94	Portrait, Zurich	c. late 1950's	4.13	2.95
95	Portrait, Zurich	c. late 1950's	4.13	2.95
96	Portrait, Zurich	c. late 1950's	4.13	2.95
97	Portrait, Zurich	c. late 1950's	4.13	2.95
98	Portrait, Zurich	c. early 1960's	4.13	2.95
99	Portrait, Zurich	c. early 1960's	4.13	2.95
100	Portrait, Zurich	c. early 1960's	4.13	2.95
101	Portrait, Zurich	c. early 1960's	4.13	2.95
102	Portrait, Zurich	c. early 1960's	4.13	2.95
103	Portrait, Zurich	c. early 1960's	4.13	2.95
104	Portrait, Zurich	c. early 1960's	4.13	2.95
105	Portrait, Zurich	c. early 1960's	4.13	2.95
106	Portrait, Zurich	c. early 1960's	4.13	2.95
107	Portrait, Zurich	c. early 1960's	4.13	2.95
108	Portrait, Zurich	c. early 1960's	4.13	2.95
109	Portrait, Zurich	c. early 1960's	4.13	2.95
110	Portrait, Zurich	c. early 1960's	4.13	2.95
111	Portrait, Zurich	c. early 1960's	4.13	2.95

PAGE	TITLE	DATE	SIZE H (inches)	SIZE W (inches)
112	Portrait, Zurich	c. early 1960's	4.13	2.95
113	Portrait, Zurich	c. early 1960's	4.13	2.95
114	Portrait, Zurich	c. early 1960's	4.13	2.95
115	Portrait, Zurich	c. early 1960's	4.13	2.95
116	Portrait, Zurich	c. mid 1960's	4.13	2.95
117	Portrait, Zurich	c. mid 1960's	4.13	2.95
118	Portrait, Zurich	c. mid 1960's	4.13	2.95
119	Portrait, Zurich	c. mid 1960's	4.13	2.95
120	Portrait, Zurich	c. mid 1960's	4.13	2.95
121	Portrait, Zurich	c. mid 1960's	4.13	2.95
122	Portrait, Zurich	c. mid 1960's	4.13	2.95
123	Portrait, Zurich	c. mid 1960's	4.13	2.95
124	Portrait, Zurich	c. mid 1960's	4.13	2.95
125	Portrait, Zurich	c. mid 1960's	4.13	2.95
126	Portrait, Zurich	c. mid 1960's	4.13	2.95
127	Portrait, Zurich	c. mid 1960's	4.13	2.95
128	Portrait, Zurich	c. mid 1960's	4.13	2.95
129	Portrait, Zurich	c. mid 1960's	4.13	2.95
130	Portrait, Zurich	c. mid 1960's	4.1a3	2.95
131	Portrait, Zurich	c. mid 1960's	4.13	2.95
132	Portrait, Zurich	c. mid 1960's	4.13	2.95
133	Portrait, East Berlin	c. mid 1960's	4.13	2.95
134	Portrait, East Berlin	c. mid 1960's	4.13	2.95
135	Portrait, East Berlin	c. mid 1960's	4.13	2.95
136	Portrait, East Berlin	c. mid 1960's	4.13	2.95
137	Portrait, East Berlin	c. mid 1960's	4.13	2.95
138	Portrait, East Berlin	c. mid 1960's	4.13	2.95
139	Portrait, Zurich	c. mid 1960's	4.13	2.95
140	Portrait, Zurich	c. mid 1960's	4.13	2.95
141	Portrait, Zurich	c. mid 1960's	4.13	2.95
142	Portrait, Zurich	c. mid 1960's	4.13	2.95
143	Portrait, Zurich	c. mid 1960's	4.13	2.95
144	Portrait, Zurich	c. mid 1960's	4.13	2.95
145	Portrait, Zurich	c. mid 1960's	4.13	2.95
146	Portrait, Zurich	c. mid 1960's	4.13	2.95
147	Portrait, Zurich	c. mid 1960's	4.13	2.95
148	Portrait, Zurich	c. mid 1960's	4.13	2.95
149	Portrait, Zurich	c. mid 1960's	4.13	2.95
150	Portrait, Zurich	c. mid 1960's	4.13	2.95
151	Portrait, Zurich	c. mid 1960's	4.13	2.95

PAGE	TITLE	DATE	SIZE H (inches)	SIZE W (inches)
152	Portrait, Zurich	c. mid 1960's	4.13	2.95
153	Portrait, Zurich	c. mid 1960's	4.13	2.95
154	Portrait, Zurich	c. mid 1960's	4.13	2.95
155	Portrait, Zurich	c. mid 1960's	4.13	2.95
156	Portrait, Zurich	c. late 1970's	7.08	5.11
157	Portrait, Zurich	c. mid 1960's	4.13	2.95
158	Portrait, Zurich	c. mid 1960's	4.13	2.95
159	Portrait, Zurich	c. mid 1960's	4.13	2.95
160	Portrait, Zurich	c. mid 1960's	4.13	2.95
161	Portrait, Zurich	c. early 1970's	4.13	2.95
162	Portrait, Zurich	c. early 1970's	4.13	2.95
163	Portrait, Zurich	c. early 1970's	4.13	2.95
164	Portrait, Zurich	c. early 1970's	4.13	2.95
165	Portrait, Zurich	c. early 1970's	4.13	2.95
166	Portrait, Zurich	c. early 1970's	4.13	2.95
167	Portrait, Zurich	c. early 1970's	4.13	2.95
168	Portrait, Zurich	c. early 1970's	4.13	2.95
169	Portrait, Zurich	c. early 1970's	4.13	2.95
170	Portrait, Zurich	c. mid 1960's	4.13	2.95
171	Portrait, Zurich	c. mid 1960's	4.13	2.95
172	Portrait, Zurich	c. mid 1960's	4.13	2.95
173	Portrait, Zurich	c. mid 1960's	4.13	2.95
174	Portrait, Zurich	c. mid 1960's	4.13	2.95
175	Portrait, Zurich	c. mid 1960's	4.13	2.95
176	Portrait, Zurich	c. mid 1960's	4.13	2.95
177	Portrait, Zurich	c. mid 1960's	4.13	2.95
178	Portrait, Zurich	c. mid 1960's	4.13	2.95
179	Portrait, Zurich	c. mid 1960's	4.13	2.95
180	Portrait, Zurich	c. mid 1960's	4.13	2.95
181	Portrait, Zurich	c. mid 1960's	4.13	2.95
182	Portrait, Zurich	c. mid 1960's	4.13	2.95
183	Portrait, Zurich	c. mid 1960's	4.13	2.95
184	Portrait, East Berlin	c. mid 1960's	4.13	2.95
185	Portrait, East Berlin	c. mid 1960's	4.13	2.95
186	Portrait, Zurich	c. mid 1960's	4.13	2.95
187	Portrait, Zurich	c. mid 1960's	4.13	2.95
188	Portrait, Zurich	c. mid 1970's	4.13	2.95
189	Portrait, Zurich	c. mid 1970's	4.13	2.95
190	Portrait, Zurich	c. mid 1970's	4.13	2.95
191	Portrait, Zurich	c. mid 1970's	4.13	2.95

PAGE	TITLE	DATE	SIZE H (inches)	SIZE W (inches)
192	Portrait, Zurich	c. mid 1970's	7.08	4.72
193	Portrait, Zurich	c. mid 1970's	7.08	4.72
194	Portrait, Zurich	c. mid 1970's	7.08	4.52
195	Portrait, Zurich	c. mid 1970's	7.08	4.72
196	Portrait, Zurich	c. mid 1970's	7.08	4.52
197	Portrait, Zurich	c. mid 1970's	7.08	4.72
198	Portrait, Zurich	c. mid 1970's	7.08	4.52
199	Portrait, Zurich	c. mid 1970's	7.08	4.72
200	Portrait, Zurich	c. mid 1970's	7.08	4.42
201	Portrait, Zurich	c. mid 1970's	7.08	4.52
202	Portrait, Zurich	c. mid 1970's	7.08	4.52
203	Portrait, Zurich	c. mid 1970's	7.08	4.52
204	Portrait, Zurich	c. mid 1970's	7.08	4.72
205	Portrait, Zurich	c. mid 1970's	7.08	4.72
206	Portrait, Zurich	c. mid 1970's	7.08	4.72
207	Portrait, Zurich	c. mid 1970's	4.13	2.95
208	Portrait, Zurich	c. mid 1970's	4.13	2.95
209	Portrait, Zurich	c. mid 1970's	4.13	2.95
210	Portrait, Zurich	c. mid 1970's	4.13	2.95
211	Portrait, Zurich	c. mid 1960's	4.13	2.95
212	Portrait, Zurich	c. mid 1960's	4.13	2.95
213	Portrait, Zurich	c. mid 1960's	4.13	2.95
214	Portrait, Zurich	c. mid 1960's	4.13	2.95
215	Portrait, Zurich	c. mid 1960's	4.13	2.95
216	Portrait, Zurich	c. mid 1960's	4.13	2.95

OTHER TITLES FROM THE SONG CAVE:

1. *A Dark Dreambox of Another Kind* by **Alfred Starr Hamilton**
2. *My Enemies* by **Jane Gregory**
3. *Rude Woods* by **Nate Klug**
4. *Georges Braque and Others* by **Trevor Winkfield**
5. *The Living Method* by **Sara Nicholson**
6. *Splash State* by **Todd Colby**
7. *Essay Stanzas* by **Thomas Meyer**
8. *Illustrated Games of Patience* by **Ben Estes**
9. *Dark Green* by **Emily Hunt**
10. *Honest James* by **Christian Schlegel**
11. *M* by **Hannah Brooks-Motl**
12. *What the Lyric Is* by **Sara Nicholson**
13. *The Hermit* by **Lucy Ives**
14. *The Orchid Stories* by **Kenward Elmslie**
15. *Do Not Be a Gentleman When You Say Goodnight* by **Mitch Sisskind**
16. *HAIRDO* by **Rachel B. Glaser**
17. *Motor Maids across the Continent* by **Ron Padgett**
18. *Songs for Schizoid Siblings* by **Lionel Ziprin**
19. *Professionals of Hope*, The Selected Writings of **Subcomandante Marcos**
20. *Fort Not* by **Emily Skillings**
21. *Riddles, Etc.* by **Geoffrey Hilsabeck**

22. *CHARAS: The Improbable Dome Builders*, by **Syeus Mottel** (Co-published with Pioneer Works)
23. *YEAH NO* by **Jane Gregory**
24. *Nioque of the Early-Spring* by **Francis Ponge**
25. *Smudgy and Lossy* by **John Myers**
26. *The Desert* by **Brandon Shimoda**
27. *Scardanelli* by **Friederike Mayröcker**
28. *The Alley of Fireflies and other stories* by **Raymond Roussel**
29. *CHANGES: Notes on Choreography* by **Merce Cunningham** (Co-published with the Merce Cunningham Trust)
30. *My Mother Laughs* by **Chantal Akerman**
31. *Earth* by **Hannah Brooks-Motl**
32. *Everything and Other Poems* by **Charles North**
33. *Paper Bells* by **Phan Nhiên Hạo**